For Barbara, by far the best
Harrison cook. I'm sure you
have experienced many an
impulse to gesture...

Simon

(05.05.2019, Waddington)

The Impulse to Gesture

Gestures are central to the way people use language when they interact. This book places our impulse to gesture at the very heart of linguistic structure: grammar. Based on the phenomenon of negation – a linguistic universal with clear grammatical and gestural manifestations – Simon Harrison argues that linguistic concepts are fundamentally multimodal and shows how they lead to recurrent bindings between grammar and gesture when people speak. Studying how speakers express negation multimodally in a range of social and professional contexts, Harrison explores how and when people gesture, what people achieve linguistically and discursively with their gestures, and why we find similar uses of gesture in different languages (including spoken and signed language). Establishing the inseparability of grammar and gesture, this book is an important reference for any researcher interested in the relation between language, gesture, and cognition.

SIMON HARRISON is Assistant Professor of Applied Linguistics in the School of English at the University of Nottingham Ningbo China. His research has played a vital role in bridging the divide between grammar and gesture.

The Impulse to Gesture

Where Language, Minds, and Bodies Intersect

Simon Harrison

University of Nottingham Ningbo China

CAMBRIDGE
UNIVERSITY PRESS

University Printing House, Cambridge CB2 8BS, United Kingdom

One Liberty Plaza, 20th Floor, New York, NY 10006, USA

477 Williamstown Road, Port Melbourne, VIC 3207, Australia

314–321, 3rd Floor, Plot 3, Splendor Forum, Jasola District Centre,
New Delhi – 110025, India

79 Anson Road, #06–04/06, Singapore 079906

Cambridge University Press is part of the University of Cambridge.

It furthers the University's mission by disseminating knowledge in the pursuit of
education, learning, and research at the highest international levels of excellence.

www.cambridge.org
Information on this title: www.cambridge.org/9781108417204
DOI: 10.1017/9781108265065

© Cambridge University Press 2018

First published 2018

Printed and bound in Great Britain by Clays Ltd, Elcograf S.p.A.

A catalogue record for this publication is available from the British Library.

ISBN 978-1-108-41720-4 Hardback

In loving memory of Christine Anne Harrison, devoted Mum and dedicated teacher. Thank you for the roots to call home and the wings to fly far.

The Cloths of Heaven
Had I the heaven's embroided cloths,
Enwrought with golden and silver light,
The blue and the dim and the dark cloths
Of night and light and the half-light;
I would spread the cloths under your feet:
But I, being poor, have only my dreams;
I have spread my dreams under your feet;
Tread softly because you tread on my dreams.   *W. B. Yeats*

Contents

Figures

Tables

Preface

When we talk, how aware are we of our gestures, or indeed, whether we are gesturing at all? Sometimes gestures can be deliberate as with emblematic gestures like the well-known 'thumbs up' gesture. But sometimes we seem to be less aware of the gestures we use when we converse, argue, and collaborate with others in social and professional interaction. If you are unconvinced as to whether you or others gesture in these everyday settings, pause for a moment and watch people speaking. You will notice that they often repeat certain gestures as they put across or defend their point of view. This book explains what determines, shapes, and organises these gestures that keep recurring, what I refer to as *the impulse to gesture*.

Our impulse to gesture is intricately connected to what we say, what we mean, and what we aim to achieve with language in spoken interaction. Repeatedly viewing videos of people conversing and using methods to analyse different aspects of their gestures shows that the timing, form, and meaning of our gesturing hands coordinate systematically with the linguistic structures and pragmatic functions of speech. The type of gestures that are integral to the form and function of utterances can be grouped together and labelled 'recurrent gestures'. These are gestures that we use conventionally but in diverse and intriguing ways.

One of the most fascinating gestures is the family of gestural forms associated with expressing negation. As all linguists will know, negation involves lexical and grammatical patterns that determine word order and operate on the semantics of an utterance, such as 'not' in English, 'ne pas' in French, and 不 (bù) in Chinese. What is perhaps less well known, but will soon become clear, is that speakers of these languages also express negation with gestures that exhibit an open hand shape either raised vertically with the palm oriented towards the addressee or turned palm down and swept along the horizontal axis. When speakers coordinate these linguistic and gestural resources in rejecting offers, refusing suggestions, denying assertions, and negating unwanted implications, they are expressing negation multimodally.

The multimodal expression of negation is what I have been studying for the past ten years and is the primary focus of this book. It leads us to discover the 'grammar–gesture nexus' – recurrent bindings of linguistic and gestural forms at the level of the utterance, with ramifications for discourse and interaction. This is an understudied but central feature of gesturing, and this book is designed to help show and understand its importance. Gestures are often viewed as free and spontaneous, but the nexus illustrates that even seemingly spontaneous gestures are constrained in ways that shed light on the relation between language, minds, and bodies.

Over eighty examples culled from hours of recorded spoken interactions in diverse contexts will show that when we gesture in relation to negation, we shape, orient, position, and move our hands in a reproducible way. How we prepare, release, and hold our gesture in space respects the ordering principles that negative forms and constructs impose on utterances. The form of these gestures is motivated by the thoughts, images, and actions that we associate with negation, such as removal, exclusion, and absence. On a discourse level, our gestures are constrained by the desire to maintain cohesion and coherence in relation to not only what we want to say but also what we want to do, our communicative aims in a particular interaction. Though inseparable within a given gestural impulse, the sequentiality of chapters in the book reflects the nesting of these different constraints.

The multimodality of a linguistic universal such as negation raises important questions about both gesture and 'linguistic' or 'grammatical' concepts. What is the relation between gesture and grammar? Why are some gestures shared within and across linguistic communities? Are these gestures similar to the signs we find in sign languages? In view of the centrality of gestures to linguistic structures, what then is the nature of language itself? This book on the 'Impulse Theory' of gesture brings us closer to answering some of these questions.

Acknowledgements

This book was possible thanks to an elaborate support system of mentors, colleagues, friends, and family. I wish to thank first and foremost Jean-Rémi Lapaire for introducing me to cognitive linguistics, to gesture studies, and to the 'grammar–gesture nexus' – a concept at the heart of this book. The focus on negation was suggested by Cornelia Müller and Ellen Fricke, whose insights have had a bearing on the current work since its inception. Within the same *Towards a Grammar of Gesture* group, I must thank Silva Ladewig and Jana Bressem for their training in methods of gesture analysis and unreserved discussions of this work. The influence of Adam Kendon should be made clear from the outset too – the ideas in his book *Gesture* were my entry point to this discipline and his comments on this project at earlier stages have proven invaluable. Mats Andrén, Dominique Boutet, Alan Cienki, Camille Debras, Vito Evola, Sukeshini Grandhi, Julius Hassemer, Gina Joue, Leland McCleary, Irene Mittelberg, Aliyah Morgenstern, Mark Tutton, Eve Sweetser, and Robert Williams have similarly invested generously in helping me understand the ideas that grew into this book.

In addition to these foundations, I am grateful to several experts who have helped bring the current text to fruition. I could not have hoped for a better writing partner for a book on gestures than Heather Brookes – her questions and comments have greatly improved the chapters that follow. To Leland McCleary, I owe what became the title, and consequently, the frame for the whole book – hopefully the ideas herein will prolong our enjoyable discussions. Svenja Adolphs, Geneviève Calbris, Laura Hildago Downing, Geoff Hall, Daryl Johnson, Stefan Kopp, Pierre Larrivée, Steven Schoonjans, Michael Stevens, Levi Stutzman, Gunnel Tottie, and Robert Williams also kindly provided feedback on manuscripts, outlines, and proposals that culminated in this text. Feedback from two anonymous reviewers have helped me to clarify aspects of the work.

A sabbatical semester was granted by the University of Nottingham Ningbo China at the perfect moment – I thank my colleagues in the School of English for facilitating this leave, and my students for sounding out some of the ideas that follow. Li Meng, Zhenghui Shen, and Magali Kerbellec helped substantially with transcriptions, translations, and edits of the Chinese and French spoken data. I thank the patience and hard work of three artists for the excellent illustrations: Esther Stutzman, Virginia Reitzel, and Eshwar Prasad. My gratitude for last-minute technical support goes to Amarpreet Gill.

A number of people have been crucial to the completion of this work without ever seeing the text, not least the anonymous conversationalists whose speech and gestures animate the pages that ensue. The friendship of two scholars, Logan Connors and David Fleming, has been an ongoing source of intellectual stimulation. The love and support from 陈星超 (Chen Xingchao), my *merveilleux quotidian*, has been invaluable; my deadlines became her deadlines and finishing the book became a team effort, with overwhelming support from her family in Ninghai. A walk across northern Spain with my brother and Dad – James and Mark Harrison – helped put things into perspective, as their company always does. 'Time and interest' are what children need, as my Dad often says. So finally, I thank my parents for their lifelong investment – for spreading their dreams under my feet.

Notational Conventions

Following Kendon (2004), the below conventions are adopted for gestural action unless otherwise specified.

Abc	speech is transcribed with conventional orthography
NOT	all capitals used to show stressed syllables (when relevant)
|	start/end of gestural action
~~	preparation phase
***	stroke phase
.-.-.-	retraction phase
<u>*****</u>	gestural action underlined is held
***/**	a forward slash indicates a new stroke
(rh/lh)	right hand/left hand (if relevant, when two hands are being used)

Additionally, a number of other conventions have been adopted:

(...)	pauses in speech are indicated with series of full stops inside parentheses
(.)	micro-pause
(3)	lengthy pauses are given in seconds
[]	square parentheses indicate overlapping speech of different speakers
[1]	these numbers in the text and the transcripts refer to gestures being described

Code names provided with each example correspond to the video clips in my corpus. For example, 'G_K gm 11.40 no one around' is an example of the expression 'no one around', which occurred eleven minutes forty seconds into a recording of a conversation between two speakers 'GJ' and 'K' playing a board game ('gm').

1 The Impulse to Gesture
Spontaneous but Constrained

1.1   The Impulse to Gesture

The idea of an *impulse* to gesture while speaking is an ideal starting point for
this book. First of all, it captures an everyday view of gesturing as something
uncontrollable and subconscious. I am not alone among gesture researchers to
have made an addressee, upon mentioning this research area, suddenly claim
heightened self-awareness of her gestures. Some people report immunity to this
impulse – they say they 'never' gesture – whilst others are apparently overwhelmed by it – they 'always' gesture. In both cases, I observe a steady stream
of recognisable gesture forms coherently organised and deployed as they speak.
At the same time, the idea of an impulse to gesture captures a view of gestures
that has arguably shaped the field of contemporary gesture studies; namely, the
view that gestures are primarily a cognitive impulse, a spontaneous, unwitting,
and idiosyncratic manifestation of thought (McNeill 1992, 2005, 2012, 2016).

The goal of this book is to explore a much lesser known side of the impulse to
gesture. By 'recognisable gesture forms', I am not referring to emblematic
gestures such as 'thumbs up' or to sustained body postures such as 'arms
crossed' – for a dictionary combining emblems and postures see Morris
(1994). I am referring to gestures that routinely connect with grammatical
concepts in speech, and in the nature of that connection, exhibit regularity in
their form, organisation, and function. This book is about those regularities.
It is about the form and organisation of our impulse to gesture in connection
with a particular grammatical concept in speech. My case will be based on
negation.

Negation is a linguistic universal with clear grammatical and gestural manifestations. In grammar, a range of verbal particles and affixes explicitly
express negation; they operate on the polarity of an utterance, and they impose
positional constraints on syntax through negative node, scope, and focus – this
understanding has been established for decades through various strands of
linguistic, psycholinguistic, and logical–philosophical research (Horn 1989).
Meanwhile in gesture, the head shake is a famous expression of negation

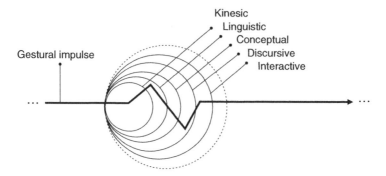

Figure 1.1 The impulse to gesture

(partly because of its notorious cultural variations; Harrison 2013). People are also aware of an array of manual gestures associated with negation that appear to block, wipe away, or push against imaginary objects – and some of these have received scholarly attention since antiquity (Kendon 2004). By exploring the connection between grammatical and gestural manifestations of negation at the micro-level of utterances in face-to-face conversation, a novel understanding of the impulse to gesture emerges.

A decade of research into these connections in natural spoken language interaction shows that our impulse to gesture is constrained by kinesic, linguistic, conceptual, discursive, and interactive structures (Figure 1.1).

These different layers of structure are inseparable within any one instance of gestural impulse. But they offer unique analytical angles to address gestures qualitatively and therefore constitute the sequentiality of chapters in this book. Furthermore, the identification of constraints in gesture through increasingly broad levels of structure stems from a methodological procedure for qualitative bottom-up gesture analysis developed within the *Towards a Grammar of Gesture* framework (henceforth 'ToGoG'; Müller, Bressem, and Ladewig 2013). The research underpinning this book was crucially shaped through a series of ToGoG workshops and conference panels, and my main methodology for gesture description and analysis draws from ToGoG's *Linguistic Annotation System for Gestures* (Bressem et al. 2013). For ToGoG, gesture analysis is a 'procedure of discovery' where each level of form description provides an empirical basis for the analysis of meaning. This book takes stock of my own discovery of the impulse to gesture through its connection to negation in speech.

In this introduction, I will begin by describing the origin of the project and its centrality to the cognitive linguistics framework. Then I will situate the work within the context of contemporary gesture studies and contextualise the approach I have adopted theoretically and methodologically, focusing on a particular type of gesture form and function. Next I will introduce the spoken language corpora that serve as the primary data source for this exploration and explain the software I have used to analyse them (ELAN annotation software). Finally, I will offer a synopsis of each chapter to help readers navigate the book.

1.2   *Grammar in Motion* and the Grammar–Gesture Nexus

The research underpinning this book began in the countryside surrounding Bordeaux, France with a project in applied cognitive linguistics called *Grammar in Motion* (Lapaire 2005; see also Lapaire 2013, 2016). Contracted by Hachette Education and collaborating with a choreographer, Jean-Rémi Lapaire designed and filmed a series of gestural sequences designed to help English language teachers in France explain how English grammar works. Lapaire's gesture creation and choreography were based on embodied approaches to grammar within the field of cognitive linguistics.

In cognitive linguistics, researchers analysing evidence from linguistic usage patterns have found that seemingly 'abstract' or 'semantically empty' grammatical markers, processes, and structures actually encode rich and dynamic patterns of conceptualisation (Langacker 1987, 1991a, 1991b, 2008; Lapaire 2007). For Langacker (1991a), grammatical structures are not empty but meaningful and 'inherently symbolic, providing for the structuring and conventional symbolization of conceptual content' (p. 1). The patterns of conceptualisation reflected in grammar shed light on embodied reasoning and schematic structures derived from experience and body-based interaction in the world (Heine 1997; Lakoff and Johnson 1999). Bodily interaction with space, time, matter, and other bodies gives rise to conceptual metaphors (Lakoff and Johnson 1980), image schemas (Beate 2005; Johnson 1987; Lakoff and Johnson 1999), mappings (Fauconnier 1997), blends (Fauconnier and Turner 2000), and other body-based conceptualisation structures (Heine 1997), all of which are consequently structured and symbolised by grammar.

In *Grammar in Motion*, Lapaire (2005) examined the body-based conceptualisation patterns underpinning well-researched areas of English grammar to elaborate a theory of *Kinegrams*. According to Lapaire (2007), Kinegrams (from *kinesis* and *gram*) are 'postural and gestural analogues of core grammatical phenomena', created based on image-schematic, metaphoric, and conceptual blending analyses of grammatical meaning and processes (p. 7). The Kinegrams created for the *Grammar in Motion* project therefore visualise or '"act out" the semantic configurations and pragmatic mechanisms typically associated with selected grams or constructions' (ibid.). For example, addressing the English modal verbs Lapaire (2007) wrote:

In the kinegrammatic performance that accompanies remarks on the socio-cognitive properties of deontic *must*, one of the manipulator's hands is shown pressing on the manipulee's back to obtain forced motion towards the target action. Likewise, the weaker force-dynamic but stronger directional properties of deontic *should* in *You should behave yourself* or *You should see a doctor* become more apparent as the manipulator is shown exerting lighter pressure on the manipulee's back with one hand, while 'showing the right way' with the other to indicate 'the appropriate course of action'. (p. 23)

Kinegrams such as those for the modal verbs establish an important theoretical link between grammar and gesture. For me, they opened a space for empirical investigation into real-time dynamic connections between grammar and gesture in spoken language discourse and interaction.

The existence of a 'grammar–gesture nexus' – a systematic binding of grammatical and gestural form – challenges a mainstream view that gestures are primarily spontaneous, unwitting, and idiosyncratic manifestations of thought (McNeill 1992, 2005, 2012, 2016). In McNeill's (1992) original 'speech-gesture nexus' (p. 9), the temporal and semantic coordination between speech and gesture in spoken language discourse has nothing to do with grammar but instead reflects a psychological 'growth point'. This growth point is 'the initial unit of thinking for speaking out of which a dynamic process of organisation emerges' (McNeill 2005: 17). Within the growth point, a 'real-time dialectic' occurs between static and dynamic modes of thought. The static mode of thought consequently manifests itself through conventional, linear, syntactic structures in speech – grammar – while the dynamic mode of thought manifests itself through imagery – gestures. Gestures are thus spontaneous creations based on unfiltered conceptual content, diametrically opposed to the 'static structures' or 'chunks' of linguistic structure (McNeill 2016) provided conventionally by grammar.

In the grammar–gesture nexus, 'grammar' is not a set of disembodied static structures. Grammar is a symbolic resource for speakers to shape and share embodied conceptualisation. Grammatical patterns construe thought patterns (Langacker 1987, 1991a, 1991b), and those thought patterns also motivate the gesture forms and functions that accompany speech. Grammar in the grammar–gesture nexus thus has salient symbolic and functional dimensions, both of which connect explicitly with gesture symbolism and function. By shaping and sharing conceptual content in particular ways, speakers 'use' grammar to achieve a range of functions. Speakers use grammar to hypothesise (conditionality), to request (question marking), to affirm (assertion), and to reject, oppose, and deny (negation). Following Givón (1993), from this perspective grammar is both a symbolic resource and 'a set of strategies that one employs in order to produce coherent communication' (p. 1). In focusing on the embodied, symbolic, and functional dimensions of grammar, similarities between grammar and gesture begin to emerge.

First, both grammar and gesture are embodied. Gesture is embodied not only in the literal sense that gesture involves the body, but also because the hands are an evolutionary source of embodied conceptualisation (Streeck 2009). As Streeck (2009) notes, 'no part of our body (except the eyes) is as important as the hand in providing us knowledge of the world' (p. 4). The hands are thus a central tool for distributing and extending human cognition (Hutchins 1995). As we interact manually with our world, for example, 'fingers capable of grasping objects sort and categorise stimuli' through peripheral neuron systems (Wilson and Folia 2017; cf. Pruszynski and Johansson 2014). Second, both grammar and gesture are symbolic structures that speakers deploy for coherent communication. McNeill (1992) notes that 'gesture is a symbol in that it represents something other than itself' (p. 20). Like grammatical symbolism, gestural symbolism also involves the pairing of physical form with conceptualisation. Langacker (2008) explicitly includes '[u]nder the rubric phonological structure … not only sounds but also gestures' (p. 29), consequently speculating elsewhere 'whether such gesture should itself be considered linguistic in nature, that is, an inherent aspect of language structure' (p. 249). Third, both grammar and gesture have a salient functional dimension. Speakers also 'use' gestures to achieve an array of communicative functions. As Kendon (2004) observes, people may show 'through visible bodily actions, that they are asking a question, making a plea, proposing an hypothesis, doubting the word of another, denying something or indicating agreement about it' (p. 1).

By investigating these connections between grammar and gesture, this book describes the kinesic, linguistic, conceptual, discursive, and interactive structures that shape our impulse to gesture in interaction. The focus shifts from the raw cognitive–psychological side of gestural impulses to the systematic forms, organisation patterns, and functions that gestures exhibit in co-occurrence with core grammatical concepts structuring speech.

1.3 Gesture Form, Organisation, and Function

Gesture form refers to a salient kinesic feature of gestures: what they look like and how we can describe their appearance. Looking at a gesturing hand, gesture form can be described as the simultaneous combination of at least four form features. Every gesture has a handshape, a palm orientation, and a location in space; and most have a movement pattern (Bressem 2013). The result of this combination is perceived holistically as 'a gesture form' and is only broken down for initial analytical purposes. This rudimentary level of gesture form can also be described in terms of form dimensions (Hassemer 2015) or egocentrically, that is, from the perspective of physiological mechanism (Boutet 2010).

Gesture organisation refers to the temporal unfolding of gestures. Every gesture exhibits a basic temporal sequence akin to a beginning, middle, and end. More technically, phases of gestural action include a preparation phase, a stroke phase, various hold phases, and a retraction phase (Kendon 1980, 2004). The preparation phase occurs at the beginning of gesture performance when the speaker's hands are initially mobilised to perform a gesture. This initial movement often begins from a position of rest or 'home position' into a visible space immediately in front of the speaker's body (Sacks and Schegloff 2002). Then, the stroke phase is characterised by clear and visible form features; movements are part of the gesture's form as opposed to being a means to situate the gesture in a particular location; and the stroke is generally accepted as the moment when a gesture's meaning is expressed and its functions are achieved (Kendon 2004). Hold phases are moments where a phase of gestural action is momentarily interrupted or paused – the hands are still but tense. The retraction phase occurs as the hands return to their position of rest. Together, these phases coordinate the unfolding of any particular gesture and orchestrate its momentum in relation to speech. Though the stroke is often seen as carrying the gesture's meaning, all phases are potentially meaningful and provide speakers with interactive resources in face-to-face communication (see, for example, Cibulka 2015).

Gesture forms and organisation patterns allow speakers to achieve an array of different functions through gesturing while speaking. To report a sample of well-understood functions, gestures have been shown to add informational content to utterances (Beattie and Shovelton 1999), assist speakers in lexical retrieval and other production processes (Hadar 1989), guide intrapersonal thinking processes (Goldin-Meadow 2003), convey source domains of conceptual metaphors (Cienki and Müller 2008; Sweetser 1998), replace words (Kendon 1988; McNeill 1992), mark up discourse structures, such as topic–comment (Kendon 1995, 2004), connect speech to material structures in the local environment (Goodwin 2007), create cohesion over stretches of discourse (Chui 2009; McNeill 1992), manage the interaction and distribution of turns (Bavelas et al. 1992), and contribute to speech act performance (Kendon 2004; Müller 2004; Streeck 2009). While recent handbooks serve testimony to this diversity of gesture functions (Müller et al. 2013b, 2014), Kendon's (2004) distinction between the referential and pragmatic functions of gesture is most relevant here.

Kendon (2004) observed that gesture functions could broadly be categorised into referential and pragmatic functions. When a gesture nuances, enhances, elaborates on, illustrates, depicts, or otherwise represents aspects of the co-occurring speech, gestures function 'referentially'. In such cases, these are 'gestures that are part of the referential content of their respective utterances' (p. 158). When a gesture frames, presents, interprets, and structures aspects of the co-occurring speech, often in relation to the broader interaction, then gestures function 'pragmatically'. Gestures that function pragmatically are 'gestures that indicate something about the speaker's attitude to the referential meaning or that contribute to the interpretive framework in terms of which this meaning should be treated' (ibid.). Kendon (2004) observed that gestures with pragmatic functions 'serve to indicate the type of "act" or "move" the speaker is engaged in, how the speaker regards the utterance, or how the discourse is to be structured' (p. 359).

Speech act performance, modality, and discourse structure emerge as functional dimensions shared by both grammar and gesture. Symbolic structures in grammar can be identified that speakers use to perform speech acts, adopt stance, and structure discourse; and likewise, symbolic structures in gesture have been identified that achieve those functions by shaping and sharing conceptual content in particular ways in the gestural modality. It is those structures within the gestural modality that I referred to earlier as 'recognisable gesture forms'. Gestures that achieve pragmatic functions are recognisable because they have undergone conventionalisation. As Kendon (2004) explains:

If so-called 'pragmatic' gestures appear conventionalised, this perhaps is not very surprising. Whereas what may comprise the substantive content of any utterance is without limits, and whereas how aspects of this content may be expressed gesturally may be a highly variable matter, the kinds of speech acts that there are, the types of organisational structures in turn-taking, and the ways in which discourse may be structured are much more limited. If any aspect of conversational gesture is to become stylised, we might expect those aspects that function pragmatically would become stylised first. (p. 282)

Gesture forms and functions thus range from spontaneous and idiosyncratic (i.e. 'improvised'; Streeck 2009) to routine and conventionalised. Based on grammatical analysis, Langacker (1987) has argued that '[l]anguage is a mixture of regularity and idiosyncrasy' (p. 411). The co-existence of referential and pragmatic functions in gesture suggests that the mix observed for grammar is also characteristic of gesture. Within a grammar–gesture nexus, it is not that grammar is the regular dimension and gestures are the idiosyncratic dimension of language. Symbolic structures in *both* grammar and gesture exhibit a continuum between regularity and idiosyncrasy depending on their function in spoken discourse. While idiosyncrasy has primarily been studied through the imagistic function of gestures, the regularity of gesture has been explored, identified and documented most saliently in studies of 'recurrent gestures' (Ladewig 2011, 2014b) and 'gesture families' (Kendon 2004).

1.4 Recurrent Gestures and Gesture Families

Recurrency is a major feature of the impulse to gesture and thus a central theme of this book. Generally speaking, recurrency characterises the impulse to

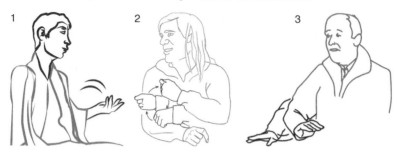

Figure 1.2 Examples of recurrent gestures: 'Palm Presenting' [1], 'Cyclic' [2], and 'Horizontal Palm' [3]

gesture because gestures continuously occur whenever people speak. Gestures have been observed to occur across speakers, contexts, languages, and cultures. More specifically, recurrency is a dimension of gesture form and function that leads to the repeated performance of similar gestures to achieve similar functions by different speakers in different contexts.

Any stream of gestures that accompanies speech will be populated with 'recurrent gestures' (Ladewig 2011, 2014b). Ladewig (2014b) defined the 'recurrent gesture' as a 'stable form-meaning unit [that] recurs in different contexts of use over different speakers in a particular speech community' (pp. 1559–60). The stability of recurrent gestures arises in the conventional pairing of a 'formational core' with a 'semantic core' that also often corresponds to a discursive function. Repertoires of recurrent gestures may be identified for a given linguistic community, such as German (Bressem and Müller 2014b) and French (Calbris 1990). The formational core of a recurrent gesture can be described as a relatively fixed combination of gesture form features, and the semantic core can be described as the associated meaning or function that the combination conventionally encodes and achieves.

Several recurrent gestures are now well documented in the gesture studies literature (Figure 1.2). Examples include the 'Palm Up Open Hand' or 'Palm Presenting' gesture ([1]); the 'Brushing Aside' gesture; the 'Cyclic' gesture ([2]); and the 'Horizontal Palm' gesture ([3]). To describe them briefly, the Palm Up Open Hand or Palm Presenting gesture connects with speech acts of offering, presenting, and suggesting, and at the level of discourse the gesture can mark the introduction of a new topic (Kendon 2004; Müller 2004). The Brushing Aside gesture has been observed among German and Spanish speakers to connect with rejections (Bressem and Müller 2014b; Teßendorf 2014). The Cyclic gesture can represent ongoing activity referentially but also extends metaphorically to connect with elicitations, requests, and turn-holding (Ladewig 2011, 2014a).

Finally, the Horizontal Palm gesture is a recurrent gesture associated with negation and may indicate the speaker's refusal (Calbris 2003; Harrison 2010; Kendon 2004).

Studies of recurrent gestures present an array of conventionalised symbolic structures in the gestural modality that occur repeatedly, that is, they recur in spoken language discourse data. Recurrent gestures were absent from the widely adopted 'Kendon's continuum' – a continuum used to distinguish between various gesture types developed by McNeill (1992) and credited to research conducted by Kendon (1988). However, researchers have since inserted recurrent gestures between gesticulation and emblems (Cienki 2012; Ladewig 2014a). Any one stretch of spoken language discourse will be populated by such recognisable gesture forms, and they are contrasted with more idiosyncratic forms of gestural expression that may be termed 'singular gestures' (Müller 2010). Following Müller (2010), Ladewig (2014b: 1559) describes the distinction as follows:

Singular gestures have been described as spontaneous creations, which are used co-expressively with a certain speech segment and, as such, are part of the propositional content of an utterance. Recurrent gestures often fulfil performative functions, act upon speech, and form a repertoire of gestures that is shared within a culture.

Recurrent gestures thus comprise a formational and semantic core. This core is typically based on or derived from schematised re-enactments of everyday manual actions (Calbris 1990, 2011; Kendon 2004; Ladewig 2014b; Morris 2002; Müller 2004; Müller et al. 2013a; Streeck 2009). As Bressem et al. (2013) write: 'Gestures often constitute re-enactments of basic mundane actions, grounding the gestures' communicative actions in real world actions' (p. 1106; McNeill's 2016 critique of this view is addressed in Chapter 7). In addition to the formational core, recurrent gestures tend to exhibit a number of form-variants. The precise performance of a recurrent gesture may vary depending on context and lead to utterance-specific or 'local' meanings (Kendon 2004). Form variants arise usually from variations in form parameters other than those that constitute the core, especially movement pattern and location. Form-variants are determined by context and lead to subtle semantic variations for each gesture in interaction with specific utterances (Kendon 2004; Calbris 2003, 2011; Ladewig 2014b).

A recurrent gesture and its form-variants together constitute what Kendon (2004) has called a 'gesture family'. According to Kendon (2004), gesture families are:

groupings of gestural expressions that have in common one or more kinesic or formational characteristics ... [W]ithin each family, the different forms that may be recognised in most cases are distinguished in terms of the different movement patterns that are employed ... [E]ach family not only shares in a distinct set of kinesic features but each is also distinct in its semantic themes. The forms within these families, distinguished as they are kinesically, also tend to differ semantically although, within a given family, all forms share in a common semantic theme. (p. 227)

Gesture families are thus collections of form variants centred around a formational core. A gesture family structures and symbolises meaning conventionally in connection with a salient domain of speech act performance, modality, and discourse structure. The focus in this book is a particular gesture family associated with negation.

1.5   Negation and the Open Hand Prone Gesture Family

Recurrent gestures associated with negation were previously described in Kendon's (2004) context-of-use studies of gestures with 'pragmatic' functions. Kendon (2004) studied gestures of the Open Hand and first identified two gesture families: Open Hand Supine and Open Hand Prone gestures. In the Open Hand Supine gesture family, the hand is open and the wrist is supine so that the palm is facing upwards. Gestures in the Open Hand Supine family were found to occur in contexts where the speaker was presenting, offering, or suggesting ideas (Müller 2004). Gestures associated with negation, however, were described as part of the Open Hand Prone family.

In the Open Hand Prone family, according to Kendon (2004) 'the forearm is always in a prone position so that the palm of the hand faces either toward the ground or away from the speaker, depending upon how the elbow is bent' (p. 248). Gestures where the palm of the hand faces towards the ground were called 'Horizontal Palm' or 'ZP' gestures, and these also involved an abrupt horizontal movement along the lateral axis. ZP gestures are apparently derived from the act of knocking something aside with the hand or using the open hand to cut through (Calbris 2003). Open Hand Prone gestures where the palm of the hand faces away from the speaker were called 'Vertical Palm' or 'VP' gestures. With VP gestures, the hand re-enacts a stopping action. When analysing the contribution of Open Hand Prone gestures to the utterances they were part of, Kendon (2004) found that the gestures applied a 'semantic theme of stopping or interrupting a line of action that is in progress' (pp. 248–9). He found all gestures in this family to be performed 'in contexts where something is being denied, negated, interrupted or stopped, whether explicitly or by implication' (p. 248). Kendon (2004) thus established a connection between Open Hand Prone gestures and negation in terms of context-of-use.

Gestures in the Open Hand Prone family have also been described by other gesture researchers. Connections between Open Hand Prone gestures and the expression of negation have now been observed from semiotic (Calbris 1990,

2005, 2011), praxeological (Streeck 2009), and conceptual perspectives (Bressem and Müller 2014a; Calbris 2003; Harrison 2009a).

1.6 Corpus of Spoken Language Interactions

The primary corpus for research in this book contains conversations between Anglophones collected with their permission between 2007 and 2008 in both laboratory-like and natural settings. For the laboratory-like data, I invited pairs of speakers living in Bordeaux whose first language was English into a comfortable apartment setting to take part in a study. The participants were aged between twenty-three and thirty from North America, Canada, Ireland, and England. They included men and women, and in all but one case, the pairs knew each other prior to arriving at the apartment.

To stimulate conversation, each pair was asked to play a board game called *Half-Minute Topics*. The game required participants to take turns throwing a dice, then accordingly move a counter along a winding path of squares on the board. Each square contained a topic of conversation and the pair was instructed that upon landing in a given square, whoever threw the dice had to strike up a conversation with their partner based on that square's topic. I took this game from an English Language Teaching resource pack for a lesson aimed at teaching aspects of English grammar, in particular negation and conditionals. Some of the topics had therefore been designed specifically to elicit negative speech acts. For example, a number of topics required participants to engage in discussions about unpleasant topics, such as boring household chores, annoying habits, and general dislikes.

Although the pairs sometimes began this task with an artificial conversation opener (e.g. 'OK, your turn, tell me about … '), the stimulus quickly led to spontaneous conversations about a multitude of topics that extended beyond those prescribed by the board game. When often the pairs digressed, I made no attempt to restrain conversations or to re-direct attention back to the game, and I allowed participants to converse for as long as they wanted. When they finished playing, I also asked the pairs to discuss whether they thought the game they had played would be suitable for English Language Teaching (a number of participants where also part-time English teachers). The goal of this add-on session was to collect a further 20 to 30 minutes of spoken interaction data from each pair. The participants agreed to take part in the research, but the design of the game and the focus of the study were not discussed. The overall amount of data collected in this laboratory-like setting comprised approximately four and a half hours of conversation between five pairs of English speakers (the interactions typically lasted between 45 and 60 minutes).

Added to this experimental data are recordings from various speakers collected in a diverse array of settings:

- natural interactions in English during summer 2007 on and around a campsite in southwest France, particular of one surfer in his late twenties interacting with friends at the campsite bar (approximately two hours);
- stories I recorded of an English man in his mid-sixties, whilst he cooked in his kitchen at home or on camping holidays (approximately four hours);
- two group discussions in English among students at the coffee shop of a British university campus in China (approximately two hours).

This 12-hour plus corpus of conversations in spoken English provides the primary basis for Chapters 2, 3, 4, and 5 of this book, each of which investigates a particular dimension of the impulse to gesture among English speakers. Chapters 6 and 7 continue to investigate the impulse to gesture but extend the study to include episodes of interaction in French, Chinese, and French Sign Language. Accordingly, those chapters are based on an additional three hours of recording:

- an informal business meeting in French between myself and a colleague in France as we prepared for a project in industry (approximately 90 minutes);
- an episode of interaction between lifeguards on a beach in southwest France (five minutes, extracted from author's larger corpus of workplace interactions);
- an episode of interaction between a new home-owner and her builder in a newly constructed tower of apartments in China (approximately 30 minutes);
- a French sign language class (one hour).

In all cases, I avoided rearranging or disturbing the subjects requested permission, and followed Kendon (2004) in aiming for recordings of 'ordinary settings of people talking together, in most cases while they were in pursuit of their own purposes' (p. 365). Recordings were all made with a camera on a tripod or hand held. The total data set of spoken interaction is therefore in the region of 15 hours and includes interactions between over thirty-five speakers. Added to this, I conducted two retrospective interviews with participants from the corpus and two focus groups about negation with undergraduate students at a university in China – these are reported in Chapter 8. Finally, Chapter 2 and 3 both include one example taken from video-recorded lectures publically available on YouTube.

1.7   Identifying the Grammar–Gesture Nexus

The goal of this book is to characterise the impulse to gesture through specific bindings of grammatical and gestural form that occur when English speakers conceptualise and express negation. In this grammar–gesture nexus, the speech involves utterances structured explicitly by linguistic negation including a grammatical particle like NO, NOT, and NOTHING, as well as syntactic processes such as negative node, scope, and focus (Horn 1989). The gestures involve a subset of recurrent forms belonging to the Open Hand Prone gesture family described by Kendon (2004) that have been observed in connection with negation in a number of empirical studies (Bressem and Müller 2014a; Calbris 1990, 2003, 2005, 2011; Harrison 2009b, 2010, 2015; Kendon 2004; Streeck 2009). This specific grammar–gesture nexus is key to understanding the kinesic, linguistic, cognitive, and discursive structures that shape the impulse to gesture in spoken language interaction.

To identify utterances structured by linguistic negation, I followed what Horn (1989) describes as 'the traditional criteria for negativity – the presence of a negative particle, its appearance in a specified syntactic location, and so forth' (p. 34). As Huddleston and Pullum (2005) write, negation in English is 'marked by individual words (such as *no, not, never*) or by affixes within a word (such as *-n't, un-, non-*)' (p. 149; original emphasis). I initially ignored cognitively more complex types of negation such as implicit or inherent negation (Leech and Svartvik 1994), however, they will be discussed where relevant; as will linguistic phenomena such as multiple negation and Negative Polarity Items (Lawler 2005; Horn and Wansing 2017).

To create a corpus of negative utterances, I viewed the video recordings in ELAN annotation software (www.mpi.com). The graphical user interface of ELAN presents the video feed and options for creating analytical tiers. In a tier I called 'speech', I made annotations for each utterance that contained linguistic negation, effectively compiling a corpus of 'negative utterances'. To then identify gestures associated with negation, I used the video feed to examine all the negative utterances and selected those utterances with which the speaker gestured for further study. Within those utterances, I followed Kendon's (2004) distinction between gestures with referential functions and gestures with pragmatic functions, then set out to identify gesture forms with form properties of gestures in the Open Hand Prone family: both the Vertical Palm and the Horizontal Palm manifestations first identified by Kendon (2004). To illustrate this process, examples (i) through (v) below were initially identified in the corpus as negative utterances co-occurring with gestures:

(i) I don't like getting my nose punched.
(ii) They are not real rocks.
(iii) They don't broadcast it.
(iv) I don't have to pay for that night.
(v) I don't know.

Utterances (i) to (v) all contain grammatical forms of negation and therefore qualified to be in the initial corpus. More specifically here, they each contain the negative particle *not* or its clitic *n't*, and these negative nodes are introduced either by an auxiliary *are* or so-called *do*-support. Syntactically the nodes are

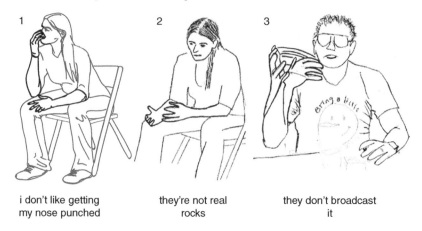

| i don't like getting | they're not real | they don't broadcast |
| my nose punched | rocks | it |

Figure 1.3 Gestures with [1] 'nose', [2] 'rocks', [3] 'broadcast'

located immediately after the grammatical subject, and they project a negative scope over the predicate that follows. Thus in (i) the speaker negates any desire to be punched on the nose when boxing, while in (ii) it is the authenticity of rocks used on an indoor climbing wall that is being negated. The speaker in (iii) negates broadcasting information as a metaphor for talking publicly about private information, while the speaker in (iv) negates the obligation to pay a particular night's fees on the campsite. The speaker in (v) negates having knowledge on a specific topic, in this case gender equality in France. Regardless of this variation, the grammatical forms and processes in these negative utterances conventionally encode negation and allow the speaker to negate a particular proposition.

Turning to the video feed, the speakers all perform gestures with their negative utterance so all instances were also included in the gesture corpus. However, the kinds of gestures they performed determined whether they would be included for further study into the relationship between gesture and negation. Only examples (iv) and (v) exhibited forms resembling members of the Open Hand Prone family, while examples (i), (ii), and (iii) exhibited forms that varied depending on the referential content of the utterance (Figure 1.3). Thus in example (i), as the speaker negates any desire to be punched on the nose when boxing, she brings her right hand up to her face and with an open hand makes contact with her nose [1]. The speaker's gesture can be understood as connecting with the concept of nose expressed in speech, perhaps referring to her own nose. Importantly though, the gesture form does not refer to the linguistic negation in any way. Likewise in example (ii), as the speaker says 'They are not real rocks' she moves her open hands into the gesture space

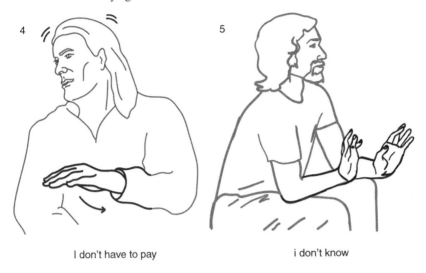

I don't have to pay   i don't know

Figure 1.4 Gestures that connect to [4] 'don't' and [5] 'don't'

cupped with the palms facing upward, as if to enact holding a rock [2]. In example (iii), as the speaker says 'They don't broadcast it' (using 'broadcast' metaphorically to mean 'talk about'), he raises an open hand with the fingers extended into his upper right gesture space, and with the palm lateral, moves this hand away from his body twice [3].

Examples (i) to (iii) illustrate ways the gesture forms connect to the variable content of the negative utterances and the difference in gesture forms reflect that variability. However, in example (iv), as the speaker says 'don't', he moves an open hand turned palm down abruptly along the horizontal axis (Figure 1.4 [4]). This gesture is recognisable as the 'Horizontal Palm' observed in the Open Hand Prone family to occur in contexts where negation is being expressed (Kendon 2004); it co-occurs specifically with the node of negation (Harrison 2010) and researchers agree that the Horizontal Palm encodes negation via an underlying action of cutting or sweeping aside (Calbris 2003; Kendon 2004). When the speaker in example (v) says 'I don't know', he raises both hands with open palms vertical into the gesture space and holds them there for the entirety of his utterance (Figure 1.4[5]). This gesture is recognisable as the 'Vertical Palm' gesture, also observed in the Open Hand Prone family to occur in contexts where negation is being expressed (Kendon 2004). The Vertical Palm also co-occurs specifically with the negative node (Harrison 2014b) and likewise can be related semantically to negation via an underlying action of blocking, stopping, or holding away (Bressem and Müller 2014a; Calbris 2011; Kendon 2004).

These five examples capture the broad distinction between the referential and pragmatic functions of gestures and they exemplify gestures in the Open Hand Prone family. Examples (i) to (iii) illustrate how the form of gestures that connect to referential content of the negative utterances varies depending on the nature of the object being negated. Examples (iv) and (v) illustrate the horizontal and vertical variants of Open Hand Prone forms that gestures exhibit when they connect to the negation in the utterance. Gestures connecting to the referential content of the utterances can be said to reflect the spontaneous, unwitting, and idiosyncratic side of the impulse to gesture, with each form potentially reflecting the speaker's individual experience, viewpoint, and understanding. Gestures explicitly connecting to negation, on the other hand, exhibit recognisable forms that are coordinated temporally with the negative particle. They capture the systematic and constrained side of the impulse to gesture, and they constitute a basis for analysing the grammar–gesture nexus.

1.8   Methods of Gesture Analysis

The over-arching research methodology and paradigmatic stance towards gestures throughout this book stems from a 'form-based view' or 'linguistic approach' to gestures (Bressem 2013; Bressem et al. 2013; Müller et al. 2013a). A number of research content and practical considerations will be offered to introduce this approach.

The underlying approach to gestures adopted here can be considered 'form-based' because it 'gives [gesture] form a prominent role in the process of description and analysis' (Bressem et al. 2013: 1100). The description and analysis of each gesture associated with negation began with an in-depth description of the gesture form along with an interpretation of the kinds of meanings the form could produce (i.e. bottom-up). Although the presence of grammatical negation in the co-occurring speech was a key criterion to identify utterances for the grammar–gesture corpus, the details of this verbal context were then not taken into account during the first critical stages of gesture analysis. The initial focus of gesture analysis was the form features, organisational structures, and possible semantic derivations of the gesture as a meaningful action.

To describe gesture form, organisation, and derivation, I adopted Bressem et al.'s (2013) *Linguistic Annotation System for Gestures* which proposes a sequence of steps to take when analysing gestures:

The structure of the *Linguistic Annotation System for Gestures* is determined by the focus of form aspects of gestures. It first provides for the description and motivation of gestural forms (modes of representation, image schemas, motor patterns, and actions). Afterwards it addresses gestures in relation to speech on a range of levels of linguistic description for speech, that is prosody, syntax, semantics, and pragmatics. (p. 1101)

The first stage of description of gesture form focuses on the four salient parameters: Handshape, Orientation, Position, Movement type (Bressem 2013). Recall that gestures in the grammar–gesture nexus corpus were initially selected because of their potential family resemblance to gestures in the Open Hand Prone family (Kendon 2004). Carrying out a form feature analysis served to verify the formational core of each gesture in the corpus and identify and describe variations in form along the different parameters. Based on that analysis, a more detailed understanding of the formational core was possible and a number of gestural variations were identified for both vertical and horizontal manifestations of the gesture.

Each variation was then examined with the goal of discerning the motivation of the gesture forms. The *Linguistic Annotation System for Gestures* takes into account the mode of representation, underlying action, and salient image schema. Examining the mode of representation involves asking what kind of action are the hands engaged in when they gesture and offers insight to potential meanings of the gesture. Müller et al. (2013a) proposed four modes of representation – 'the hand *acts*, the hand *molds*, the hand *draws* (or *traces*), and the hand *represents*' (p. 712). Identifying the mode of representation leads naturally to proposing an underlying action. While moulding, drawing, and representing can constitute underlying actions, when the hand 'acts', further speculation is required about what kind of action the gesture seems to be performing.

The fine-grained description and analysis of the gesture form provided by this approach results in a vocabulary for talking about the gestures in non-semantic terms regardless of the verbal utterance they are part of. An empirical basis is thus provided to consider the gesture as a communicative action itself rather than a mode of expression dependent on speech (Müller 2013). Within the form-based approach, this empirical basis is a prerequisite to then analyse how the form interacts in specific instances or 'locally' as an integral part of speech, which depending on the research questions can focus on the level of prosody, syntax, semantics, and pragmatics (Bressem et al. 2013). As Bressem et al. (2013) state, with this method 'a gesture's meaning is determined in a (widely) context-free analysis of its form, which grounds the later context-sensitive analysis of gestures' (p. 1100). This grounding process is highly qualitative with the initial categories developed during context-free analysis then reiteratively pursued, evaluated, and revised in order to find a 'goodness of fit' with the contextualised data (Dörnyei 2007).

1.9   Road Map

The sequentiality of the chapters in this book is guided by the logic of the ToGoG form-based or linguistic approach to gesture (Müller et al. 2013a). Generally speaking, the chapters move from the micro-level of identifying and describing recurrent patterns at the utterance level (Chapter 2), to issues of linguistic organisation (Chapter 3), conceptualisation (Chapter 4), discourse cohesion (Chapter 5), discourse coherence (Chapter 6) and interaction (Chapter 7). Each level sheds light on the various principles and constraints that lead to the centrality of recurrent co-occurrences between grammatical form and gesture form to spoken language interaction, allowing the book to end with an Impulse Theory of how, when, and why we gesture (Chapter 8). The different contributions of each chapter may be summarised as follows.

Chapter 1. The Impulse to Gesture: Spontaneous but Constrained. This chapter has introduced the idea of an impulse to gesture and described the genesis of the grammar–gesture nexus in association with the conceptualisation and expression of negation. The chapter narrowed down the focus of gesture studies to a particular subset of gestures called recurrent gestures and gave an overview of previous work on the Open Hand Prone gesture family related to negation. Finally, the corpora used in this research were presented and the methodology was described.

Chapter 2. The Grammar–Gesture Nexus: A Mechanism for Regularity in Gesture. Chapter 2 develops the notion of a grammar–gesture nexus – systematic recurrent bindings between grammatical and gestural form that constitute a mechanism for the regularity we observe in spontaneous co-speech gesture. Three grammar–gesture nexus are identified and presented. They each illustrate the conventional pairing of a negative grammatical form or construction with a variant of the Horizontal Palm gesture. Variations in the gesture form stem from variations in the different manual action they reproduce, which connects to the co-occurring linguistic segment in terms of joint realisation of meaning and/or function. The variants reproduce actions I describe as 'striking aside', 'clearing a space', and 'cutting through' that bind respectively with clausal negations (NOT), exclusions (with the adverbial JUST), and rejections (with negative adjectives and adverbs in the construction *It's X*).

Chapter 3. Sync Points in Speech: Evidence of Grammatical Affiliation for Gesture. Chapter 3 posits the grammar of linguistic concepts as an organisational principle for the impulse to gesture. We illustrate how gestures associated with negation may occur with a range of elements in the utterance, including negative particles and elements in the scope they project, such as Negative Polarity Items and focused elements. Examining how speakers prepare, perform, hold, and retract their gestures in relation to these elements reveals a grammatical affiliation between speech and gesture, with the grammar of negation yielding sync points that constrain the organisation of gesture in relation to speech.

Chapter 4. Gesture as Construal: Blockage, Force, and Distance in Space and Mind. Moving from the mechanics of the grammar–gesture nexus to its cognitive basis, Chapter 4 adopts a cognitive-linguistic perspective on a class of gestures associated with negation and views them as tools for dynamic construal operations with speech. The Vertical Palm gesture may reproduce various embodied actions including blocking, stopping, pushing, throwing, and wiping away. When speakers perform this gesture in conjunction with negative structures and speech acts, they construe their negation in terms of the physical action they reproduce. A conceptual semantic analysis of such multimodal utterances shows how gestures operate on a similar conceptual basis to the negative construals identified by linguists working with speech. Speakers use gesture in physical space to construe negation and their negative speech act as expressions of distance, force, and absence in conceptual space. Furthermore, their construals of space are sensitive to the position of their addressee(s) in the real-time interactive space.

Chapter 5. Gesture Sequences: Wrist as Hinge for Shifts in Discourse. Chapter 5 extends the concept of a grammar–gesture nexus from individual bindings at the utterance level to a mechanism for cohesion across linguistic segments at the level of discourse. We focus on a particular sequence of recurrent gestures that speakers use to frame their verbal content and indicate linguistic, logical, and rhetorical links between otherwise separate elements in the co-occurring speech. The basic sequence invariably involves a Palm Up gesture and a Palm Down gesture, specifically the Palm Presenting gesture and the Horizontal or Vertical Palm gesture. In sequencing, the rotation of the wrist(s) between the two gestures is key as it relates to the shift in discourse underway. These discourse shifts may include, for example, a logical consequence or the resolution of a conflict. Palm Up and Palm Down gestures have previously been isolated and opposed, but this study of their sequencing sheds light on a gesture-based construction that operates on co-occurring speech, regardless of its content.

Chapter 6. Patterns of Gesturing: The Business of 'Horizontal Palming'. Taking an entire interaction as the analytical unit now, Chapter 6 examines the impact of genre, style, and identity on the impulse to gesture. Maintaining a focus on gestures associated with negation but shifting language to French, we scrutinise one speaker's repeated use of the Horizontal Palm gesture over the course of a 90-minute informal business meeting. Our analysis starts from the micro-kinesic context of individual occurrences of the gestures at the utterance level upwards (and outwards) by considering the increasingly broad semantic, pragmatic, and discursive structures that operate reflexively on the speaker's impulse to gesture. The broader communicative purpose of the interaction, the role the speaker was adopting, and the position of this interaction within a chain of related interactions (inter-textuality) are shown to be essential elements shaping a 'gestural genre' that accounts for the recurrency of gestures associated with negation at the micro-level. The chapter invites us to view recurrency not only as a product that leads to 'recurrent gestures', but also as a dynamic process that results in 'recurrent gesturing'.

Chapter 7. Wiping Away: Embodied Interaction in Speech and Sign. Chapter 7 puts the impulse to gesture within more complex ecological contexts of situated activity in order to examine the embodied actions motivating gestures associated with negation. To do this, we study interactive contexts in which the real-world action of 'wiping away' – using the open palm to remove or eliminate something from a surface – plays a central role in the ongoing interaction. These contexts showcase how such actions acquire communicative properties in interaction, as well as how they connect to the gestures associated with negation that continue to occur with the ongoing speech. These observations provide the basis to then explore the wiping away gesture as a tool for embodied interaction, both in spoken language and in sign language. The relation between action, gesture, and language emerges as inseparable over the course of this chapter.

Chapter 8. Impulse Theory: How, When, and Why We Gesture. The recurrent form-function pairings studied throughout this book raise important questions about the nature of gesture and its relation to linguistic structure in interaction. Chapter 8 presents Impulse Theory to account for how, when, and why, we gesture in this conventional and systematic way. Based on conclusions from the previous chapters, it begins by answering the question of what is the impulse to gesture. This answer involves several key constructs addressed throughout the book – the grammar–gesture nexus, sync points in speech, conventionality, gestural competence, and the action–gesture–grammar link – each of which provides connection points to evaluate how current approaches diverge and converge. Having situated Impulse Theory, we evaluate it with reports of interview and focus groups held with the conversationalists from our corpora. We then extend the theory by illustrating its application to examine other linguistic concepts multi-modally – namely, progressive aspect – before concluding the book with some ongoing challenges for research into the impulse to gesture.

2 The Grammar–Gesture Nexus
A Mechanism for Regularity in Gesture

Language is a mixture of regularity and idiosyncrasy.

—Ronald Langacker (1987: 411)

2.1   Introduction

Langacker's (1987) observation that 'language is a mixture of regularity and idiosyncrasy' (p. 411) is not only a central tenet of his *Foundations of Cognitive Grammar*, but also a statement with profound implications for our understanding of gestures. Gestures are integral components of language (Kendon 2004; Calbris 2011; McNeill 2016), so they should exhibit a mixture of regularity and idiosyncrasy too. We know much more about the spontaneity of gestural expression than about its regularity, yet regularity is key to understanding what determines, shapes, and organises our universal impulse to gesture with speech.

In one of the most influential monographs ever written on gesture, McNeill (1992) defined gestures as 'idiosyncratic spontaneous movements of the hands and arms accompanying speech' (p. 37). This definition has played a central role in the development of our understanding of gesture and led to an emphasis on gestural spontaneity in major fields of cognitive and social-scientific enquiry (including cognitive neuroscience, second language acquisition, and sign language linguistics). The definition is challenged by a straightforward observation though: the form and organisation of gesture is highly systematic. As Kendon (1994) put it, 'people are far more consistent in what they do gesturally than this "idiosyncrasy" claim would lead one to imagine'. Speakers share practices or modes of meaning-making in gesture (Enfield 2009; Streeck 2009; Müller 2014). Families of gestural expressions with similar forms and meanings can be identified (Kendon 2004). Speakers reproduce the same gestures in different contexts (Ladewig 2014). Repertoires of such gestures can be established (Bressem and Müller 2014b). And so on. Evidence that gesture exhibits a mixture of spontaneity and regularity abounds.

What does this mixture tell us about the impulse to gesture? To answer this question, we need to take a close look at when, why, and how people gesture when they speak. Building on the previous chapter, we develop our argument that linguistic constructs in speech cause, determine, and shape the impulse to gesture. We focus on one of the recurrent gestures from the Open Hand Prone gesture family – the 'Horizontal Palm' (Kendon 2004). Speakers perform this gesture in a variety of ways with a variety of meanings (Calbris 2003, 2011). But its performance is often bound to the speaker's expression of negation, structured verbally in English by grammatical forms like *no, not, never* and *none*. This systematic binding of grammatical and gestural form creates what we have called a 'grammar–gesture nexus'. This chapter illustrates how the grammar–gesture nexus are mechanisms for the regularity we observe when people spontaneously gesture.

2.2   The Horizontal Palm Gesture

In his study of gesture families of the Open Hand, Kendon (2004) observed that people commonly use a gesture in which the forearm is prone and the hand is open so that the palm is turned downward and moved rapidly along the horizontal axis, hence he called it the 'Horizontal Palm' (Figure 2.1).

The usage of the Horizontal Palm gesture is widespread in Europe, with observations attested among speakers of French (Calbris 1990, 2003, 2011), Italian (Kendon 1995, 2004), English (Kendon 2004; Harrison 2009b, 2010), Spanish (Prieto et al. 2013), and German (Streeck 2009; Bressem and Müller 2014a, 2014b). Furthermore, the gesture is common between speakers of English from Britain, Ireland, the USA, Canada, and Australia (Harrison 2009b). Examples later in this book attest to the gesture in China.

The Horizontal Palm gesture occurs around the globe for at least three reasons. First, it is related to the expression of negation, which is a linguistic universal (Dahl 1979; Horn 1989). Second, the Horizontal Palm is reportedly derived from a 'basic mundane action' of the hand (Bressem

Figure 2.1 Example illustrations of the 'Horizontal Palm' gesture

et al. 2013), namely sweeping aside (Calbris 2011; Kendon 2004). And third, the gesture is diverse and useful. As a 'polysemous gesture' (Calbris 2011), it expresses a variety of meanings and functions that are central to language and interaction, such as halting a topic (Kendon 2004). Different meanings often lead to variations in the precise articulation of the gesture. These three features – relation to negation, basis in action, and variation in form – provide the starting points to consider mechanisms for regularity in relation to this gesture.

2.2.1 The Horizontal Palm and the Expression of Negation

In defining the expression of negation, grammarians focus on language and argue that negation in English 'is marked by individual words (such as *no, not, never*) or by affixes within a word (such as *·n't, un·, non·*)' (Huddleston and Pullum 2005: 149). Beyond these explicit forms of negation, 'there are certain words which are negative in meaning and behavior although they do not appear negative in form' (Leech and Svartvick 1994: 308). Implicit negation can be expressed with verbs (e.g. *ignore*) nouns (e.g. *divorce*), adjectives (e.g. *false*), and adverbs (e.g. *horribly*). A broad view on negation includes both explicitly negative forms and 'elements of negativity implicit in some meanings and their presuppositions contained in the structures that have no surface linguistic negation at all' (Lewandowska-Tomaszczyk 2006: 379; Horn 1989).

The Horizontal Palm gesture is related to this linguistic expression of negation. First, people often produce the Horizontal Palm gesture when they utter both explicit and implicit verbal expressions of negation (Kendon 2004; Harrison 2009b; Calbris 2011). Second, the gesture has also been observed to occur in discourse contexts where, according to Kendon (2004), the speakers are referring 'to some line of action that is being suspended, interrupted, or cut off' (p. 255). In referring to this suspension, interrupting, or cutting off, speakers use the gestures to convey meanings and achieve discourse functions that are similar to those of negation. Furthermore, Calbris (2011) pin-pointed a specific meaning of the gesture as 'negation-refusal' and explained that 'the absolute character of the negation expressed by this gesture is confirmed by the terms accompanying it: "nothing; no; never; no more"' (p. 180). The gesture has been specifically included in a number of language-specific typologies of gestural forms associated with negation, such as for French speakers (Calbris 2005) and for English speakers (Harrison 2009b).

The Horizontal Palm is related to the expression of negation on linguistic, semantic, and discursive levels, and this relation is salient in cultural repertoires associated with people's communicative practices.

Figure 2.2 A person uses her palm to remove crumbs from the tabletop

2.2.2   *Basis in Everyday Action*

The regularity of the Horizontal Palm gesture stems not only from the contexts in which it is performed and how it relates to linguistic negation, but also from its basis in an everyday action. Bressem et al. (2013) enunciate a widely shared view about gestures when they claim that 'gestures often constitute re-enactments of basic mundane actions, grounding the gestures' communicative actions in real world actions' (p. 1106; Morris 2002; Calbris 1990; Kendon 2004; Streeck 2009). For the Horizontal Palm, Kendon (2004) specified that these gestures 'perhaps derive from the action of cutting something through, knocking something away, or sweeping away irregularities on a surface' (p. 263). This action occurs in the real world when we use our hand shaped in the same way as a Horizontal Palm gesture – open, flat, palm turned down – to remove crumbs off the surface of a table, as I observed the person in Figure 2.2 to do.

Everyday actions like this are available to speakers to reproduce as gestures in face-to-face communication. The embodied experience of sweeping away crumbs provides the basis for a gesture related to the expression of negation. Rather than sweeping away crumbs (or other unwanted objects) off a surface, speakers perform the action as a gesture in the space in front of them to 'sweep away' unwanted elements relating to the symbolic world of language and discourse. If crumbs cause people to sweep their hands off the table, then it is unwanted elements in language and discourse that cause people to perform the action as a Horizontal Palm gesture in interaction. Exactly how they perform the gesture is determined by the grammar of negation and may influence the exact kind of sweeping away action they hope their gesture to achieve.

2.2.3   Variation in Articulation of the Horizontal Palm

People perform the Horizontal Palm in a wide variety of ways. They vary the speed, amplitude, and number of strokes of the gesture's movement. They may perform single or repeated strokes, movements ranging from slow to rapid, and amplitudes restricted to enlarged. The articulation of the gesture also varies in exactitude: from fluffy to crisp, wishy-washy to mechanical. One hand or two hands may be used. Such variations in the Horizontal Palm gesture can always be explained with evidence observable in the surrounding linguistic structures, discourse, and interactive context.

Beyond the richness of individual variation, however, certain differences in how people perform this gesture systematically reflect differences in the corresponding type of negation or negative speech act. Such form-function correspondences are a defining characteristic of recurrent gestures (Ladewig 2014a, 2014b). Precisely how people perform their Horizontal Palm gesture may correspond to variations in the linguistic and discursive context of their utterance.

The kinesic form of three such variants of the Horizontal Palm gesture may be described as follows. The variations occur first of all between whether the speaker uses one hand or two hands to perform the gesture. When the speaker only uses one hand, I will refer to the variant as the 'palm down horizontal across body' variant or the 'PDA' (see Figure 2.1). This variant usually reproduces 'sweeping away'.

When speakers use two hands, the variation lies between where the speaker places her hands at the beginning of the gesture. The arms are either crossed so that both hands are 'across body' (on opposite sides) or the hands are drawn together at the thumbs so as to be at the midline of the body when the gesture begins. The different starting points have consequences for the type and direction of movement. When the hands begin at the midline, they move outward along the horizontal axis. I will refer to this second variant as the 'two palms down horizontal from mid body' variant or the '2PDmid' gesture (Figure 2.3). This variant reproduces 'clearing aside' or 'clearing away'.

When the hands begin their stroke from the across body position, the trajectory of movement is diagonal down. At the beginning of the stroke, the arms are crossed and the palms are facing down. For the stroke, the arms uncross so that the hands move outwards on a diagonally downward trajectory.

Figure 2.3 Examples of 'clearing aside' (2-Palms Down Mid)

Figure 2.4 Examples of 'cutting through' (2-Palms Down Across)

During this movement, the ulna or 'pinkie' edges of the hands converge, before moving away from each other to a greater or lesser extent. I will refer to this variant as the 'two palms down diagonal across body' variant or the '2PDA' (Figure 2.4). Following Morris (1994), this gesture reproduces an action of 'cutting through'.

The 'sweeping away' (Palm Down Across), the 'clearing aside' (2-Palms Down Mid), and the 'cutting through' (2-Palms Down Across) can be viewed as form variants of the Horizontal Palm gesture. They suggest that rather than one action of 'sweeping away', occurrences of the Horizontal Palm gesture may be based on a category of actions involved in the removal, exclusion, and obliteration of unwanted objects.

2.3   Grammar–Gesture Nexus of the Horizontal Palm

Grammar–Gesture Nexus constitute mechanisms for the regularity that we observe when people gesture. They are specific bindings of grammatical and gestural form that occur when speakers use particular types of linguistic negations or perform certain negative speech acts. Three Grammar–Gesture

Nexus illustrate how a linguistic construct determines the way we gesture when we speak. They are based on the different variants of Horizontal Palm gesture in conjunction with a type of negation or negative speech act.

2.3.1 Clausal Negation and 'Sweeping Away' (the Palm Down Across)

When speakers wish to say that something *didn't* happen or *was not* the case, they structure their verbal utterance with a clausal negation. Clausal negations modify the main verb or a related item and result in the clause being negated (Huddleston and Pullum 2005: 152). Examples we will consider include a speaker saying 'I don't have to pay' and 'they don't speak any of the language'. With such utterances, speakers may perform a Horizontal Palm gesture and coordinate it explicitly with the negative form. The negative forms in our examples include the particle 'not' cliticised as 'n't' as well as the particle 'no'. The gestures are all instances of 'sweeping away' – the Palm Down Across variant. Four examples serve to illustrate this mechanism.

The first example illustrates the natural correspondence between clausal negations and the Sweeping Away gesture. A surfer called D is on a campsite explaining to his friend a special deal he has brokered with the campsite owners. D can occupy a spot on the grounds with his belongings but does not have to pay for that pitch unless he sleeps the night in his tent. He explains this as follows: 'I only have to pay for five nights ... these guys are really cool. If I'm not here, I don't have to pay for that night.' He gestures coherently with each one of these utterances (Figure 2.5). As he says 'five nights', he raises a hand towards his addressee with the five fingers spread out [1]. When he says 'these guys', his gesture transforms into a thumb point to a location behind him, possibly towards the reception area where the campsite managers often convene [2]. He now explains the deal and with 'if I'm not here' he locates a 'cupped' hand palm down in the space in front of him to refer to 'here' [3]. With 'I don't have to pay', he performs a Palm Down Across variant of the Horizontal Palm gesture, that is, 'sweeping away' [4].

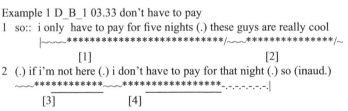

Example 1 D_B_1 03.33 don't have to pay
1 so:: i only have to pay for five nights (.) these guys are really cool
         |~~~~✱✱✱✱✱✱✱✱✱✱✱✱✱✱✱✱✱✱✱✱✱✱✱✱✱✱✱✱✱/~~~✱✱✱✱✱✱✱✱✱✱✱✱✱✱/~
                       [1]   [2]
2 (.) if i'm not here (.) i don't have to pay for that night (.) so (inaud.)
   ~~~✱✱✱✱✱✱✱✱✱✱✱~~~✱✱✱✱✱✱✱✱✱✱✱✱✱✱✱_.-.-.-.-.-.|
        [3]   [4]

[1] All fingers and the thumb are outstretched to represent '5', [2] thumb point to a region behind him, [3] 'cupped' hand palm down in the space in front of him to refer to 'here', [4] Palm Down Across gesture.

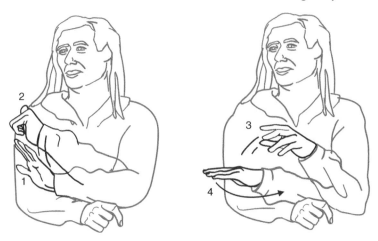

Figure 2.5 'Five' – 'these guys' – 'not here' – 'don't have to pay'

As this speaker explained the deal he had brokered, he performed a number of different gestures. The form of each gesture connected coherently with what he was saying: a 'five' handshape with 'five nights', a 'thumb point' behind him with 'these guys', and so on. The Palm Down Across gesture is coherent to produce with a clausal negation because it reproduces the act of sweeping away, which is consistent with the linguistic function of his clausal negation in speech.

Our second example illustrates the extent of binding between linguistic and gestural form within a grammar–gesture nexus. S has been describing a time when he and his family played the board game *Cluedo*, which involves several players collaborating to solve a murder mystery. S is explaining to his addressee how he cunningly managed to stop his younger brother from winning. The grammar–gesture nexus occurs when he performs the Sweeping Away gesture with the negation 'he couldn't win'. The speaker had first described his strategy (lines 1–3), then introduced the negative outcomes of his plan for his brother. As part of those outcomes, he says 'and so it was a complete waste of time if you follow me' (line 4). He is now pointing to a space in front of him with an index finger extended from a fist turned palm down [1]. As he finishes this utterance, he flattens out his handshape and moves this hand across his body to prepare the Sweeping Away gesture. He then says 'so he couldn't' (line 5) and synchronises the stroke of his gesture specifically with 'couldn't' [2]. He then pauses and repeats 'he couldn't' (Figure 2.6). With this repetition in speech, he also re-prepares and repeats the stroke of his gesture. After a short pause, he utters the rest of his utterance 'he couldn't err win and eventually he got so fed up and despondent'. With this stretch of language he is beating his gesture with salient points in speech. He maintains the gesture hold as he reveals that he and his mother were in hysterics (line 6), then explains how he subsequently dashed across the room to win (line 7) and represents this successful trajectory with a tracing gesture [3]. His addressee N responds at this point with a laugh (line 8).

Example 2 S_N gm 25.31 he couldn't win
1   S and i kept dragging him back into a different room
2   be it the dining room or the ball room
3   knowing that i had that room or that he was going to show me the card
4   and so it was a complete waste of time (.) if you follow me
     /**/~~
                    [1]
5   so he COuldn't (.) he COuldn't err WIn and eVENtually he got so FEd up
     ~~***********~~~_~***
        [2]   [2]   beat   beat   beat
6   and deSPONdent and i was in hysterics and my mother was
     ****
            beat
7   and eventually i just like made a zoom across the room and i think i won
     /~~~~~~~~~~~~~~~~~~~~************_._._._._._._._._._._._._._._._.|
                        [3]
8 N ha

[1] Pointing gesture used to indicate different rooms is held, [2] Palm Down Across, [3] resumes index finger point illustrates a trajectory away from his body.

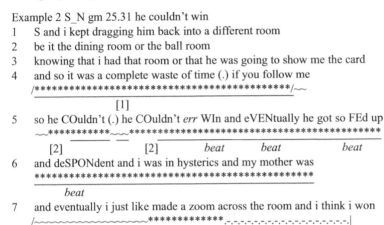

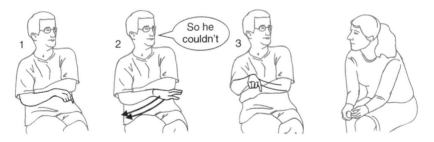

Figure 2.6 A speaker negates his brother's attempt to win at *Cluedo*

So inseparable are the grammatical and gestural forms in this example, that when the speaker repeats his negation, he also repeats his gesture. He may be repeating for emphasis or buying time to formulate the object of his negation. But the stroke of 'sweeping away' is firmly bound to the utterance of the negated modal 'couldn't'. The answer to what determined the form and organisation of his gesture in this example, therefore, is saliently the expression of negation.

A third example now illustrates the mechanics of this grammar–gesture nexus and emphasises one of its interactive functions too. An American student at a British university in China, A, has been asked to clarify 'what is the so-what factor?' of his research project by one of his Chinese peers, B. He explains he is interested in how 'people can live in another country when they don't speak any of the language'. As he says 'people can live in another country' (line 2), he performs a gesture in the direction of his peer [1] in which the palm is open and 'addressed' to his peer (cf. Kendon 2004: 271–3). He then begins to prepare a Sweeping Away gesture with 'when they' [2]. He completes this preparation then pauses in speech for half a second. During this pause, his gesture is cocked in a pre-stroke hold position. As he resumes speech with 'don't speak' he releases the stroke of the gesture [3]. He maintains a post-stroke hold of the gesture as he utters 'any of the language'. He continues this hold over a brief moment of interaction where his addressee agrees 'yeh' and he responds 'right' (lines 3–4). After this episode of interaction, he partially retracts his gesture. He now says 'and I think I'm interested in how people can do that' (line 5). With this utterance he performs a form of inward cyclic gesture that could reflect his ongoing reasoning and indicate a cohesive link back to his first expression of 'interest' in line 1 [4] (Figure 2.7).

Example 3 A3b 19.32 don't speak any language
1 A   well i think it's very really interesting to me because (.)
2   i think people can live in another country (.5)
        |~*********************************
                   [1]
3   when the::y (.5) don't speak any of the language [(.)] right/
        /~~~~~~~~~~*********************************
                [2]   [3]
4 B: [yeh]
5 A: and i think i'm interested in how people can do that
        -.-./~~~~~~*****************************-.-.|
                   [4]

[1] Palm Addressed, [2] prepares Palm Down Across, [3] performs Palm Down Across, [4] form of inward cyclic.

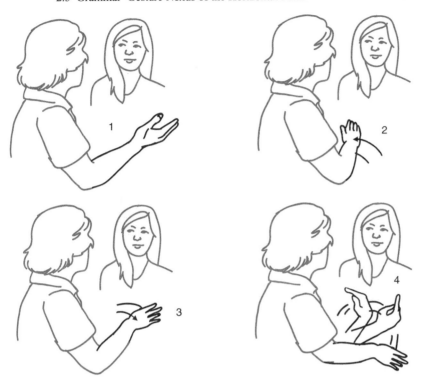

Figure 2.7 Palm Addressed – preparing and sweeping away – inward cyclic gesture

Cocking, releasing, and holding the Palm Down Across gesture stroke are central features of this grammar–gesture nexus. The speaker above knows how he wants to gesture and what he wants to say, but he does not know exactly how he wants to say it. The speaker initially cocks his gesture to foreshadow the clausal negation in his upcoming speech, but momentarily pauses to formulate the clause he intends to negate. The cocked Palm Down gesture is destined for a clausal negation in speech. This is prepared for as early as the subordinating 'when' that introduces his clause. And by maintaining the gesture in space after its performance, he is able to solicit an acknowledgement of his opinion from his addressee.

The next example situates the grammar–gesture nexus within a more elaborate sequence of gestures and illustrates the role it can play in the structure of the speaker's broader narrative. The speaker is describing how as a teenager he broke up with his girlfriend in order to 'put myself out there', which he admits 'was the dumbest thing in the world' (lines 1–2). Developing on why the plan was 'dumb', he performs a Palm Presenting gesture [1] and says 'because every girl in the school knew that I was Sally's man Sally's ex-boyfriend' (lines 3–4). He now utters the dire consequence of his actions: 'so I was like... I was like no-go territory'. As the transcript shows, he begins to prepare a Palm Down Across gesture at the outset of his utterance with the discourse marker 'so'. He is thus bringing his forearm across the body and orienting the palm downward during the first 'I was like', so that when he then pauses for a second and repeats 'I was like', he has a Palm Down gesture cocked in a pre-stroke hold position. As he says 'no-go', he releases the stroke of this gesture across his body and performs a post-stroke hold with 'territory' ([2], line 5). In his following utterance, he develops on why this was a dumb idea, saying 'there was no way that any other girl in that school was gonna go near me' (line 7). With 'no way' he performs a precision grip gesture which involves a hand transition from precision-to-open [3] (cf. Kendon 2004: 241), then with the rest of his conclusion he is performing another Palm Presenting gesture [4] (Figure 2.8).

Example 4 DLC_5 11.55 no go territory
1   D   i should probably just break up with sally and put myself out there
2   which was the dumbest thing in the world
3   because every girl in that school knew that i was sally's man
                                      /**************
                                      ‾‾‾‾‾‾‾‾‾‾‾‾‾
                                            [1]

4   sally's ex-boyfriend
         ****
         ‾‾‾‾‾‾‾‾‾‾‾‾‾‾‾
5   so i was like.. . . .. i was like NO-go territory (.)
         /∼∼∼∼∼∼∼∼∼∼∼∼∼∼∼∼∼∼∼∼**************/
                 ‾‾‾‾‾‾‾‾‾‾‾‾‾   ‾‾‾‾‾‾‾‾‾‾‾‾‾
                        [2]

6 S   yeh
7   (.) there was no way that any other girl in that school was gonna go near me
         ∼∼∼∼∼*******/∼*******************-.-.-.-.-.-.-.-.|
             ‾‾‾‾‾   ‾‾‾‾‾‾‾‾‾‾‾‾‾‾‾‾‾‾‾‾
             [3]   [4]

[1] Palm Presenting gesture, [2] Palm Down Across, [3] precision grip-to-open, [4] Palm Presenting gesture.

Figure 2.8 Palm Presenting – Palm Down Across – precision release – Palm Presenting

The speaker coordinates the stroke of his Palm Down Across gesture meticulously with the negative expression 'no'. According to McNeill (2005), '[a] prestroke hold delays the stroke until a specific linguistic segment is ready to be articulated' (p. 32). However, this speaker is not delaying gesture for speech to catch up; the linguistic material during the hold is not a catch-up but a repeat. He is delaying both speech and gesture to create suspense in the crux of his narrative. It is not that the stroke is delayed – the stroke is cocked, which is as much a mechanism for ensuring co-expressivity of the gesture and the particle as it is a strategy for creating suspense. People attend to gestures to help interpret verbal expressions of negation (Prieto et al. 2013). Cocking the Palm Down Across gesture can indicate that a negation is forthcoming.

Summing up, the binding together of clausal negation and the Palm Down Across gesture illustrates our first grammar–gesture nexus in English spoken discourse. Examples of speakers discussing different topics show how the conditions for the occurrence of this nexus transcend the content of the individuals' speech. The grammar–gesture nexus occurs because of the move that the speaker is making in speech. The coherence between the particular linguistic pattern and the gestural action based on 'sweeping away' is that *both* are motivated by the speaker's goal to remove an unwanted element or implication from the discourse; for example, staying at the campsite *but* not having to pay, playing a game *but* not being able to win, living in a country *but* not speaking a language.

The coherence of binding in the nexus stems from the relation between the linguistic function of the clausal negation and the underlying action reproduced by the gesture, namely negating and sweeping away or striking aside. While the position of the negative particle is pre-determined by the syntax of negation, the release of the gesture stroke is determined by the position of the negative particle. The impulse to gesture is thus constrained by the potentiality of these grammar–gesture nexus in speech, which constitute mechanisms for regularity in spontaneous gesturing.

2.3.2 Exclusions and 'Clearing Aside' (the 2-Palms Down Mid)

Specific bindings or 'nexus' of grammatical and gestural form lead to regularity in a flow of spontaneous gesturing. A second nexus that we can regularly observe when people express negation in everyday spoken discourse provides further support for this view. Speakers describing a preference, a favourite, or a situation they find ideal can use the adverb JUST along with explicit verbal particles of negation. When asked what his favourite food is, for example, one speaker says '*just* sushi, *no* prawns though'. As Horn (1989) writes, 'every description necessarily implies a limitation or exclusion' (p. 41). Speakers use

JUST to explicitly impose that limitation on the state of affairs they are describing. Linguists often paraphrase this function of JUST as a minimiser meaning 'nothing else' or 'only' (cf. Carter and McCarthy 2006). Others argue more broadly that JUST 'indicates the goodness of fit of the modified item, the fact that it does not exceed the limits of its target in any way, shape or form' (Duffley and Larrivée 2012: 38). Negative particles in the same utterance may expand on JUST by using negative particles to specifically exclude elements that jeopardise this goodness of fit, that is, elements whose absence is a condition for the situation to be favourite, ideal, preferred, and so on.

The current nexus occurs when speakers perform a 'two palms down horizontal from mid body' variant of the Horizontal Palm gesture with JUST or the negation particles in the utterance. The variation in form of the gesture indicates a variation in the everyday action that it reproduces. Related to 'sweeping away', the lateral movement of both palms horizontally from the midline is based on the real-world action of 'clearing aside': using the flat palms to clear a space (i.e. to move things out of the way) on the surface in front of you. The coherence between the real-world removal and the exclusion of JUST motivate the occurrence of this grammar–gesture nexus.

Our first example illustrates how the exclusivity of JUST is embodied by the co-occurring Horizontal Palm gesture. A speaker is describing how his 'philosophy' towards sport has changed as he has matured. In the lead up to the segment I have transcribed, the speaker has explained that he 'used to be more competitive' and even occasionally get involved in 'fights', whereas now he likes 'to get serious and competitive but not like get mental'. In line 1, he is developing on this by saying 'no there's no reason for me to ever get like aggressive to anybody or pissed off'. Then he says 'but I prefer, you know, just, a good game' (line 3). As he introduces his preference with 'I prefer', he performs a Palm Presenting gesture [1]. When he then says 'just a good game', he prepares, performs, and holds a 2-Palms Down Mid gesture [2]. Finally, he explicitly excludes cheating from this preference by repeatedly pointing to his chest [3] and saying 'you know I don't wanna cheat myself' (line 7) (Figure 2.9).

Example 5 K_C gm1 06:32 a good game
1 K   no there's no reason for me to ever get like aggressive to anybody or pissed off
2   if someone has a bad attitude that changes the whole game
3   but i prefer you know (.) just (.) a GOod game
         |~*****-| |~**************-|
                                 ‾‾‾‾‾‾‾‾‾‾‾‾‾‾‾
           [1]   [2]
4 C   yeh yeh yeh
7 K   you know i don't wanna cheat myself
        |~*************************-|
                  [3]

[1] Cupped hands palms up, [2] 2PDMid, [3] repeatedly pointing to his own chest.

Figure 2.9 Offering up preference – 2-Palms Down Mid – repeated self point

A closer look at the coordination of gesture and speech in this example helps appreciate the inner workings of a grammar–gesture nexus. The speaker prepares his Horizontal Palm gesture with 'just' then pauses in speech and releases the gesture stroke; this stroke is then held while he utters 'a good game'. By reproducing an action of 'clearing aside', the stroke of the gesture achieves the meaning of JUST that it follows – it expresses exclusion and limitation via an embodied action. The gesture hold then indicates the element to which the exclusivity applies to, namely, 'a good game'. Our ability to identify this sequentiality, however, should not overshadow the simultaneity of the elements in the nexus. By reproducing an action of exclusion, the gesture applies the exclusivity of 'just' to his idea of what constitutes a good game, namely no aggression, no bad attitudes, and no cheating.

The grammar–gesture nexus may also occur in response to unwanted elements added to a description by the addressee. This occurs, for example, when two colleagues are discussing what constitutes their ideal evening. S first describes his ideal evening as involving 'some nice restaurants and some nice wine' (line 1), but then referring to the buskers that frequent his local restaurants, he specifies 'not too many of these people strumming away with their guitars' (line 2), while sarcastically adding 'not too early into the meal' and performing a Vertical Palm gesture off to his side [1]. N responds by paraphrasing 'so for you it would be more of a quiet sort of romantic', then pauses (line 4). Before she can finish her utterance, S says 'well, just a quiet evening' and performs a 2-Palms Down Mid gesture [2] (Figure 2.10).

Example 6 S_N 18.13 just a quiet evening
1 S   some nice restaurants and some nice wine and er
2   not too many of these people strumming away with their guitars
3   and things not not too early into the meal
       |~~~~****************_.|
              [1]
4 N   aha ok (.) so for you it would be more of a quiet sort of romantic (.)
5 S   well, just a quiet evening
       |~~~~~~****************_.|
              [2]
[1] Palm Vertical (with some oscillation), [2] 2-Palms Down Mid.

Figure 2.10 Palm Vertical gesture then 2-Palms Down Mid gesture

In S's uptake of his addressee's description, he specifically excludes the word 'romantic' by using *just* to say 'well just a quiet evening'. N has added an element into S's description that does not fit with his conceptualisation of an ideal evening, so he excludes it with a grammar–gesture nexus. In S's uptake of his addressee's description, he specifically excludes the word 'romantic' by using *just* to say 'well just a quiet evening'. The action of clearing things aside reproduced by the gesture performed concurrently applies to the addressee's unwanted addition to his ideal description. His performance of a Vertical Palm gesture earlier in the utterance was also indicative of his desire to narrow the scope of his evening. In a later chapter, I illustrate similar uses of that gesture to construe negation as absence and distance, as the speaker does here by placing the gesture away from the interactive space (cf. Chapter 4).

The precise organisation of elements within the nexus often exhibits some flexibility. In the following example, the Horizontal Palm gesture occurs with the negative expression which precedes the clause with JUST. Two visitors to the campsite are playing the board game and have landed on the square 'something you like doing in winter' (line 1). K immediately answers snowboarding (line 2). As G is thinking about his answer (line 3), K offers an alternative to his own answer with 'or' and describes a situation 'when it's pissing down and really cold outside and you're just chilling in with a home fire' (lines 4–5). When G acknowledges this with 'yeh that's what I was going to say' (line 6), K continues to add elements to his description that would make it enjoyable for him. These include 'a glass of red wine and no one around' (line 7). As he says 'no one around' he performs the Horizontal Palm gesture [1]. Then he adds 'you're just by yourself', flinging both hands outwards and upwards [2] (Figure 2.11).

Example 7 G_K gm 11.40 no one around
1 G something you like doing in winter?
2 K snowboarding
3 G yeh? e:::::::m
4 K or (.) when it's PIssing down and really cold outside
5   and you're just CHilling in with a home fire
6 G yeh [that's what i was going to say]
7   [and a glass of red wine] and NO one around you're just by yourself
                      /~~************/~************|
                      [1]   [2]

Figure 2.11 Clearing aside – flinging up

The nexus here highlights a triangular relation between the gesture ('clearing aside'), the verbal negation ('no one'), and the JUST-clause ('just by yourself'). It also shows different actions that may be relevant to the nexus, such as the upwards fling of the hands as if to let any other elements go, while punctuating the individuality of being 'just by yourself' and ending the turn.

The grammar–gesture nexus can also be situated within a broader complex or sequence of gestures. A discussion between two men about what would be 'their ideal job' illustrates how the embedding of a grammar–gesture nexus takes place. Based on a question in the board game, C has asked K 'what job would you like to have?' K begins his answer by saying 'this is actually (.) a conditional question' (line 1). When he then says 'I'm kind of going into the career I'm going into . . . because of the state of things' (line 4), he is referring to his current studies into political science, where 'the state of things' refers to an an earlier discussion about illegitimate and unfair forms of government. As he says 'the state of things', he raises both of his hands in open palm formations faced away from the body as if to 'hold up' 'things' [1]. Continuing to refer to these things, he now says 'but if that didn't exist and the world was in perfect harmony' (line 5). When he says 'but if that didn't exist', he transforms his hands from the 'holding up' position to a gesture of closing the hands then opening them and moving them outwards, with the affect of appearing to push what was being held up away [2]. Then with 'and the world was in perfect harmony', he performs a 2-Palms Down Mid gesture centrally in the space in front of him [3]. He partially retracts this gesture whilst saying 'I'd love to work in' (line 7), then performs a Palm Presenting gesture as he says 'possibly Hawaii' [4] (Figure 2.12).

Example 8 K_C gm2 00.31 perfect harmony
1 C this is actually (.) a conditional question
2   it all depends on the state of things
3   i'm kind of going into the career I'm going into
4   which I've already somewhat explained because of the state of things
                                          /~****************** ____
                                                    [1]
5   but if THAt didn't exist and the WOrld was in perfect harmony (.)
       /~*************/~*********************************_.-./
            [2]   [3]
6 K right
7 C i'd love to work in:: (.) possibly Hawaii (.)
       -.-.-.-.-.-.-.-.-.-.-.-./~~~********** ____
                                     [4]
8 K doing?
9 C (.) erm (.) i wanna use my languages
       -.-.-.-|

[1] Vertical palms raised high in gesture space, [2] opening up and pushing outward, [3] 2-Palms Down Mid, [4] Palm Presenting gesture.

Figure 2.12 Holding up – pushing away – clearing aside – offering

The speaker's early announcement of a 'conditional question' set the scene for a number of exclusions inherent to the description of his ideal job. These conditions involved the current state of things not existing and the world being in perfect harmony. Once these had been 'cleared away', 'Hawaii' was introduced as a potentially perfect place to work. This discursive move motivated a grammar–gesture nexus that allowed the speaker to accomplish his exclusions – it followed a gestural logic with the moves both before and after it. The example shows how the actions accomplished by the exclusion fit coherently within a sequence of actions in which the speaker appears to be 'speech handling' (Streeck 2009) – each gesture connects to the logic of what the speaker is using speech to accomplish.

The examples illustrate how this second grammar–gesture nexus is flexibile, interactive, and embedded. For a situation to be ideal, favourite, or preferred, certain elements must necessarily be excluded. In three of the examples, the adverb 'just' was an important trigger or cue for the Horizontal Palm gesture. In all examples, explicit forms of grammatical negation were also central to the description being offered by the speaker. The recurrent coordination of the JUST-adverbial, negative particles, and the 'clearing aside' gesture provides another instance of regularity within the impulse to gesture.

2.3.3   Rejections and 'Cutting Through' (2-Palms Down Across)

Observing how people gesture when they characterise a situation in negative terms as unsuitable has given rise to a third grammar–gesture nexus. We will consider examples now that include speakers referring to a situation and exclaiming 'it's wrong!' or even 'it's fucked!' Rejections like this go hand in hand with the 2-Palms Down Across gesture. The gesture stroke of this variation starts when the hands are crossed over, in a position on opposite sides of the body, from where they move diagonally downwards through the gesture space as the arms uncross. Morris (1994) called this gesture the 'hands scissor' because '[t]he hands are crossed over one another and then forcibly sliced apart' (p. 137). He noted how this gesture is used 'when a speaker wishes to finish an argument' and means 'That is finished!' (p. 137). For Morris, the meaning of the gesture arises because it is 'as if [the hands] are the blades of a large pair of scissors' (p. 137). Without distinguishing such a form variation, Kendon (2004) found the Horizontal Palm gesture to occur in a similar discourse setting, where '[r]eference to circumstances that render the execution or continuation of some action or project impossible' (pp. 256–8). Though the blades of scissors do not move apart like the hands in this gesture (Kendon, personal communication), as the hands converge during the stroke they nevertheless achieve the 'forcible slice' consistent with their verbal rejection.

A speaker's irritation to the point of exasperation illustrates an occurrence of this third nexus. An Australian surfer at the campsite in France is ranting about how difficult it is to contact his bank back home because of the time zone differences – a situation he goes on to dismiss as 'fucked'. This rant involves several utterances that all involve gestures. D first sets the scene by explaining 'I need to ring Australia during business hours which is like the complete opposite you know' (lines 1–2). With the word 'complete' he enacts rotating a spherical object 180 degrees, that is, 'upside down', which begins to illustrate a situation potentially in chaos [1]. Referring to the bank, he then explains that he must 'ring them between 1 o'clock in the morning and 9 o'clock in the morning' (line 3). He enumerates these options gesturally by coordinating his right hand with a finger on his left hand once with '1 o'clock' and once with '9 o'clock' [2]. He now concludes this situation as 'so it's fucked!' (line 4). With this evaluation, he performs the 2-Palms Down Across gesture [3] (Figure 2.13).

Example 9 D_B_1 05.31 calling the bank
1   i need to ring australia during business hours
2   which is like the complete opposite you know
    /~~~~~~~~~**********_-_-_-_-_-_-_-_-_-_-_-/~
              [1]
3   i have to ring between 1 o'clock in the morning and 9 o'clock in the morning
    ~~***/***********************/
          [2]
4   so it's f::ucked
    ~~~~*****_-.|
      [3]

[1] Enacts rotating a spherical object 180 degrees (i.e. upside down), [2] right hand making contact with fingers on left hand to count, [3] 2PDA.

Figure 2.13 Rotating – enumerating – striking/cutting through

Here we have a situation about which the speaker can do very little that culminates in the specific coordination of verbal and gestural resources for rejecting. The inner workings of this nexus are revealing. He begins to prepare his gesture with the conjunction 'so' in order to have the hands in place with 'it's'. He then releases the stroke with the first syllable of 'fucked', which he prolongs ('f::u'), so that the stroke is finished and in a post-stroke held with the rest of the word. By 'cutting through', the gesture expresses the same content as the expletive – what should be a simple task is rendered impossible, indeed beyond repair.

Part of the flexibility of the grammar–gesture nexus involves being able to elaborate on the verbal and gestural components that it includes. We see this in Example 10 when a professor performs the nexus at a key point during his lecture on YouTube (see www.youtube.com/watch?v=0KmimDq4cSU). Nobel Prize-winning physicist Richard Feynman is teaching an audience of students about the scientific method. Having described how to create and test a hypothesis, he explains that 'if it disagrees with experiment it's wrong'. He picks up on this point and proceeds to explain why this is what he calls 'the key to science', which he says whilst waving a Grappolo gesture (Kendon 2004: 229) in front of him [1]. He then lists a number of features that may influence the outcome of an experiment but that should not, saying 'it doesn't matter how beautiful your guess is, it doesn't make a difference how smart you are, who made the guess or what his name is', producing another precision grip ring gesture with this last condition [2]. Pointing at the board [3], he now repeats 'if it disagrees with experiment ... it's wrong' (line 6). In the pause in between those two utterances, he performs a large 2-Palms Down Across gesture [4]. He then adds 'that's all there is to it'. At this point the camera pans to the audience, several of whom are laughing (line 7) (Figure 2.14).

Example 10 RF 0.38 Scientific method wrong
1 if it disagrees with experiment it's wrong.
2 in that simple statement is the key to science.
   |~~~~****************/**************
                       [1]
3 it doesn't matter how beautiful your guess is
4 it doesn't make a difference how smart you are
5 who made the guess or what his name is.
   /~~~~**************/~~~~*****-.|
              [...]   [2]
6 if it disagrees with experiment (.5) it's wro::ng ... that's all there is to it
   |~~~~***************/~~~~***-.|
            [3]   [4]
7 (laughter from the audience)

[1] Precision grip Grappolo, [2] precision grip ring, [3] pointing to board, 2-Palms Down Across gesture.

Figure 2.14 Two precision grip gestures – pointing to board – 2-Palms Down Across

The speaker repeats the expression 'it's wrong' twice over the course of this segment – first without the gesture then second with it. In between the two instances, there is a crescendo in the discourse in which the speaker sets up the elements he is going to reject. In setting up, he produces several gestures to specify, including Grappolo and Ring forms (Kendon 2004) as well as pointing towards the equations on his blackboard. The impossibility of this situation being anything other than wrong is captured by the large 'cutting through' gesture, as well as by the verbal add on 'that's all there is to it'. The clarity and size of articulation of this gesture suggests it is done for additional rhetorical effect, an interpretation supported by the laughter its performance achieves from the audience.

Our next example illustrates the deliberateness with which people in conversation may deploy a given nexus. The speaker is describing a surprising revisit to a pub during a group holiday to Scotland. Having visited the pub previously and found it empty, the group he was with later 'got back to the pub at about eight o'clock' (line 1). With an expression of surprise on his face, the speaker then says 'and er we walked in and it was like the Wild West' (line 2). Up until this point, the speaker's hands have been in his pockets. But as he now describes the scene of the pub as 'it was absolutely heaving', he takes his hands out from his pocket [2], and prepares then performs a big 2-Palms Down Across gesture [3/4]. The stroke of the gesture coincides with the adjective 'heaving'. He holds the gesture as he adds imagery to the scene by specifying 'there were already some people fighting', then retracts his gesture and concludes 'scots guys I mean they go mad the scots after a few drinks' (line 4) (Figure 2.15).

Example 11 E Arran 09.37 absolutely heaving
1 so we got back to the pub at about eight o'clock
2 ((laughing)) and er we walked in and it was like the wild west
3 (.) it was absolutely heaving there were already some people fighting in there
   |⁓⁓⁓/⁓⁓⁓⁓⁓***********************************_.|
       [2]   [3]   [4]
4 scots guys i mean they go mad the scots after a few drinks

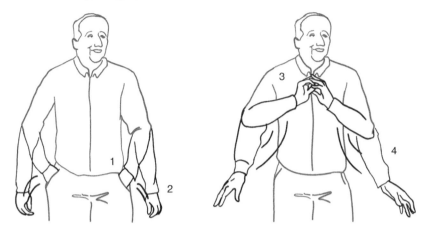

Figure 2.15 Out of the pockets, up to chest, 2-Palms Down Across gesture

The speaker's removal of his hands from his pockets in order to gesture is worth dwelling on here. In order to coordinate the gesture with the expression 'heaving', the speaker first brings his hands out of his pockets with 'it was'. Note that he is not preparing the gesture yet; he is *preparing to gesture*, which involves moving his hands to a starting point that is lower than his actual pockets. This important distinction suggests that, in this instance, the large preparation phase in which the hands are brought up to chest level is also a part of the gesture's performativity. In removing his hands from his pockets and lowering them, the speaker prepares to prepare. The preparation phase must be considered a meaningful part of the gesture in this instance.

Finally, the negative evaluation that gives rise to a grammar–gesture nexus may be part of a normative stance towards a state-of-affairs. Two participants in our last example are discussing the pros and cons of the board game they have just played. They are going through each question on the board and giving their opinion on whether or not they think the question would be suitable for starting a conversation between students in an English as a Foreign Language class. One of the speakers comes across the topic 'favorite type of food'. She reacts strongly by pointing at the board and repeating the phrase 'Hate that question' (line 1). She argues that 'it needs to be divided up into six questions', which she then comically begins to state whilst making counting gestures with her hands: 'favorite type of ice cream' (line 4). Her addressee laughs and says 'oh' as a sign she understands the speaker is not being serious (line 5). The speaker then interrupts her list and adopts a more serious tone, saying 'Because, like, I don't know, you can't, *eww*, hate that question' (line 7). With this utterance, she performs a sequence of four gestures. With 'because like' she points at the board [1], then with 'I don't know' she performs a Palms Presenting gesture [2]. As she says 'you can't', she performs the 'cutting through' gesture [3], then oscillates a Vertical Palm Lateral gesture with the interjection 'eww!' [4] (Figure 2.16).

Example 12 B_T ds 12.15 favourite food
1 T   favourite food . . . hate that question, hate that question.
2   it needs to be divided up into six questions.
3 B   really?
4 T   favourite type of ice-cream
5 B   oh ha ha ha
6 T   favourite type of- ha ha
7   because like i don't know (.) you CAn't (.) eww hate that question
       /~*********/~********_.||~*********/~*****-.-.-.|
          [1]   [2]   [3]   [4]

[1] Index finger points to board, [2] Palms Presenting gesture, [3] 2PDA, [4] palms lateral with vertical oscillations as if to agitate something.

Figure 2.16 Pointing – Palm Presenting – 2-Palms Down Across – shake/ throttle

Albeit in a joking manner, the speaker is appalled by the idea of clumping together 'food' into one category. With her speech and gesture she rejects the legitimacy of such a question. The negated modal 'can't' binds together with the abrupt scissor action of her gesture. Her negative interjection *eew!* supports this interpretation, as it may be a form of 'oral gesture' of negation, such as those observed by Calbris and Porcher (1989) and by Kendon (2002) as *tzt!*

Our examples support Morris's (1994) finding that this type of 'cutting through' gesture may occur 'when a speaker wishes to finish an argument' (ibid.) and means 'That is finished!' (p. 137). Additionally, our examples indicate the gesture may have additional meanings and especially bind with negative evaluations in a nexus to characterise a situation as negative or adopt a negative stance. Its performance exhibits variation in size and extent, which may also correspond to the communicative purpose the speaker intends and the role of the gesture in a particular sequence of gestures. This nexus lies at the intersection between a speech act, a set of linguistic structures, and a particular variant of the Horizontal Palm gesture.

2.4   Discussion

Like language, gesture exhibits a mixture of regularity and idiosyncrasy. The grammar–gesture nexus is a mechanism for the regularity that we observe when people spontaneously gesture. These are specific bindings of grammatical and gestural form that occur when speakers express negation. The genesis of a grammar–gesture nexus in spoken language is the established linguistic conventions of negation on the one hand, and the corresponding actions that gestures may reproduce on the other.

The three gesture variants we studied in this chapter are among a set of gestural forms that combine with grammar in speech to express negation or elements of negativity. These gestures reproduce everyday manual actions that are coherent to use as gestures when expressing negation in speech. The gestures are tailored to different types of negative expressions and the functions they achieve in discourse through variations in form that reproduce different types of actions; for example, sweeping aside, clearing a space, and cutting through. The gestures constitute a repertoire of embodied actions that are integral to the linguistic expression of negation. A salient dimension of regularity in gesture stems from the conventional binding of grammar and gesture into a nexus in this way.

The embodied actions in gestures are inherent to the forms of negative expression in speech. They are the gestural dimension of grammar that may be activated during a particular segment of discourse in interaction. The exact content and purpose of the speaker's utterance will determine subtle variations in the gestures in terms of timing and kinesic variation (amplitude, speed, extent, etc.) – this may constitute idiosyncrasy of gesture. However, the coordination with negative expression of gestural actions that reproduce sweeping aside, clearing a space, and cutting through – as well as the embodied knowledge and experience of those actions that people have – constitutes regularity in the impulse to gesture.

3   Sync Points in Speech
Evidence of Grammatical Affiliation for Gesture

So, the question is, where is the negation concept in the surface structure of speech? One may argue that it is in fact distributed across a whole clause, which thus should yield the *sync points* for the gesture.   —Stefan Kopp

3.1   Introduction

The term 'sync points' in Stefan Kopp's valuable advice diverges from the way many people think about gestures. For a long time, we have thought of speakers performing gestures in relation to a single linguistic segment of their verbal utterance, usually a word or phrase (i.e. the 'lexical affiliate'; Schegloff 1984). This is especially the case when gesture embodies imagery expressed by nouns, verbs, and adjectives in the co-occurring speech. Gestures must be 'co-expressive' with those segments and accordingly synchronise with them (McNeill 1992). But grammar imposes different organisational properties on gestures than do lexical affiliates in speech.

Negation may be distributed across a whole clause, as Kopp points out (echoing pioneers of negation such as Jespersen and Horn). The exact distribution of negation within the clause continues to animate debates in linguistics (see Horn 2010; Larrivée and Lee 2016; Horn and Wansing 2017). But the issue can be simplified for our purposes here. The negative sentences in this chapter all contain a grammatical particle called the negative node. Nodes of negation are explicitly negative forms such as *not, no, never,* and *none*. They constitute an observable location of negation and may be multiplied throughout the utterance. Particles are not the only locations for negation though. Nodes project a semantic influence over other elements in the utterance that lie in their 'scope'. The scope of negation generates the occurrence of Negative Polarity Items (like *any, only,* and *even*) and may 'focus' negation on to other parts of speech, including nouns, adverbs, and adjectives. Particles, polarity items, and focused elements are all potential sync points for gestures associated with negation.

This chapter posits the grammar of linguistic concepts as an organisation principle for the impulse to gesture. We take an array of utterances with similar

47

surface negation and examine how speakers organise their gestures differentially with the potential sync points in speech. When speakers prepare, release, hold, and repeat their gesture in relation to the node, scope, and focus of negation, they evidence a grammatical affiliation that determines how and why people gesture when they speak. Before considering evidence for grammatical affiliates of gestures, we first introduce the negative constructs we use when we speak and then layout the principles of temporal coordination between gesture and speech.

3.1.1   Node, Scope, and Focus of Negation

Negative particles in speech are like 'nodes' – a term borrowed from botany that denotes 'the part of a plant or stem from which one or more branches emerge' (*Oxford Concise English Dictionary*, 9th edn). Comparing utterances momentarily to plants, negation may emerge from the negative particle and spread across the linguistic elements that follow. An initial node of negation may lead to negation sprouting up in the rest of the utterance. This sprouting or 'multiple negation' is based on a simple and apparently universal observation: speakers express negation then reinforce it. Referring to the negation-marking morpheme 'ne-' at the base of many negators in English, Jespersen (1924) historically formulated this observation as follows:

> The insignificance of these initial (negative) sounds or weakly stressed syllables makes it desirable to multiply them in a sentence so as to prevent their being overlooked. Under the influence of strong feeling the speaker wants to make absolutely sure that the negative sense will be fully apprehended; he therefore attaches it not only to the verb, but also to any other part of the sentence that can be easily made negative: he will, as it were, spread a layer of negative colouring over the whole sentence instead of confining it to one single place. (p. 333)

Which parts of an utterance 'can be easily made negative'? Pullum (2012) observed 'multiple marking of a single negation at all relevant points in the negated clause – roughly, at all the indefinite determiners and quantifiers, including quantificational adverbs' (Pullum 2012). He exemplifies this with the hypothetical utterance '*I didn't never mean no harm to nobody or nothin*'', where bold font indicates the 'relevant points' at which the initial negation from 'don't' is systematically reinforced as the utterance unfolds. Negation has been incorporated here to determiners (*no*), quantifiers (*nothing*), and pronouns (*nobody*). Rather than cancelling each other out, multiple negatives in informal spoken language reinforce each other (cf. *I can't get no satisfaction*; Horn and Wansing 2017).

Multiple negation is related to the spread of negation that follows a negative particle, called the 'scope of negation'. Huddleston and Pullum (2005) define scope as 'the part of the sentence that the negative applies to semantically' (p. 156). For Celce-Murica and Larsen-Freeman (1999) it is 'everything that comes after the negative particle until the end of the clause' (cf. Downing and Locke 2006: 25). Constraints operating in scope become evident when we consider Horn's (1989) finding that some words 'can only occur felicitously within the scope of negation', such as *any, ever,* and *yet* (p. 49):

(1)   He {isn't / *is} eating any meat tonight.
(1')   I {can't / *can} ever seem to make any progress.
(1")   She {hasn't / *has} been to Casablanca yet.

Words such as *any, ever,* and *yet* belong to a category of linguistic items called Negative Polarity Items or 'NPIs' (Lawler 2005). NPIs 'almost always follow the negator that licenses them' (Larrivée 2017: 456), and they indicate an expression of negation in the utterance in addition to the negator they follow.

The presence of an NPI in negative scope affects the spread or influence of negation across the rest of the clause. The examples in (2) from Quirk et al. (2000: 226) illustrate this, because the presence of *any* (as opposed to *some*) extends negation across the entire clause (as opposed to restricting it to the verb). Extensions of negation are indicated by underlining the stretch of language 'lying' in negative scope:

(2)   I didn't listen to some of the speakers.
(2')   I didn't listen to any of the speakers.

In (2) the influence of negation can be interpreted as ending at 'listen', since we can infer that the negation of the subject's listening does not extend to all of 'the speakers' – if she didn't listen to some, then she also *did* listen to some. Conversely, the presence of the Negative Polarity Item *any* ensures that negation is applied to the whole clause: the relationship between the subject, her listening, and all the speakers available to be listened to is completely negated. Scopes of negation thus have a 'close connection with the ordering of elements' (Quirk et al. 2000: 85). How the speaker locates the node determines how he structures the rest of the utterance. He will place elements in reach of scope to negate them; for example, with a Negative Polarity Item such as *any*. And he will remove or 'shield' them from scope to affirm them (Givón 2001).

The process of signalling elements in scope that are negated is called *negative focus*. Beyond the placement of an NPI, Quirk et al. (2000) remark that '[t]he focus is signalled in speech by the placement of a nuclear stress, which indicates that the contrast of meaning implicit in the negation is located at that spot while the rest of the clause can be understood in a positive sense' (p. 227). Examples (3a) to (3f), again from Quirk et al. (2000: 227), illustrate this with large capitals to indicate the stressed syllable and underlining to indicate the relevant application of negative scope:

(3)

(a) I didn't take Joan to swim in the PÒOL today. – I forgot to do so.

(b) I didn't take JŎAN to swim in the pool today. – It was Mary.

(c) I didn't take Joan to SWĬM in the pool today. – Just to see it.

(d) I didn't take Joan to swim in the PŎOL today. – I took her to the seaside.

(e) I didn't take Joan to swim in the pool TODĂY. – It was last week that I did so.

(f) Ĭ didn't take Joan to swim in the pool today. – It was my brother who took her.

Negation from the particle may be applied to whole stretches of language, as in (a). Or depending on negative focus in (b) to (f), negation may apply to noun phrases ('Joan'), prepositional phrases ('in the pool'), and temporal adverbs ('today'). This 'pragmatic focus' occurs when 'the predicate can be inferred to be the case but for one element in its scope' (Larrivée 2017: 59). The examples also illustrate what Larrivée (2017) calls the 'isomorphy principle', that is, 'negation precedes the item it focuses on; an item that precedes the negative is not focused by it' (p. 459). In certain cases such as (f), however, the negation from the particle may retroactively be applied to elements that were uttered before it (the so-called 'left periphery negative scope'; Larrivée 2001: 50–1). Huddleston and Pullum (2002) summarise that '[t]he scope of negation is the part of the meaning that is negated. The focus is the part of that scope that is most prominently or explicitly negated' (p. 790).

Negation particles, Negative Polarity Items, and focused elements lying in negative scope offer one answer to Kopp's question 'where is the negation concept in the surface structure of speech?' They constitute potential sync points for gestures associated with negation and provide clues about how speakers might deploy such gestures when they speak. The bold fonts, capitalisation, and underlining used to track the expression of negation even look similar to annotations of how gestures unfold temporally in relation to speech.

3.1.2   *Temporal Coordination of Gesture and Speech*

A quick glance at someone talking may give the impression that gestures flash fleetingly in and out of existence. But on closer inspection, speakers prepare, perform, and retract each gesture methodically with relevant segments of their co-occurring speech (Kendon 2004). They may hold, postpone, abandon, and reinstate their gestures as they speak and interact (Cibulka 2015; Haddington et al. 2014). Speakers often insert gestures into specific gaps in the syntax of speech (McNeill 2005; de Brabanter 2007; Ladewig 2012), or they may start an utterance verbally then complete it entirely with gesture (Olsher 2004; Mori and Hayashi 2006). Speakers often perform gestures in sequences or use different articulators to perform gestures simultaneously too (Calbris 2011).

The rich complexity of how gestures unfold amounts to what McNeill (2005) has called the 'lifetime' of a gesture (p. 34). Kendon (2004) refers to this lifetime as the 'Gesture Unit'. It is 'the entire movement excursion, which commences the moment the gesturing limb or limbs begin to leave their position of rest or relaxation, and which finishes only when the limbs are once again relaxed' (p. 124). During this excursion, a person's gesture may transition through a number of phases, defined in Chapter 1 as phases of preparation, stroke, hold, and retraction (cf. Kendon 1980; Kita et al. 1998; Kendon 2004). These phases are like different stages in the life of a gesture – they may all be meaningful in the way they orchestrate with speech.

Since Schegloff's (1984) micro-analyses of gesture in video-recorded inter-actions, studies of the temporal coordination of gesture with speech have focused on representational gestures in relation to their 'lexical affiliate' (e.g. Nobe 2000; Chui 2005; Ferré 2010; Bergmann et al. 2011). The semantic connection between gestures and speech determines the way speakers coordinate their gestures to occur with (or even momentarily before) a semantically congruent word or phrase. However, McNeill (2005) emphasises that 'a co-expressive linguistic segment might be a lexical affiliate, but there is no necessity for it to be' (p. 37). Earlier, he argued that 'synchrony arises in the form of the thought itself' (McNeill 1998), which leads to a 'conceptual affiliation' between speech and gesture that goes beyond individual linguistic segments (de Ruiter 2000; Kirchhof 2011, 2017). The organisation of gesture units with speech is therefore determined by aspects of conceptualisation, or what Langacker (1987) called 'the internal structure of such phenomena as thoughts, concepts, perceptions, images, and mental experience in general' (pp. 97–8).

Conceptual descriptions of the temporal coordination between speech and gesture miss how people organise gestures associated with negation. The gestures may link to speech through a semantic link with a negative form (Calbris 1990, 2011), but they may also link to the pragmatic function associated with negative speech acts (Kendon 2004; Harrison 2009b; Calbris 2011; Bressem et al. 2015). Speakers may use gesture to pre-empt, add, overlay, or achieve a function relating to the negation expressed verbally, and accordingly perform the gesture in advance of the utterance, after it, or as an utterance on its own. Consider Kendon's (2002) finding that 'the head shake can be prepositioned in relation to a unit of discourse and so can express in anticipation the negation that the discourse contains. It can also be placed after the unit of discourse, serving as a sort of 'tag' to the spoken component of the utterance, as a comment by the speaker on what has been said' (p. 180; cf. Harrison 2014b). In some contexts, manual gestures in the Open Hand Prone family may also exhibit such flexibility and accordingly express negation in advance of, after, or in absence of a negation in speech (Calbris 2011; Kendon 2004). In other contexts, however, the way speakers organise Open Hand Prone gestures is constrained by the negative constructs structuring speech.

3.1.3   Grammatical Affiliates for Gesture

As people gesture when they speak, the phases of their gestures inevitably relate to the grammatical structures underpinning speech. Based on the grammar of negation, this chapter presents evidence of grammatical affiliates for gestures in speech and demonstrates how these affiliations influence the way people gesture when they speak.

Negation may be located in a single word, or spread out across an utterance through negative scope and focus. Gestures associated with negation thus provide a case study to examine how the organisation of gestures relates to the organisation of grammar. Our study begins with negative particles, default synchronisation points for gestures associated with negation. Continuing to focus on Horizontal Palm gestures, we first examine how speakers prepare and perform their gesture in relation to particles such as NOT, NO, and NEVER, as these also project a scope of negation that influences gesture organisation. Coordination of gestures with elements in negative scope are then examined, including Negative Polarity Items and focused elements.

3.2   Negative Particles

Negative particles are default sync points in speech for gestures associated with negation, so the position of the particle determines how people organise their gesture when they speak. Speakers prepare their gesture *before* the negative particle (preparation phase), release the gesture *with* the negative particle (stroke phase), then *maintain* their gesture in space as they utter the language lying in scope (post-stroke hold). This organisation principle is systematic but influenced by the content and length of individual utterances, the communicative goals of the speaker, and the dialogic context of the utterance. We illustrate this variation now by examining our corpus of multimodal negative utterances, first those with the negative particle NOT and then examining NO and NEVER.

3.2.1   NOT (Sentential Negation)

When the utterance contains a sentential negative, the gesture stroke synchronises with the negative particle. Speakers may hold the gesture after this stroke, with the length of the post-stroke hold corresponding to the extent of verbal material lying in scope (cf. Harrison 2010, 2014a). This organisation varies depending on the specifics of each utterance and may additionally serve different functions.

Two examples from the previous chapter provide an initial illustration of this organisation. Recall Example 1, in which the speaker was explaining a privileged relationship he had with the owners of the campground. Unlike other clients, the speaker could occupy a tent-pitch without having to pay unless he actually slept there. When the speaker said 'I don't have to pay for that night', he prepared a Horizontal Palm gesture in advance of the negative particle, released the stroke of the gesture with the particle, then maintained a post-stroke hold of the gesture as he uttered elements lying in negative scope ('have to pay').

Example 13 (prev. Example 1 D_B_1 03.33. don't have to pay)
2 (.) if i'm not here (.) i don't have to pay for that night (.) so (inaud.)
   ~~~***********~~~****************-.-.-.-.-.-.-.-.|
     [1]   [2]
[1] Deictic, [2] Horizontal Palm (PDA).

A second example from Chapter 2 demonstrates almost identical organisational principles, and additionally illustrates the interactive function of post-stroke holds. Recall Example 3, in which the speaker was referring to people who live in foreign countries (line 2), then said 'they don't speak any of the language' (line 3). He used a negative particle with *do*-support to negate the relation between 'they' (people who live in another country) and 'speak any of the language' (a property he wishes to negate of those people). He prepared a Horizontal Palm gesture as he said 'when they', pausing both speech and gesture momentarily before releasing the stroke with 'don't speak' (line 3). He then maintained a post-stroke hold through negative scope 'any of the language', which includes the Negative Polarity Item 'any'. He maintains the gesture hold as his addressee backchannels 'yeh' (line 4), which the speaker acknowledges 'right', only then retracting his gesture.

Example 14 (prev. Example 3 A3b 19.32 don't speak any language)
3 A: when the::y (.5) don't speak any of the language [(.)] right/
      /~~~~~~~***********************************
        [2]   [3]
4 B: [yeh]
5 B: And . . .
    -.-./ . . .

[2] prepares Palm Down Across, [3] performs Palm Down Across

In addition to synchronising with the particle 'don't' and aligning with negative scope, the speaker in this example uses a post-stroke hold to mobilise the addressee's response, agreement, or confirmation that she has understood his utterance. The post-stroke hold may thus be maintained beyond scope as part of managing the interaction.

The post-stroke hold may also be discontinued before the end of scope. The speaker in our next example again synchronises the stroke of his gesture with the negative particle then maintains a post-stroke hold through scope. However, he releases his gesture from the hold before the end of scope in order to prepare a gesture for the utterance that follows. The speaker is explaining the difficulties of communication in his previous employment that required him to interact with people with whom he did not share a common language. He uses a negative particle to negate the relation between a subject 'we' (now referring to himself and international customers to his shop) and its predicate 'speak the same language'. As he says 'even though we don't speak the same language', he prepares a Horizontal Palm gesture with 'even though we'. He performs the gesture stroke with 'don't' then maintains a post-stroke hold with the stretch of language in negative scope 'speak any of the language'. Before finishing the word 'language', however, he interrupts his gesture hold to prepare an iconic gesture of cutting related to 'how they want the food', which then also transitions into a Palm Presenting gesture.

Example 15 A3b 23.18 we don't speak any of the language
1   it would always be me and them trying to explain to each other

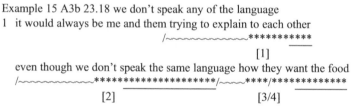

[1] Palms lateral held, [2] Horizontal Palm (PDA), [3/4] Iconic/Palm Presenting gesture.

This example suggests that length of holds may be influenced by scope but also depend on the type of gesture being performed next. Following synchronisation with a negative particle, the stroke can be maintained until the end of scope unless the speaker needs to prepare a gesture to occur with the beginning of the next utterance or linguistic segment.

If there is no linguistic material lying in scope, then the speaker will not perform a post-stroke hold following the particle (unless for interactive reasons as previously). This is exemplified when 'don't' is used as a negative tag without projecting a scope. The speaker in Example 16 is talking about her rock climbing hobby and says 'I wish I had the time on Tuesdays to go twice but I don't'. She prepares and synchronises her Horizontal Palm gesture with the negative 'don't', then immediately retracts her gesture.

Example 16 B_T gm 21.05. Wish had time but don't
1 B i wish i HAd the time on TUEsDAys to go TWIce but i DOn't…. uuuhm.
                                                    |~****-.-.-|
                                                       [1]

[1] Horizontal Palm (2PDmid).

In this example, negative meaning is expressed prior to the particle 'don't'. The speaker's verb *wish* indicates 'an environment expressing an unrealized event' (Larrivée 2017: 452) and prompts the addressee to build relations of counterfactuality (cf. Steen and Turner 2013: 267). This sets the scene for her subsequent negative tag 'but I don't'. Because the object of negation (have the time to go twice on Tuesdays) is elided from that tag, there is no linguistic material with which a post-stroke hold could co-occur.

How speakers gesture in relation to negation may also reflect the speaker's rhetorical aims, and the gesture form features may be influenced by their position among other gestures in a gesture unit. In our final example of NOT-negation, the speaker is reporting part of a motivational speech that he gave at his local scout group. At one point, he tells how he specifically addressed the girl scouts of the group and sought to elevate their aspirations. Referring to a mural in the scout hut of the sky with a moon, he reports that he first said 'and by the way girls, there's no woman ever set foot on the moon, but there will be one day, and just maybe it could be one of you girls'. He apparently then said 'the world's your oyster, in fact it's not just the world now, the universe is your oyster' (lines 1–3). As he reports this rousing segment, he performs a sequence of three Open Hand Prone gestures. The palm is oriented similarly for each instance between vertical (away body) and horizontal (down). But with each performance it is swiped across the gesture space to a different extent. With 'the world is your oyster', the palm is moved horizontally across his entire frontal gesture space [1]. With 'in fact it's not just the world now', he performs a second, much shorter gesture that starts from the end point of the previous one and moves abruptly along the horizontal axis in his right periphery [2]. A third gesture of even bigger spatial extent than the first gesture is then prepared [3] and produced as he says 'the universe is your oyster' [4] (Figure 3.1).

Example 17 20.12.2015 MTS 18 37.30 the world is your oyster
1 you know i said the world is your oyster in fact it's not just the world now
           |~~~~~**********~~~~~**************/
                     [1]   [2]
2 (breath in) the universe is *ha* your *ha* oyster
  /~~~~~~~**********-.-.-.-|
     [3]   [4]
3 so i want you to remember that

[1] Vertical/Horizontal Palm gesture (PDA) from central to right periphery, [2]Vertical/ Horizontal Palm gesture (PDA) in right periphery, [3] preparation of [4] Horizontal Palm gesture (PDA) from centre to extreme upper periphery.

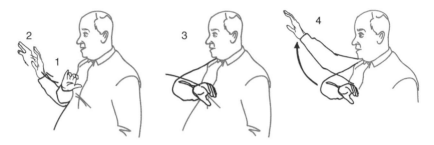

Figure 3.1 Embedding of a Horizontal Palm (meta-linguistic negation)

Having used the idiom 'the world is your oyster' and produced a Horizontal/ Vertical Palm gesture to convey a 'panoramic' of possibilities (Calbris 1990), this speaker immediately determined that the global scale of possibilities was unsuitable for the message he was hoping to convey. He thus negated an element of his own speech ('it's not just the world') and replaced it on the fly with a more suitable expression in the utterance that followed ('the universe'). The pattern of this 'meta-linguistic negation' (Pullum 2012; Horn and Wansing 2017) determines the form and organisation of the co-occurring gestures. The preparation and performance of the second gesture is orchestrated with the node and scope of his clausal negation, showing how the embedding of a meta-linguistic negation is verbal and gestural, achieved multimodally. Such manipulation of linguistic and gestural patterns could evidence aspects of this particular speaker's communicative competence, whose laughter suggests a degree of delight at the multimodal utterance he has achieved (line 2).

Five examples of NOT-negation have been introduced. They illustrate how nodes of negation and the scopes they project influence the temporal coordination of gestures associated with negation in speech. Negative nodes yield sync points for the gesture strokes, whilst scopes determine the maintenance (or absence) of a post-stroke hold. The post-stroke holds are not co-expressive with the content of the linguistic material in scope, however. They are co-expressive with the grammatical relation between that material and the negative particle earlier in the utterance. Rather than showing that aspects of gesture connect referentially to the elements in speech, they indicate that negation is still being applied, regardless of the specific elements in scope. The way we organise these gestures seems therefore to be based not only on conceptual and pragmatic relations between speech and gesture, but also on the grammatical relations that hold between different parts of the utterance. These NOT-negations thus evidence how there may be a grammatical affiliation between speech and gesture.

3.2.2 NO *and* NEVER

Briefly re-examining two examples from Chapter 1 in the context of this chapter will start our study of NO-negation. The first example is with the negative pronoun NO ONE. Recall how a speaker from the campsite described his preference for activities in winter as staying inside and drinking wine with 'no one around, you're just by yourself' (line 1). He coordinated the stroke of his Horizontal Palm gesture with 'no one around' [1], then flung his hands upwards with 'you're just by yourself' [2].

Example 18 (previously Example 7 G_K gm 11.40 no one around)
yeh [that's what i was going to say]
  [and a glass of red wine] and NO one around you're just by yourself
         /~~*************/~***************|
                 [1]   [2]
[1] Horizontal Palm (2PDmid), [2]abrupt upwards 'fling' of hands (see Chapter 2 for illustrations; Figure 2.11).

The second example that we borrow from the previous chapter illustrates how 'no' used as an adjective solicits the synchronisation of a Horizontal Palm gesture. The speaker reported the result of his disastrous plan to break up with his high school sweetheart in order to 'get with other girls in the school'. Because those other girls were friends with his ex-girlfriend, he said that he 'was like no-go territory'. He began preparing his gesture with the discourse marker 'so', continued to prepare it with 'I was like', then withheld the stroke while he repeated 'I was like' again. He performed the stroke of the gesture with 'no-go' then held the stroke with 'territory'.

Example 19 (previously Example 4 DLC_5 11.55 no go territory)
1 so i was like.. .... i was like NO-go territory (.)
  /~~~~~~~~~~~~~~~~~~~~~~_____************/

                      [4]

Gesture organisation with node and scope here occurs within the confines of a noun phrase. The organisation of gesture therefore reflects a 'sub-clausal negation', where '[t]he negation only affects a phrase' (Pullum 2012).

NO can also be used in a way similar to clausal negation, in which case the scope it projects may determine the organisation of a post-stroke hold. An example from an online lecture by Noam Chomsky illustrates this similarity (see www.youtube.com/watch?v=_tvPkSveevA). Chomsky is responding to a question from the audience about 'the mind-body problem'. He first describes why he believes this problem no longer exists, referring back to Newton and comparing the term to an 'honorific word' (lines 1–4). Then he ends his answer with 'but there's no further concept of physical, material, or body' (line 5). He prepares a Horizontal Palm gesture (2PDmid) in advance of the node 'no', releases the stroke as he utters 'no' [1], then performs a post stroke hold with 'further concept of physical material or body'. He imposes three beats onto this hold when he utters the words 'physical', 'material', and 'body'. As he concludes 'so there can't be a mind body problem' (line 6), his Open Hand Prone gesture transitions into an upwards fling of the hands [2], possibly a form of Palm Presenting gesture that retains the speaker's negative stance.

Example 20 Chomsky ML 02.35 no further concept
See www.youtube.com/watch?v=_tvPkSveevA, occurs towards the end of the clip.
1   there hasn't been any concept of body since newton (. . .)
2   so there is no concept of physical (.) the term physical is just kind of like an
3   honorific word
4   so to say that something's physical today just means you gotta take it seriously
5   but there's no further concept of physical material or body
      /~~~~~~***********************************/
            [1] ————————————————————————————————
                              beat   beat   beat
6   so there can't be a mind body problem.
      ********************/
                  [2]

[1] Horizontal Palms (2PDmid) (large beats correspond to physical + material + body),
[2] Palm Presenting upwards movement gesture.

This speaker specifies the kind of concepts that no longer exist by holding the gesture after the negative particle and 'beating' it with each mention of a concept he wishes to reject – a pragmatic underlining function of a post-stroke hold. The form and function of the gesture occur regardless of the concepts he is discussing. Instead they perform a focusing function of the negation from the negative particle 'no' onto each of the elements being rejected. Furthermore, Chomsky is not rejecting concepts in general . He is rejecting the type of concepts that he is arguing do not exist. The way he organises gesture reflects this important distinction, because the gesture hold suggests that 'no further concept of' is one chunk, while the beats indicate that 'physical, material or body' is another. By beating the gesture with each of those concepts, the speaker indicates to which concepts the negation from that gesture applies. In this sense, the speaker may beat the gesture during the hold to 'reactivate' the meaning first expressed in the stroke (Mats Andrén, personal communication).

NEVER is another negative particle in contemporary English. As Cheshire (1999) has observed, this particle can either occur with 'standard' universal temporal reference ('Sally never eats meat') or with informal simple negation to refer to the past ('you never went to school today'), in which case its meaning is similar to 'not'. NEVER often therefore projects a scope of negation too, so these particles also determine a co-occurrence pattern based on a grammatical affiliation between speech and gesture.

The first example illustrates how a speaker gestures with NEVER as a simple negator that functions similar to NOT. Describing his research focus, a student explains he is interested in the fact that 'some people can live in another country for a very long time and they never learn very much of the language' (lines 4–6). The speaker begins to prepare his Horizontal Palm gesture (2PDmid) as he introduces this utterance with 'and they'. He performs the stroke of this gesture with 'never' [1]. He performs a post-stroke hold over 'learn', the brief pause that follows, and very much of the language', with which he shakes his head [2]. He continues to hold the gesture during a pause after his utterance, during which his interlocutors respond with various forms of back channelling (lines 7–9), including a head nod [2]. Following this, the speaker says 'right so they can just communicate with things like gestures' (line 7) and performs a gesture unrelated to negation in which the hands circle inwards around each other [3] (Figure 3.2).

Example 21 A3b 05.15 Never learn the language

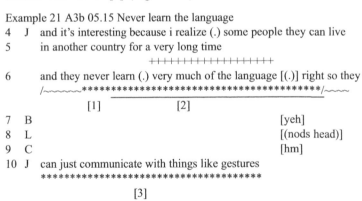

[1] Horizontal Palm gesture (2PDmid), [2] post-stroke hold coordinated with head shake (+++++), [3] inward cyclic gesture possibly illustrating the sequentiality of his reasoning (cf. 'so').

Figure 3.2 Post-stroke hold coordinates with head shake and solicits addressee head nod

Gesture organisation here is integral to the internal structure of the negative utterance. The pause after 'never learn' (line 6) might suggest that 'never learn' and 'very much of the language' are distinct linguistic segments (cf. Dahlmann and Adolphs 2009). But the stroke of the Horizontal Palm gesture is held over the pause and into scope, while the head shake gesture specifically (and uniquely) indicates the influence of negation with 'very much of the language'. This sustained post-stroke hold and negative head shake illustrate that despite the pause, the elements in scope are grammatically inseparable from the initial negator (cf. Larrivée 2017).

Other kinds of hitches in the negative utterance have ramifications for the way speakers organise their gestures. Gestural organisation in the next example illustrates how the speaker's use of 'really' as a hedge influences his execution of a Horizontal Palm gesture. The man is describing a principle of the way he does business as a claims manager, which is to avoid raising people's hopes unnecessarily when working on a claim for them. He begins to formulate this maxim by saying 'if there's any doubt about' (line 1) but then restarts with 'that's why I never really I never say to people on the claims side' (line 2). He prepares and performs a Horizontal Palm gesture with 'that's why I never' [1], but then retracts his gesture as he interrupts his utterance with the hedge 'really'. When he then repeats the negation with the full utterance 'I never say to people', he does not repeat the gesture. He only gestures again with 'on the claims side', and accordingly performs a Palm Presenting gesture to indicate he is adding a specification [2] (cf. Kendon 2004) (Figure 3.3).

Example 22 EC 22.20 never say to people
1   if there's any doubt about
                    +++++++++
2   that's why i never really i never say to people (.) on the claims side
    |~~~~~~~~~***-.-.-.| |~~*****-.-.-.-.-.|
              [1]   [2]

[1] Horizontal Palm gesture (PDA), [2] Palm Presenting gesture.

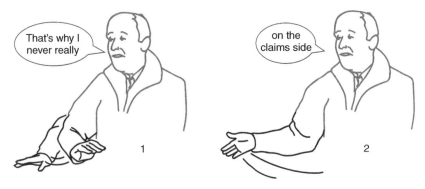

Figure 3.3 Horizontal Palm with NEVER interrupted with hedge

The stroke of Horizontal Palm gesture in this example emerges as a feature of the negative particle, since the speaker can perform and retract it before uttering the verb to which the negation applies. The effect is to emphasise the expression of negation at the main sync point, rather than embody the structure of his clausal negation. However, note how his hedge and repetition of the negation are nevertheless accompanied with a cohesive head shake.

These examples of utterances with NO and NEVER reinforce the claim that negative particles determine how people gesture when they speak. Like NOT, speakers prepare and coordinate gestures from the Open Hand Prone family with the particles NO and NEVER. The different ways the gesture is held or retracted can be explained in relation to the constituent structures of the negations it occurs with.

3.2.3 Strokes, Holds, Hitches, and Beats

Negative particles determine how people gesture with entire stretches of language, including before, with, and after a negative particle. The coordination patterns between the grammatical and gestural structures may be evident as early as the discourse markers that introduce the negative speech act underway (e.g. SO, EVEN THOUGH, and BUT). We have seen how speakers prepare the gesture stroke well in advance of the negation. They synchronise the stroke of their gesture with the particle. This synchronisation constitutes the nucleus of co-expressivity for speech and gesture within the negative utterance.

Yet the influence extends after the particle, because speakers also maintain their gesture with a post-stroke hold as they utter the linguistic elements to which their negation applies. These post-stroke holds are not co-expressive with the content of co-occurring speech but rather with its grammatical relation to the negation expressed by the particle earlier in the utterance. This is emphasised when speakers 'beat' their hold to highlight (or pragmatically underline) the objects of their negation. Additionally, speakers may maintain the stroke of a gesture associated with negation beyond the scope for interactive reasons, such as to mobilise a response from the addressee (Stivers and Rossano 2010). They may discontinue their gesture before the end of scope because of hitches in the utterance (pauses, fillers, hedges, and restarts) or to release the hand to prepare for a gesture in the following utterance.

Studying how speakers gesture with utterances structured by NOT, NO, and NEVER therefore tells us that gestural organisation is integral to the negative constructs with which people organise their verbal utterances in face-to-face, spoken discourse. The linguistic patterns of negation determine gesture organisation and provide evidence of grammatical affiliates for gesture in speech.

3.3   Scope of Negation

Negative particles are not the only sync point for gestures associated with negation in speech. Speakers also organise their gestures to synchronise the stroke of a Horizontal Palm gesture with elements lying in negative scope. Various elements lying in scope can constitute sync points for the strokes of such gestures. These include Negative Polarity Items and focused elements.

3.3.1   Negative Polarity Items

Negative Polarity Items (NPIs) introduce a salient gestural sync point to the scope of negation. NPIs are items that speakers use to reinforce a negation in the first relevant location following a negative particle (cf. Larrivée 2017). They include words such as *any, even, ever,* and *at all* (Lawler 2005). These elements occupy the same utterances as the negative particle that they serve to reinforce, so whether speakers synchronise their gesture with the particle or the NPI in scope reflects the emphasis they aim to achieve with the utterance. Gesture organisation may also reflect the speakers' discursive aims, for example, to emphasise a negation, to introduce a contrast, or to suggest a particular stance towards the topic under discussion. In all cases, the performance of the Horizontal Palm gesture adheres to (and thereby reflects) grammatical relations between linguistically associated elements within the utterance.

As a first case study, the speaker in Example 23 performs her Horizontal Palm gesture after the negative particle to synchronise its stroke with the Negative Polarity Item ANY. B has just announced the next topic of discussion as 'programmes you like watching on TV' (line 1), when T intimates that she 'grew up without one', so for her 'this is a recent development' (lines 2–3).

B then asks T 'Do you have a television?' (line 5). T answers rhetorically by first saying 'I own the physical box' (line 6), to which B interjects 'oh ok' (line 7), then by saying 'but I don't get a single channel' (line 8). The form of her gesture is the same as we have seen so far – a Horizontal Palm gesture. However, she does not begin to prepare her gesture until well after the negative particle 'don't'. Her gesture unit is coordinated instead with the expression 'a single channel'.

Example 23 T_B gm 05.40 don't get a single channel
1 B   programs you like watching on tv
2 T   well I grew up without one (*clap!*)
3   so this is a recent development for me.
4   now erm on television because that DVDs are everything
5 B   Do you have a television?
6 T   I own the physical box . . .
7 B   Oh ok
8 T   but I don't (.) get a single CHAnnel . . . . .uhmm
             |~~************-.-|
                   [1]

[1] Horizontal Palm (PDA).

Although performed with the expression 'a single channel', the Horizontal Palm form of the gesture indicates a potential relation of this expression to the negative particle 'don't'. Indeed, negative polarity items such as 'a single' are said to be 'licensed' by the particles they follow (Horn 1989). The precise temporal coordination of the gesture with 'single channel' respects this grammatical relation while achieving the speaker's rhetorical strategy – to say that she has a television, but one without channels. A grammatical affiliation determines the organisation of gesture because 'a single' emphasises the negation expressed earlier by 'don't'.

The number of NPIs in the scope of negation may determine the number of gesture strokes that the speaker performs. As the speaker in Example 24 repeats the NPI 'at all', she also repeats the stroke of her gesture. The utterance is from a discussion between two junior teachers who are chatting about the enjoyable length of their weekends. One speaker uses the NPI 'at all' to emphasise how long her weekends are by saying 'because I don't work Friday at all or Monday at all' (Figure 3.4).

Example 24 A_J gm 07.54 P don't work at all
1 J   Yes, I like the weekends. And they're long too, like yours . . . Because
2   I DOn't WOrk FRIday at ALL or MONday at ALL.
             |~~~~****~~~~~~~*****-.-.-.-|
                   [1]

[1] Horizontal Palms (2PDmid).

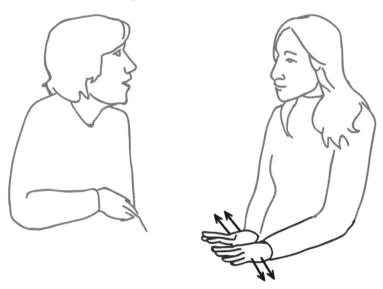

Figure 3.4 Horizontal Palm gesture repeated with each NPI

The speaker's gesture may initially appear to be detached from the negative particle 'don't', perhaps used purely to emphasise the length of her weekends. But by repeatedly performing the gesture with each NPI, the gesture shows fundamental relations to the negation expressed earlier in the clause. The gesture is only related to the expressions 'Friday at all' and 'Monday at all' by virtue of the NPIs, which are grammatically connected to or 'licensed by' the negative particle. The way the speaker organises and deploys her Horizontal Palm gestures is determined by that connection. Briefly compared to the previous example, we do not see different gestures for different NPIs. The performance of the Horizontal Palm gestures is more to do with expressing negation than with expressing the content or form of the NPI (e.g. 'single' and 'at all').

Another way that the gesture phrase may map onto the verbal utterance is when it is performed in a way that includes both the negative particle and the NPI. In the next example, the speaker starts to prepare his ZP gesture with the beginning of his negative utterance. However, he continues this preparation phase as he utters the negation and its predicate, only releasing the stroke later with the NPI 'any' lying in scope of negation. Speaking about his friend who lived in Korea without studying Korean, he says 'he he didn't learn any of the language' (line 2). He prepares his gesture while uttering 'he didn't learn', then he performs the gesture stroke with 'any of the' [1]. The entire gesture unit encompasses the entire utterance. After this initial gesture associated with the negation, he continues speaking and performs a series of Palm Presenting gestures as he clarifies that not knowing the language was not a problem for this person. For example, when he says that his friend 'still lives there' (line 4), that he 'lived there for two years' and that 'he loves it' (line 5), he is beating a Palm Presenting gesture [2]. This may seem irrelevant to the negation. But as part of this clarification he then repeats that his friend 'doesn't speak any of the language'. As he reminds his audience of this startling fact, he embeds the Palm Presenting gesture in a lateral movement [3], otherwise called a Palm Lateral gesture (Kendon 2004: 275) (Figure 3.5).

Example 25 A3b 21.30 didn't learn any language
1   i had a friend who lived there
2   he (.) he didn't learn any of the language
        |~~~~~~~~~~~********_._._._._._._.|
                        [1]
3   but he lived there really comfortably the whole year
4   and he still lives there
        |~~~~~~~~********
                 ‾‾‾‾‾‾‾‾
                 [2a]
5   lived there for two years he loves it but he doesn't speak any of the language
        /~~~~~~~~~~~~*****/********~~~~~******************_._._._._._.-|
                                                        ‾‾‾‾‾‾‾‾‾‾‾‾‾‾‾‾
             [2b]   *beat*   [3]

[1] Horizontal Palm (PDA), [2a] left-hand Palm Presenting gesture, [2b] both hand Palm Presenting gesture + beat, [3] Palms-Up are brought together then moved out on the lateral axis and held.

The speaker in this example coordinates the gesture unit of a Horizontal Palm gesture with an entire negative utterance. Like previous examples, the stroke occurs with the negative polarity item. But unlike previous examples, the whole gesture phrase unfolds during the whole utterance, so the preparation phase begins before and subsequently includes the negative particle. If a speaker wanted to perform the gesture stroke with the NPI, he or she could just begin preparing the gesture after the particle (as was the case in Examples 23 and 24). So if speakers can begin preparing their gesture at the beginning of the utterance but perform the stroke either with or after the negative particle, it suggests they are able to modify the speed at which they prepare the gesture. This indicates a specific choice and certain degree of control on behalf of the speaker to modify the speed of preparation depending on which sync point she wants the gesture to occur with. Not only is the gesture's post-stroke hold organised in relation to the negation, but also the gesture's preparation (along with any pre-stroke holds; cf. Examples 14 and 19, this chapter).

Utterances with a negative particle and a Negative Polarity Item have yet another, perhaps less obvious sync point. The student in the next example has

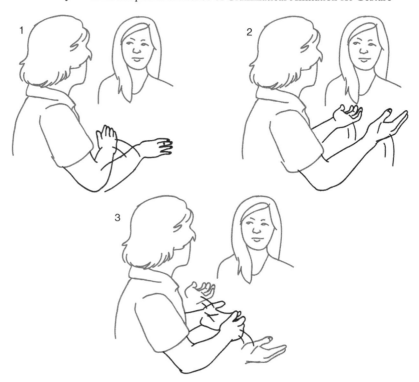

Figure 3.5 Horizontal Palm – Palm Presenting – Palm Lateral

said that in terms of finding quiet places to study she hates 'working at home' (line 1). Her addressee asks her to confirm this 'really?' (line 2), when the speaker replies 'yeh (.) I just don't get anything done' and performs an Open Hand Prone gesture. She performs this gesture not with the negative particle 'don't' or with the NPI 'anything'. She performs it immediately after her verbal utterance along with a cluck of the tongue (*cluck!*) (Figure 3.6).

Example 26 A_S gm 17.28 don't get anything done
1   S   i hate working at home
2   A   really?
3   S   yeh (.) i just don't get anything done (.) *cluck!*
                                          |~****-.|
                                              [1]
4   A   well it's true but that's why it's great

[1] Horizontal Palm (2PDmid).

Figure 3.6 Occurrence of the Horizontal Palm post-utterance with an oral *cluck!*

In this example, negation is spread through this verbal utterance, starting with the negative particle ('don't'), then marked by the NPI ('anything'), and finally expressed through the tongue click ('*cluck!*'). Calbris and Porcher (1989) observed a similar 'apico-alveolar click' among French speakers and suggested that in briefly stopping the flux of sound, the meaning of this oral gesture can be extended to express protection, refusal, or negation (p. 51; cf. Kendon 2002). Jespersen (1924) observed that the negation-marking morpheme 'ne-' is 'a primitive interjection of disgust consisting mainly in the facial gesture of contracting the muscles of the nose' (p. 335; cf. Lapaire 2006a). There are therefore three sync points for a gesture associated with negation in this utterance. The *cluck* appears to operate in a way not unlike the 'sentence final negator' observed by Larrivée (2017) in some Romance languages, such as Venetian (p. 454; citing Poletto 2008):

(10) Venetian
No la   go   **miga** magnada NO!
NEG1 3SG.F.ACC. have PRS.1SG NEG2 eat.PTCP NEG3
'I really did not eat it.' (Poletto 2008: 59)

The Negative Polarity Item is a tool with which speakers reinforce their expression of negation. If the aim of the NPI is to reinforce the negation, then one aim of the gesture may be to reinforce the NPI, which would reflect the tendency for speakers to reinforce negations in an ongoing cycle (Jespersen 1924: 333).

3.3.2   Focused Elements

Depending on the speaker's focus of negation, linguistic items including verbs, adjectives, and nouns lying in scope may all become potential sync points for gestures. These are words that express no negation of their own, but become objects of negation by virtue of the underlying grammatical construct *and* the co-occurring gesture. Because the grammatical process of focus determines the organisation of the gesture, the gesture consequently reflects the focus operations underpinning the speaker's utterance.

Our first example indicates how a speaker coordinates his gesture with an adjective to which he applies the negation from his particle. Having described why business people should avoid getting their clients' hopes up, he admits that he made 'that mistake once' with one of his clients. As soon as he has made this admission, he stresses that it was 'not not in the first instance'. Upon uttering 'not' for the second time, he begins to prepare his gesture. He then performs two strokes of the Horizontal Palm gesture. The first stroke occurs in the pause after 'not', while the second one is coordinated specifically with the adjective 'first'.

Example 27 EC 23.24 not in the first instance
1   I made that mistake with Sarah
2   Not not (...) in the FIrst instance but I did tell her on one occasion
    |~****/~~~******_.-.-|
           [1]

[1] Horizontal Palm (PDA).

With his gesture, this speaker applies the negation from 'not' to the adjective 'first'. The negation applies to 'first' in order to exclude the negation of him ever having made the mistake: he has made the mistake, but that was not in the first instance. That he did not make the mistake in the first instance is important to stress, because the client he was discussing was an important client. Making such a mistake the first time could have meant that any kind of business deals would not have been possible with this particular client, which emphasises the point of his story.

When speakers list elements onto which they focus negation, they may perform repeated strokes of Open Hand Prone gestures, each stroke corresponding specifically to an element being negated. The speaker in Example 28 has been asked what he likes to watch on television at home (line 1). He replies that he likes 'soaps' (line 4). His addressee tries to engage him in further conversation on the topic with the question 'do you like soaps?' (line 5). He gives another couple of examples of the soaps he likes, then seeks to clarify his preference by characterising the soaps he likes and dislikes. He says 'gossipy,

gossipy, light-hearted soaps, none of these heavy where everybody dies and they're probably fighting and hate each other for most of it'. The speaker is listing the characteristics of soaps he dislikes by embedding a series of undesirable qualifiers into the scope of the particle 'none of'. He coordinates a head shake with the entire utterance and repeats the stroke of a Horizontal Palm gesture with each rejected element: once with 'heavy', again with 'dies', and finally with 'fighting' (Figure 3.7).

Example 28 K_C gm 02.47 light-hearted soaps
1   K   which brings me to my next question what did you watch back home and
2   C   ER
3   K   ER
4   C   soaps
5   K   do you like soaps?
6   C   yeah eastenders coronation street
        ++++++++++++/∧∧∧∧∧∧∧∧∧∧∧∧∧∧∧∧
7   gossipy gossipy light-hearted soaps
        +++
8   none of these HEAvy where everybody DIes and they're probably FIGhting
        |~~~~~********~~~~~~~~~~~***~~~~~~~~~~~~~~~~~~******
            [1]
        +++++++++++++++++++++++++++++++++
9   and hate each other for most of it
        ~*****-._.-._.-._.-._.-._.-._.-|

[1] Horizontal Palm gesture (PDA), with three repeated strokes

Figure 3.7 Number of elements in negative focus determines repetition of gestures

The strokes of this speaker's gesture do not relate semantically to the words they accompany. There is no co-expressivity in terms of lexical semantics (though heaviness, death, and violence could evoke negative frames; Harrison 2009b). More coherently, the strokes are related to the negation expressed by the particle 'none' that occurs earlier, which the speaker is focusing onto the characteristics of soaps that he wishes to reject. The speaker's gesture is both part of achieving this focus and making it explicit.

The correspondence between number of rejected elements and repetitions of gesture strokes is not always so clear cut. The pair of speakers in the next stretch of discourse are offering up examples of chores they like. When K proposes 'cooking?' (line 1), B says 'yeah I like cooking and washing up' (line 2). However, when K then proposes 'ironing?' with a somewhat jocular laugh (line 3), B responds negatively by exclaiming 'NO', then saying 'ironing uh uh and vacuuming uh uh'. Immediately after she has said 'vacuuming', she sweeps two large strokes of a Horizontal Palm (PDA) gesture through the space in front of her (Figure 3.8).

Example 29 B_K gm 11.35 No ironing vacuuming
1 K   cooking?
2 B   yeah i like cooking and washing up
3 K   ironing ha ha?
4 B   NO::: ironing uh uh and vacuuming uh uh (inaud.)
                            |~~~~********/*********-.-.|
                                   [1]

[1] Horizontal Palm.

Figure 3.8 Two sweeps of the Horizontal Palm ('and all such other household chores')

Rather than being restricted to rejecting the two items she utters verbally ('ironing' and 'vacuuming'), the manner and extent of the speaker's repeated gesture here seems to indicate the rejection of all such similar items. The speaker's expression of negation is undeniably related to the initial negative response signal to K's suggestion of ironing. The 'no' provides a negative framework through which any discursive elements are to be understood. The vocalisation *uh uh* is made by opening and closing the glottis and, along with the *eww!* and the *cluck!* discussed earlier, may be understood as an 'oral gesture of negation' (Kendon 2002; Calbris and Porcher 1989; Harrison 2009a). Cohesion still arises between verbal and gestural forms: two unwanted household chores, two strokes of the gesture, and two oral gestures of negation.

As evidenced through the examples in this section, the stroke of gestures associated with negation must occur with the negative node or with an element that follows it, such as a Negative Polarity Item or a focused element in scope. Negative particles impose positional constraints on linguistic elements that follow them, which appears to be a multimodal principle that extends to the organisation of gestures associated with negation too.

3.3.3   An Ordering Principle for Sync Points in Speech

The examples in this chapter allow us to derive a basic ordering principle for the temporal coordination of gestures associated with negation in English grammar. Square brackets indicate stretches of language with which speakers are likely to organise their Horizontal Palm gestures, while bold type predicts location of the stroke based on the presence of elements in addition to the negation in the utterance. Underlining indicates the stretch of language with which a post-stroke hold can potentially occur.

(i)   [I **don't**]
(ii)   [I **don't** have to pay]
(iii)   [I **don't** get **a single** channel]
(iv)   [I **don't** work Friday **at all** or Monday **at all**]
(v)   [**Not** in the **first** instance]
(vi)   [None of these **heavy** where everybody **dies** and they're **fighting**]
(vii)   [I **don't** get **anything** done *******]
(viii) [***I** don't have to pay]

Based on our examples, this ordering principle predicts that if there is a negative node only, the gesture associated with negation will occur with it (i). Where a negative node projects scope over a clause, the gesture will synchronise with the node and be maintained in space through the scope (ii; cf. Harrison 2010, 2014a). A post-stroke hold synchronising with scope may be disrupted by hedges and hitches (such as cut-offs and restarts), or abandoned early to prepare another gesture. The presence of a Negative Polarity Item may indicate the speaker's emphasis or discursive aim and attract the gesture stroke accordingly (iii). If NPIs are repeated, the strokes of the gesture associated with negation may be repeated too (iv). Discourse elements targeted as the focus of negation will also attract the gesture stroke, in which case the number of focused elements may determine number of gesture strokes (v and vi). A gesture performed as part of a description of a negative state of affairs to emphasise the categorical or absolute nature of negation may be performed after the verbal utterance, as a summative expression of negation (vii). Note that in (iii), (iv), and (v), the onset of gesture does not need to synchronise with the onset of its main grammatical affiliate (the negative particle), but can be associated with grammatically related elements that occur further down the syntax. Finally, the asterisk in (viii) indicates that a gestural expression of negation that is tied in with the utterance was not found in this study to precede the main verbal negation (such as to synchronise with the grammatical subject). I propose this ordering principle as a grammatical affiliation for gestures that determines their coordination with the expression of negation in speech.

3.4   Discussion

Negative particles are a feature of all languages (Dahl 1979). They constitute a node for negation and exert semantic and syntactic influence over linguistic segments that lie in their scope (Horn 1989). These elements include Negative Polarity Items (Lawler 2005; Larrivée 2017) and focused elements (Quirk et al. 2000). Negation is thus spread across the surface of an utterance (Jespersen 1924), which yields a number of sync points for the organisation of gestures. What do these sync points tell us about the way people gesture when they speak?

Gestures are supposed to be 'co-expressive' with linguistic segments in speech. But a speaker may perform the same gesture associated with negation either with the negative particle (e.g. 'I **don't** have to pay'), a negative polarity item ('I don't work weekends **at all**'), a focused element in scope ('Not in the **first** instance'), or in a slot on its own after the verbal utterance. In these cases, it is not the referential content of the utterance that determines the co-expressivity of gesture and speech, but the form and location of the gesture is determined by the grammar of negation. Speakers may perform gestures with negative particles but also with semantically unrelated words connected by virtue of (i.e. affiliation to) the grammar of negation underpinning speech. The way people prepare, release, hold, and repeat their gestures suggests there are grammatical affiliates for gestures in speech. This chapter therefore shows that grammatical structures impose positional constraints on gestures. It also shows how the organisation of gestural units provides a mechanism for coordinating modalities in the case of a concept that is distributed across speech, such as negation.

4 Gesture as Construal

Blockage, Force, and Distance in Space and Mind

> Gesture is not only visual symbolism; it makes use of kinesthetic and haptic experiences and schemata as well. Often the gesture communicates by indexing a familiar kinesthetic or haptic experience.   —Streeck (2009: 162)

4.1 Introduction

Thinking of the mind as a region of space offers a powerful tool to describe the conceptual processes involved in language use. Concepts can be seen as domains in this space with linguistic operations constituting various actions within and upon them, such as reification, schematisation, and profiling (Langacker 1987, 1991a). Some linguistic constructs evoke, build, or open conceptual spaces (Fauconnier 1997), while others involve mappings across spaces or blending them together (Lakoff and Johnson 1980; Fauconnier and Turner 2000; Oakley and Hougaard 2008). Speaking can be viewed as a dynamic construal operation through which people tailor conceptual space for linguistic expression in communication (Langacker 1987).

As speakers shape this conceptual space linguistically, they may also shape it gesturally. Streeck (2009) views gestures with speech not only as a window onto construal processes – visual symbolism – but also as a tool for achieving those construals. When people gesture, the form of their gesture may embody a kinesthetic or haptic experience that, in its very performance, contributes to construing meaning in a particular way (pp. 160–3). These gestures may construe meaning on various levels. Streeck (2009) distinguishes between thematic construal (e.g. when gestures construe emotions, ideas, and feelings) and 'meta-pragmatic', that is, 'when they embody and visualize (and potentially enact) a communicative function or illocutionary force that is simultaneously performed by the spoken utterance that they accompany' (p. 180). How speakers use these gestures in physical space for interaction therefore sheds light on the way they are shaping thoughts in conceptual space.

To explore the conceptual basis of recurrent patterns in speech and gesture, this chapter will analyse gestures associated with negation in terms of the construal operation they achieve with specific utterances in dialogic interaction. Staying within the family of Open Hand Prone gestures, we now shift focus from the Horizontal Palm to the Vertical Palm variants. We demonstrate how variations in performance of this class of gestures constitute variations in construal operation that are integral to the conceptualisation of the co-occurring negation, on both linguistic and discursive levels. The construals of negation in interaction include construals of negation as BLOCKAGE, FORCE, and DISTANCE. Although dynamic, these construals are based on entrenched embodied cognitive routines. They are necessarily structured by image schemas and conceptual mappings consistent with those described for negation in speech: negation as absence (Fauconnier 1997; Sweetser 2006), force (Johnson 1987; Krysthaliuk 2012) and distance (Langacker 1987; Chilton 2006, 2014). Such construal operations shape the impulse to gesture and provide speakers with a powerful tool for construal in interaction.

4.1.1   Space, Force, and Distance in Conceptual Space

Linguistic concepts like negation may be analysed in terms of the contrasts, distances, forces, and blends operating in conceptual space. Mental spaces, for example, are 'small conceptual packets constructed as we think and talk for purposes of local understanding and action' (Fauconnier and Turner 2000: 40). Negation markers construct both a negative space and a positive space (Fauconnier 1997). The effect of negation arises from juxtaposing the content of the two spaces for comparison. For example, when somebody opens a refrigerator and says 'there's no milk', Sweetser (2006) explains that 'the linguistic choice of *no milk* marks the speaker as comparing the non-contents of the empty refrigerator specifically with an imagined situation where the refrigerator contains milk' (p. 315). The basic expression 'no milk' thus indexes a complex construal operation; it is the linguistic tip of a 'cognitive iceberg' (Fauconnier and Turner 2000).

Positing the absence or presence of elements in contrasting conceptual spaces is supported by image schematic treatments of negation. Johnson (1987) intended for image schemas to represent the recurrent patterns in 'human bodily movement, manipulation of objects, and perceptual interactions ... by means of which our experience manifests discernible order' (p. xix). Specifically for negation, he argued that 'either P or not-P ... has an intuitive basis with our daily experience with containment' (p. 39). A containment schema can be diagrammed to reflect this principle, where the existence of a proposition P is construed as inhabiting a bounded region of conceptual space, while not-P is construed specifically in relation to being outside of or excluded from the P space (Figure 4.1).

CONTAINMENT is one of several schemas that we use to reason when expressing negation. A sub-category of schemas associated with FORCE to

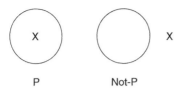

Figure 4.1 'Negation as location outside of a bounded space' (Johnson 1987: 64)

account for root senses of modal verbs, which includes the logic of negative deontic and epistemic mood, was also identified. For Johnson (1987), these force schemas are 'structures of experience that emerge from our forceful interactions in our world' (p. 48). They include COMPULSION, BLOCKAGE, COUNTERFORCE, DIVERSION, and REMOVAL OF RESTRAINT. As with other schemas, Johnson used simple shapes and vectors to represent the interplay of forces that gives rise to each different schema (pp. 45–7). BLOCKAGE, for example, was represented 'as a force vector encountering a barrier and then taking any number of any possible directions' (p. 45).

Illustrating how such models can be applied in analysis, Krysthaliuk's (2012) study of news discourse showed how force schemas affect 'the course of a person's reality conceptualization' during the expression of negation, which generates 'new opposite perceptual, force, and perceptual force relations by the transformation of one image schema into another' (p. 100). Negative markers in the text influence the ongoing construal of events through subtle cognitive operations.

Consistent with these mental space and image schematic models of negation, Langacker's (1991b) basic epistemic model situates *irrealis* as a 'region' of conceptual space 'outside' the cogniser's immediate reality or 'epistemic center' (Figure 4.2). These construals of space are built into the grammar of language. Contrasts between modal verbs such as *must* and *may*, for example, 'can be described as contrasting with one another because they situate the process at varying distances from the speaker's position at immediate known reality' (p. 246).

Building on Langacker's work, Chilton (2014) proposed a 'deictic space' theory of cognition in which cogniser's judgements of discourse referents could be plotted along a modality axis ranging from 'real/true/right' at the deictic centre ('0') to 'unreal/untrue/wrong' at the axis endpoint (Figure 4.3; cf. Chilton 2006). These discourse referents amount to 'abstract conceptual objects which semantically may be arguments of predicates' (p. 43). Specifically for negation, Chilton wrote that 'various linguistic expressions (negative particles, counterfactuals) give rise to conceptualizations that are maximally distant from S in S's discourse space' (Chilton 2006: 352). In other words, 'What is close corresponds to what is most real for S and what is

Elaborated Epistemic Model

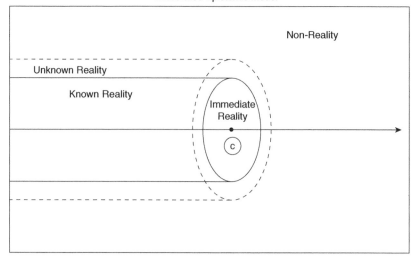

Figure 4.2 Langacker's Epistemic Model of Conceptual Space (1991b: 244)

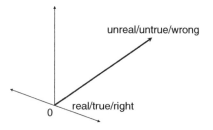

Figure 4.3 The 'modality axis' in Chilton's Deictic Space Theory (2006, 2014)

maximally distal modal corresponds to what is counterfactual, negated or unreal for S' (Chilton 2014: 39).

Offering converging evidence, Lapaire (2006) examined the etymology of terms for negative speech acts and described a ceptual script in which metonymically profiled body parts negate propositions by manipulating, removing, or destroying unwanted 'objects' from conceptual space. Consider, for example, the origin of *to object*, 'from Latin *obicere*, from *ob-* "against" + *jacere* "to throw"', or the origin of *to reject*, 'from Latin *reicere*, "to throw back," from *re-* + *jacere* "to hurl"' (Lapaire 2006a: 335fn; original emphasis).

These studies of the relation between negation and cognition map out the terrain of conceptual space associated with the expression and conceptualisation of negation. They assert the role of conceptual mappings from concrete embodied experience to abstract linguistic reasoning (Lakoff 1987; Lakoff and Johnson 1980, 1999; Sweetser 1990), and they illustrate the centrality of conceptual reification to creating and organising linguistic referents (Langacker 1987, 1991a, 1991b, 2008). However, they abstract negation away from the cogniser's actual body in interaction and therefore overlook potential insights to more dynamic, embodied dimensions of negative construal in face-to-face communication.

4.1.2 The Vertical Palm Gesture

Speakers also use gesture to construe (Streeck 2009). When they gesture with speech, the way they gesture contributes to shaping their conceptualisation as well as the interactive move they intend for it to achieve – a multimodal utterance is the expressed conceptualisation in structured and content-laden form, composed of both verbal and gestural components. The form and function of a particular gesture associated with negation serves to illustrate how gesture constitutes construal of negation consistent with the models derived from negation in speech, namely negation as absence, force, and distance.

The Vertical Palm gesture is produced when the open hand or hands are raised vertically into space with the flat palm(s) oriented away from the speaker's body (Figure 4.4).

Kendon (2004) observed that people use this gesture 'in contexts where the speaker indicates an intention to halt his or her current line of action, a wish that what is being done jointly be halted, or a wish that what is being done by the interlocutor should be halted' (p. 260). Comparing numerous examples, he concluded that the gesture expresses a 'semantic theme of stopping or interrupting a line of action that is in progress' (pp. 248–9). This finding is supported by observations of Vertical Palm performance in French (Calbris 1990, 2011),

Figure 4.4 Samples of the Vertical Palm gesture

German (Streeck 2009; Bressem and Müller 2014a), Savosavo – an Austronesian language – (Bressem et al. 2017), and English (Harrison 2009b, 2014b).

Kendon (2004) established that the formational core of this gesture was the open hand shape, vertical palm(s), and away-body orientation, and this was connected to the semantic core of stopping/interrupting a line of action. Central to the form and semantic theme of the Vertical Palm gesture is its reproduction of an everyday action related to stopping, blocking, and holding away (Kendon 2004; Calbris 2011; Bressem and Müller 2014a). Based on his analysis, Kendon (2004) argued that 'Vertical Palm (VP) gestures can be seen as derived from actions of creating a barrier against the advance of something, or pushing or sweeping something away' (p. 283). Through the semiotic mode of enacting ('the hand acts' – Müller 2014), when speakers perform a basic Vertical Palm gesture they re-enact 'stopping' (hence they generate or 'apply' a semantic theme of 'stopping or interrupting'; Kendon 2004). The hand is shaped so that the surface of the palm is displayed as if it is to come into contact with someone or something. In terms of form-meaning variations, he observed that 'where the hand is placed, relative to the speaker's body, indicates whose line of action is to be stopped' (p. 255). The Vertical Palm thus illustrates not only conceptual but also interactive influences on gesture form.

Bressem and Müller (2014a) include the Vertical Palm in their category of 'Away' gestures that is 'semantically motivated by the effect of actions of removing or keeping away of things ... annoying or otherwise unwanted objects' (p. 1596). Cognitively, they base this family on the 'semanticization of an action scheme' from real-world instances of 'holding away' to the discourse domain of 'refusal'. They write: 'Pragmatically used holding away gestures are used to reject topics of talk, to stop arguments, beliefs, ideas from intrusion into the realm of shared conversation, to stop the continuation of unwanted topics, and they qualify rejected topics as unwanted ones, in short, holding away gestures refuse and stop unwanted topics of talk' (p. 1598). For Streeck (2009), the way this and similar gestures function constitute 'speech-handling', since it evidences construal of 'talk in interaction as a transaction with physical objects' (p. 182). For gestures such as the Vertical Palm, Streeck (2009) thus emphasises the role of conceptual reification and metaphorisation of discourse objects (pp. 199–202). Earlier, Sweetser (1998) also related the motivation of Vertical Palm gestures to the source domain of a 'conduit metaphor' (Reddy 1979): speech is construed as object transfer and performing the Vertical Palm '[m]etaphorically represents a request to interlocutor not to speak now' (Sweetser 1998: 3; see also Wehling 2010).

Although cognitively oriented, these Vertical Palm studies were conducted independently of the models of linguistic negation developed in cognitive linguistics. Nevertheless, the analyses are consistent with aspects of negation and linguistic conceptual space. For example, Kendon's (2004) instantiation of a 'barrier' by the Vertical Palm relates to the BLOCKAGE schema that Johnson (1987) proposed as a force schema structuring negative modality (pp. 45–6). The centrality of the 'away' action emphasised by Bressem and Müller (2014a) is consistent with Chilton's (2014) treatment of negation as an operation that situates discourse referents at a location conceptually distant from the speaker's cognitive centre (cf. Chilton 2006). Streeck's (2009) emphasis on the role played by conceptual reification and metaphorisation of discourse entities in gestures such as the Vertical Palm is consistent with the ceptual scripts underpinning negation described by Lapaire (2006a; cf. Lapaire, 2006b). From the perspective of visual symbolism, gestures associated with negation embody these conceptual structures instantiated by the grammar of negation. In terms of gesture as construal (Streeck 2009), speakers construe their negation as real-world absence, force, and distance.

4.1.3 Where Negation, Conceptualisation, and Gesture Intersect

This chapter describes the cognitive basis of the impulse to gesture at the intersection of linguistic negation, Vertical Palm gestures, and dynamic conceptual structure. Examples of the Vertical Palm with negative utterances have been extracted from the spoken language corpus, and their analysis for this chapter integrates form-based gesture study with conceptual semantics and discourse analysis (Bressem et al. 2013; Ladewig 2011, 2014b; Müller et al. 2013a). At this intersection, context-specific variations in form of the Vertical Palm are based on a related collection of underlying actions. When these actions are reproduced as gestures, they embody the logic of a salient image schema that applies to the co-occurring linguistic segments.

4.2 Gesture Space as Conceptual Space

People use the Vertical Palm gesture in at least four main ways. Similar to the Horizontal Palm, these variants are distinguished primarily in the kind of movement pattern that the gesture involves, based on its reproduction of a different underlying action. This action corresponds to differences in conceptualisation and has ramifications for the construal operation when performed in conjunction with a negative utterance.

1. The Vertical Palm is performed with no movement (VP+Zero). In simply raising the gesture in space, speakers construe negation as blocking or stopping. Speakers locate the gesture along an interactional axis between themselves (VP+Zero+Sp) and their addressees (VP+Zero+Add.). Where they place the gesture construes the origin of the application of negation accordingly (Kendon 2004).

2. The Vertical Palm is performed with a single lateral movement (VP+Lateral), either with one hand or with both. With this gesture, the speaker construes the object of negation as something to be removed. In moving the Vertical Palm laterally, the speaker uses gesture to 'throw aside' the conceptualised objects (objects 'that do not even have to be thought of as real or existing at all', Chilton 2014: 43). Additionally, speakers may also move the Vertical Palm laterally to indicate they are 'screening' an unwanted object from view. These variants indicate that gesture space is also structured by a modality axis, whereby positions and movements away from the speaker construe negation as distance.

3. The Vertical Palm is oscillated (VP+Oscillate). The object of negation is construed as an imaginary object in gesture space, against which the surface of the palm is placed in contact and then oscillated so as to erase, rub, or wipe it away. In oscillating the Vertical Palm (repeated left–right movement), speakers construe negation as wiping away and erasing unwanted objects, such as marks left by pen on a whiteboard or stains on wallpaper.

4. The Vertical Palm is moved outwards along the sagittal axis (VP+Sagittal). Speakers construe negation as pushing an unwanted object away from them. They push the object away from both themselves and their addressees; for example, along a trajectory at diagonals to both speaker and hearer.

These variations help in understanding how linguistic structures, conceptual structure and gestures interact. They support a spatial view of conceptualisation and indicate that gestures constitute the construal operations of associated linguistic concepts in speech.

4.2.1   Blocking and Stopping

The least semiotically complex variant of the Vertical Palm gesture occurs when speakers raise a Vertical Palm into space (VP+Zero). This gesture reproduces the action of blocking (Kendon 2004), which is achieved through the semiotic mode of acting: 'in the acting mode the hands are used to mime or reenact actual manual activities' (Müller et al. 2013a: 712). With this variant of the Vertical Palm gesture, the hand or hands re-enact blocking, that is, the hand blocks. Examples include speakers performing this gesture when they use negation to end a topic of conversation, to discontinue a sexual innuendo, to refuse an offer, to exclude an undesirable implication, to correct a word that has been wrongly used, and to weaken the strength of an assertion. In performing this gesture with such utterances, the speakers construe their negation as a blockage. How they locate their gesture further construes the origin of the force they wish to block, either as themselves or as their addressees.

The first two examples present instances where the speaker's language use can be construed as applying blockage to a discursive force of which the speakers are the origin, and accordingly the speakers perform the Vertical Palm gesture with one hand located at their own bodies, that is, within personal space (Sweetser and Sizemore 2008). In the first example, the speaker has digressed from an initial conversation topic ('something you'd like to learn') into a story about a time she met several Deaf men in a bar. Having concluded that story ('all of them, were Deaf'), she begins another story which is apparently related ('Yeh and I used to know'). However, now she interrupts herself mid-sentence, performs a Vertical Palm gesture in front of her own body, utters 'anyway', and jokingly reiterates the original topic while comically scratching her head ('erm something i'd like to learn *ehum ha ha*') (Figure 4.5).

Example 30 BT gm1 11.57 anyway
1 T and yeh i ended up seeing them again later (.) it was really it was just like i went
      home
2   feeling soo (.) cool about life ha ha because i was an- we were all able to
3   communicate like people who have no idea how to use sign language and then people
4   who had no- could read lips to some extent but not you know not when i'm speaking
5   like this and er but it was still really cool
6   yeh and i used to know [. . . . . .] anyway . . . *erm* something i'd like to learn *ehum ha ha*
          |~*******-| |~*****-.| |~*************-.|
             [1]   [2]   [3]
7 B that was really cool
8 T what I'd like to learn ahem ha ha
9 A ha ha ha

[1] Palm Presenting gesture, [2] Vertical Palm gesture (VP-raise), [3] Stylised Head Scratch gesture.

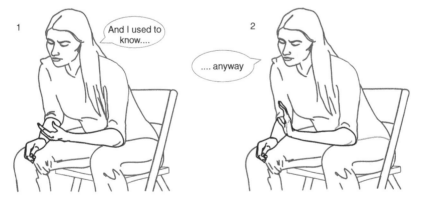

Figure 4.5 The speaker performs a VP+Zero+Sp gesture located at her own body

'Anyway' here is a discourse marker with which the speaker acknowledges her digression and indicates a return to the relevant topic. Conceptually, the speaker's digression constitutes a force vector, of which she is the origin, and the discourse marker 'anyway' imposes a conceptual barrier on that force. By enacting a 'stopping' or 'blocking' action with the hand, the speaker dynamically construes her use of 'anyway' as a barrier. By locating the gesture in personal gesture space, she construes her own action as the origin of the force to be blocked (as if to say, 'I'm going to stop myself from that story'). Having indicated this stoppage, her repeat of the original topic 'something I'd like to learn' coupled with a visibly expressive head scratch reinforces her renewed commitment to the maxim of relation.

In Example 31, the speakers have been discussing the topic 'something you like doing in winter'. Speaker 1 (K) has mentioned 'conkers' – 'a children's game in which each child has a conker on the end of a string and takes turns trying to break another's with it' (*New Oxford American Dictionary*). When the speaker boasts that he got his conker 'up to a 69-er' (line 1), meaning that his conker had beaten either sixty-nine other conkers or the equivalent value, Speaker 2 (Q) questions this ('really?'). Speaker 2 then continues and plays on a sexual innuendo with the word '69-er', which he jokingly claims makes him 'think of something else' (line 2). When Speaker 1 briefly acknowledges this claim with 'right' (line 5), Speaker 2 immediately says 'no wait maybe that's the 49-ers' (line 6). Exactly as he says this, he performs a Vertical Palm gesture in front of his own body [1] and also tilts his head back for the duration of his gesture (^–^). By pretending to have been thinking about the American football team based in San Francisco, he effectively discontinues the innuendo. His Vertical Palm gesture construes that discontinuation as a blocking of his own action. Following a brief response token from his addressee (line 7), the speaker initiates a move to change the topic completely by saying '*err* right whose turn is it?' (Figure 4.6).

Example 31 Q_K gm 19.14 69-er
1 K   mine got up to a 69-er . . . pretty good
2 Q   really? . . . 69-er hey . . .
3 K   yeh
4 Q   that makes me think of
5 K   something else right
        ^_____^

6 Q   [no wait, maybe that's the 49ers]
        |~*********************-|
             _____
                [1]
7 K   [right]
8 Q   [err] right whose turn is it?

[1] Vertical Palm with zero movement located in personal gesture space
    ^—^ Head is tilted backwards for the duration of the gesture

Figure 4.6 The speaker performs a VP+Zero+Sp gesture located at his own body

In this example, the speaker is not interrupting a line of verbal action as in Example 30, but he is interrupting a line of thought. Kendon (2004) uses the term 'line of action' to refer generally to the array of 'lines' that a Vertical Palm gesture may serve to interrupt: 'By "line of action" we mean any project that someone might be engaged in, whether this involves physical action, communicative action (such as saying something), or mental activity, such as pursuing a train of thought or assuming a certain mental attitude toward something' (p. 249). It is a line of thought – the speaker's sexual interpretation of the word '69' – that has been construed as a force vector, of which the speaker is the origin, while the linguistic negation imposes a conceptual barrier to that force. The speaker's Vertical Palm gesture enacts this instance of blocking situated at the speaker's own body. By synchronising with the negative utterance, the gestural enactment of blockage is fully integral to the conceptual one evoked by speech.

Speakers may also locate this variant of the Vertical Palm gesture towards the addressee. The movement of the gesture is not part of the gesture stroke, rather it is part of the gesture preparation in order to position the Vertical Palm form into a location towards the addressee. The speakers' use of the gesture still construes negation as blockage, however, now the addressee is construed as the origin of a force vector.

The conversational pair in Example 32 have been discussing the topic 'programmes you like watching on television'. Struggling to list the programmes she likes, one of the speakers B confesses that 'she got into *Friends*' (a popular American television sitcom). This is apparently embarrassing because she immediately admits 'sucks huh' and lowers her gaze from her addressee (line 1). The addressee T says 'oh' and also diverts her eye-gaze as if to comically disapprove (line 2). B immediately pleads with her addressee by saying 'no hold on, let me explain' (line 3). As she says this, she performs a Vertical Palm gesture towards her addressee and moves it up and down with small beat-like movements (Figure 4.7).

Example 32 B_T gm 07.22 hold on let me explain
1 B   i got into friends (.) sucks huh
2 T   oh (inaud.)
3 B   no hold on let me explain
        |~***************-|
                  [1]
4 T hahaha

[1] Vertical Palm held towards addressee

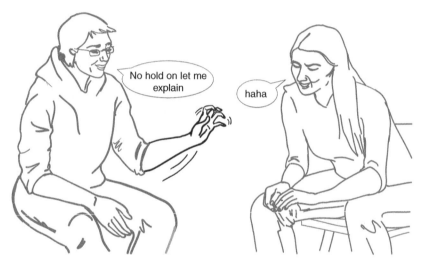

Figure 4.7 VP gesture towards addressee with 'No hold on' (VP+Zero+Add.)

In this example, the negation is part of a construal operation whereby the addressee's feigned disapproval and imminent derision constitute a force, to which the speaker's negation is deployed to apply a blockage. The performance of a Vertical Palm gesture and its positioning towards the addressee are motivated by and reinforce this construal. Furthermore, since there is a sustained period during which the addressee is laughing while the speaker is performing a Vertical Palm, the salient force schema of COUNTERFORCE is also present. The addressee's action (laughing) and the speaker's utterance ('no hold on' with Vertical Palm) illustrate the 'head-on meetings of forces' in interaction (Johnson 1987: 46).

A speaker may interrupt his own speech but perform the Vertical Palm gesture towards his addressee. This happens because the interruption serves to negate an undesirable implication that specifically concerns the addressee. In discussing the topic 'someone you'd like to meet', C has said that he would like to meet the Queen, but on the condition they could 'have a conversation' and there would be 'time to get to know one another' (lines 1–2). Now, K offers his interpretation of C's condition by saying 'stay the night' but immediately interrupts himself and says 'not with her', then continues by repeating the first part of his utterance 'but stay the night'. The expression 'stay the night' has evidently evoked an undesirable sexual interpretation that the speaker wishes to immediately rule out. As he says 'stay the night', he is maintaining a gesture in which both hands are lateral [1]. When he interrupts himself and says 'not with her', he performs a Vertical Palm gesture towards his addressee [2]. His hands return back to their original position as he continues his utterance [3] (Figure 4.8), whilst his interlocutor acknowledges the unlikely scenario with laughter (line 4).

Example 33 K_C gm1 15.21 stay the night, not with her
1 C have a cup of tea with her (.) i think go round and have a cup of tea
2   have a conversation time to get know one another
3 K (.) stay the night (.) **not with her** [but stay the night where they (.) dinner]
        /~**********/~***********/~***********/ . . .
            [1]   [2]   [3]
4 C   [ha ha ha ha]   [in Buckingham palace]
5 K yeh in the palace
6 C yeh yeh that' d be fine

Figure 4.8 VP gesture towards Addressee with meta-linguistic negation

Although the speaker interrupts himself, his performance of the Vertical Palm towards the addressee construes the addressee's potential objection to the undesirable implication as a force, to which the negation is applied. As evidenced by the laughter in the current and previous examples, the role of this gesture in evoking and blocking different forces also appears to play a role in humour.

So far, all instances of this Vertical Palm variant have been performed with one hand in lower gesture space, either situated at the speaker's body or towards the addressee's body. An example of the gesture with two hands performed in upper central gesture space will now be considered. The form variation in the gesture corresponds to a nuance in conceptualisation of the nature of blockage. The next speaker's performance of the Vertical Palm gesture with both hands located in front of his chest construes the speaker's utterance as protecting himself from the possible objections it could solicit.

Example 34 is from a discussion of gender equality in France. Comparing males and females, K tentatively expresses that he still gets 'this little sense' that gender is not equal in France (line 1). He develops on this by adopting a deep voice and saying 'it's that *I'm the man, the man's the boss*'. His addressee offers a hedged agreement by saying 'yeah I suppose they like to keep that idea don't they'. After a short pause, however, the speaker then says 'yeah ... I mean I I I don't know'. With this final utterance he uses linguistic negation to weaken his assertion and thereby protect himself from possible objections to it. As part of the utterance he performs a two-handed Vertical Palm gesture located in central gesture space (Figure 4.9).

Example 34 K_C gm3 03.14 don't know but
1 K   but still i kind of get this little sense of like you still
2   it's that i'm the man the man's the boss
3 C   yeah i suppose they like to keep that idea don't they
4 K   yeah (.) i mean i i i don't know but
          /~~~~~~~*************.-.|
                    [1]
5 C   bit of a power struggle then I suppose

[1] Speaker raises both palms open and vertical in front of chest.

Figure 4.9 Speaker raises Vertical Palms as he nuances claim about gender equality

It is the speaker's conceptualised objection to his claim from the addressee that constitutes the force vector to which the speaker applies the blockage enacted by the Vertical Palm gesture. In this case, the underlying action is a specific sub-instance of stopping, namely protecting. This interpretation is consistent with Calbris's (2011) analysis of the 'palms forward' gesture as 'signifying (self-protective) opposition' (p. 164).

Vertical Palm gestures performed with two hands also occur in lower gesture space. The following example supports the idea that verbs evoke conceptual forces as part of their semantics (Talmy 2000). Negating the meaning of a word with a so-called 'meta-linguistic negation' can be construed as blocking the force that the word exerts. The next example is taken from the discussion between K and C about 'people you would like to meet'. As mentioned in a previous example, C has said he would like to meet the Queen. The speaker K is now offering his interpretation of the conditions under which C has said he would like to meet the Queen, namely that time would be available 'to get to know her'. As K says 'I see be forced into', he is presumably about to evoke a situation where the appropriate amount of time to satisfy his addressee's condition is imposed, and his hands are in a partial rest position. However, he seems to immediately realise that the verb 'forced' indicates an inappropriate level of coercion for this context, so he immediately negates the word by saying 'not forced but', then carries on with 'into a situation'. He performs the Vertical Palm gesture with 'not forced but' [1], then a Palm Presenting gesture as he continues his utterance with 'into a situation' [2] (Figure 4.10).

Example 35 K_C gm1 15.11 be forced, not forced
1 C the queen (.) i think it'd be interesting to meet the queen
2   although it would be good to have something like this where you could get to
       know her
3 K yeh
4 C there's no point to meet her at all if it's just hello ma'am and how are you
5 K yeh
6   i see be forced in- not forced but into a situation where you have to spend
       |~~********** ~~~~*********** /...
                [1]   [2]
7 C have a cup of tea

[1] Vertical Palm gesture, [2] Palm Presenting gesture.

Figure 4.10 Speaker uses Vertical Palm during a meta-linguistic negation

The speaker's Vertical Palm gesture enacts 'stopping' as the inappropriate word is negated. The strength of coercion encoded by the verb 'force' is conceptualised as a force vector to which the speaker applies the blockage enacted by the Vertical Palm. A metaphor is at play here in which the meanings encoded in words can have a force (Lakoff and Johnson 1980), so negating a word is conceptualised as blocking the force of its meaning. Alternatively, the speech stream constitutes the force vector to which the speaker applies the blockage enacted by the Vertical Palm. In which case, this example is similar to the self-interruption in Example 30. The Vertical Palm is the gestural equivalent of stopping an utterance.

We have considered six examples of utterances containing linguistic negation and the Vertical Palm gesture with zero movement (*VP+Zero*). In all examples, the Vertical Palm construes negation as applying blockage to various forces evoked by the discourse, either explicitly or implicitly. By enacting a stopping or blocking action, the form of the Vertical Palm gestures embodies the construal of negation as blockage in situ and further illustrates aspects of a BLOCKAGE schema. Speakers construe discursive forces as originating either from the speaker or the addressee. Where the speaker locates, the Vertical Palm gesture construes who is the origin of the force. Vertical Palm gestures are located along an interactional axis running from the speaker to the addressee (Figure 4.11).

Location of gestures along this interactional axis is just one way that Vertical Palm gestures construe negation as BLOCKAGE. We also considered an example where the speaker raised a two-handed Vertical Palm gesture to his upper central gesture space, which coincided with a discourse marker serving to weaken the force of an assertion he was making. In that example, it was a potential objection to his assertion that was construed as a force, to which the blockage enacted by the Vertical Palm gesture was construed as protecting him.

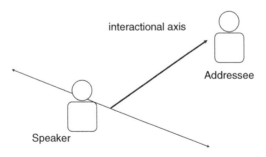

Figure 4.11 Vertical Palm gestures are located along an interactional axis

4.2.2   Throwing Aside, Separating, and Screening from View

Speakers perform the Vertical Palm gestures with a single lateral movement in the space in front of their own bodies, either with one hand or both hands (VP+Lateral). This second variant of the gesture reproduces actions related to 'throwing aside'. This action is reproduced gesturally via the semiotic mode of acting. In enacting 'throwing aside', the open palm is used as a surface which comes into contact with some object, much like blocking or stopping. But when engaged in an abrupt lateral movement with an accentuated ending, the action achieved on that object is one of 'throwing aside'.

Linguistically, this variant of the Vertical Palm gesture occurs in utterances with which the speaker is negating a proposition. A proposition has either been implied by the discourse or explicitly evoked, and the speaker utters a linguistic negation that serves to negate that proposition. The Vertical Palm gesture construes that negation as a 'throwing aside'.

Conceptually, negating propositions can also be construed as blockage, but the gesture form suggests a different image schema structuring conceptualisation, namely REMOVAL. Johnson (1987) describes a schema that he calls REMOVAL OF RESTRAINT and argues that 'the removal of a barrier or the absence of some potential restraint is a structure of experience that we encounter daily' (pp. 46–7). By reproducing a 'throwing aside' action, this variant of the Vertical Palm gesture construes negation as the removal of unwanted objects. Although subtle, this different conceptual schema has important implications for the interaction between linguistic negation, gesture form, and conceptualisation. For BLOCKAGE, negation was deployed to block forces arising from the discourse, either originating from the speaker or the addressee. For REMOVAL, negation itself is the origin of force, and this force is applied to propositions construed as objects. By including a lateral movement away from the interactional axis, the form of the gesture further suggests that negating propositions is construed as removing objects from the interactional space, either off to one side (for one-handed version) or bilaterally (for both).

Example 36 demonstrates this as a speaker describes how an expectation that he had was not met. The way the speaker gestures indicates the expectation is construed as an object, while negating that expectation amounts to removing it from the interactional space. The speaker's utterance occurs within the context of recounting highlights of a holiday he once took to Australia, and here he is directly addressing an Australian who is part of the interaction. From his discourse, we learn that the speaker was overwhelmed by the hospitality of the Australians he met, contrary to the fact he 'expected a little bit of friction' (line 4). Prior to uttering this expectation, he addresses the Australian speaker and says 'the hospitality I received', then pauses and says 'I can't fault you at all' (line 2). As he says 'the hospitality I received' he gestures so that his hand begins in an open position addressed to the addressee then during the stroke moves towards his own chest [1/2]. In the pause between this statement and 'I can't fault you at all', he performs a Vertical Palm gesture with lateral movement [3] (Figure 4.12).

Example 36 X_D 05.14 can't fault you
1 X   and oh i i you couldn't . . . .
                            +++++
2   the hospitality i received [. . . ..] i can't fault you at all
       |~~~~~~~~~~~********-.-.-.~***-.-|
              [1/2]   [3]
3 D   yeh (.) nice bunch
4 X   i expected a little bit of friction

[1/2] Open hand deictic moves from addressee to speaker, [3] VP+lateral (removal).

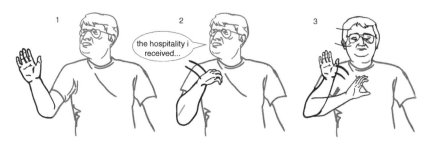

Figure 4.12   Vertical Palm+Lateral gesture

Possible faults with Australian hospitality (such as the speaker's expectation of 'a little bit of friction') constitute the conceptual object to which the speaker applies a force vector encoded by negation. The integration of a VP+Lateral gesture indicates the conceptual object is not only blocked but also removed. The movement of the gesture stroke is towards the interlocutor, however, it is not aimed at him, by turning the head away from the addressee as he performs his gesture. Since the movement involves a lateral vector from central gesture space to peripheral space, this may correspond conceptually to 'distancing' the conceptual object further away from the cognising centre.

    In Example 37, X has just explained to D that his wife is fluent in both Polish and German. D is surprised at this impressive feat and says 'Polish, I thought Polish was really dissimilar to German?' (line 1). X mishears this utterance though and believes his addressee has said 'similar' as opposed to 'dissimilar'. He replies 'no it's very ... completely different' (unaware that he is agreeing with his addressee's claim; line 2). He vigorously shakes his head with the response signal 'no::' [1] then performs the Vertical Palm lateral gesture as he says 'completely different' [2] (Figure 4.13).

Example 37 X_C 08.08 Polish German different
1 D polish? i thought it's really dissimilar to *err* german
    +++
2 X No:: it's very completely different
   [1] |~~~~*********_-_.|
                   [2]
3 D yeah it is
4 X oh no it's (.) she speaks fluent german and polish obviously
[1] Head shake, [2] 2VP+Lateral.

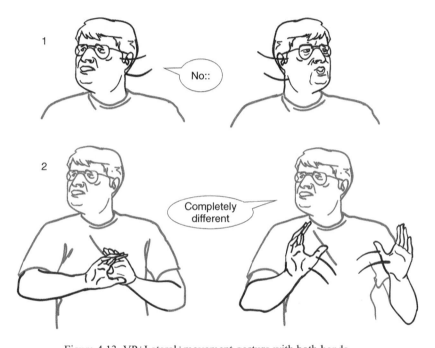

Figure 4.13 VP+Lateral+movement gesture with both hands

The speaker is rejecting the proposition that German and Polish are similar. Conceptually, this proposition constitutes the object to which the speaker applies a force vector encoded by the negation. By enacting 'throwing aside', the VP+Lateral gesture embodies this force vector and applies it to a conceptual object. Since both hands are used and move in opposite directions laterally from centre to periphery, the imaginary object is scattered from left to right. With this action, the speaker may also be experiencing difference metaphorically by moving two imaginary objects away from each other.

Example 38 demonstrates how form variations in the performance of a particular gesture variant of the Vertical Palm can be motivated by significantly different construal operations, underlying metaphors, and modes of representation.

In this example of the Vertical Palm gesture with lateral movement, the speaker prepares to perform the gesture in a location off at a diagonal axis outwards from his interactional axis with the addressee. As the stroke occurs, the lateral movement is slow rather than abrupt. The gesture no longer looks like an enactment of throwing off. Consideration of the form properties in conjunction with their linguistic context suggest the speaker is embedding a Vertical Palm form into a slow lateral movement to extend the barrier instantiated by the gesture's formational core. The two open palms raised creates a barrier (VP+Zero) and by moving the palms slowly away from each other on the lateral axis, the barrier is extended. This is an instance of moulding: 'the hands create a transient structure' (Müller, Bressem and Ladewig, 2013a: 712). The transient structure created is an extended barrier located in the gesture space. How the speaker uses this barrier depends on where he locates it and the way it relates to the function of negation in the discourse.

The speakers have been discussing the topic 'a job you'd like to have'. In the stretch of discourse leading up to the gesture, the speaker K has spoken at length about his interests in politics and how he has training in international relations, however, he also claims that he dislikes politics. His addressee C challenges this claim by saying 'if you didn't like politics, you wouldn't talk about it so much'. In response to this, K clarifies his position, explaining that he dislikes 'the way politics works' and implying this would not exclude a job in politics however, specifically stating 'my position is not to be a politician' (line 11). With 'my position is', his hands are in a partial rest position [1]. He performs a Vertical Palm gesture with lateral movement [2] and shakes his head specifically with 'not to be a politican'. He locates the gesture away from himself and his addressee at a diagonal angle from the interactional axis; the lateral movement of the hands is slow and even. Following this negation, he establishes 'my position is to make sure' and starts another gesture in which the hands begin moving to a region of space to his left [3], but opts out of finishing the verbal and gestural components of this utterance by saying 'it can get really complicated' (line 12) (Figure 4.14).

Example 38 K_C gm1 25.52 Not to be a politician
1   K   i think some of my experiences is what pushed me in this direction
2   more than i just like politics because truth is i don't like it
3   it's something i dislike which is probably why i'm paying more attention to it
4   at this point th-
5   C   but if you don't like politics you wouldn't talk about it so much
6   K   erm i don't like what's happening
7   C   okay

8   K   i don't like the way politics work which is why
9   C   okay you disagree with some of the sorry some of the
10 K   yeah i disagree definitely with the way certain things are happening
                                        ++++++++++++++++
11   So my position is NOt to be a politician (.) My position is to make sure
                        /~~~~~~~~******-_-_-_/~~~~~~~~************/ ... |
                        [1]   [2]   [3]
12   it can get really complicated
13 C   sounds like

[1] Hands in partial retraction from previous gesturing, [2] 2PV-Horizontal, [3] hands begin moving to space on left (abandoned).

Figure 4.14 VP+Lateral gesture with two hands

In previous examples of the VP+Lateral, the lateral movements were interpreted as applying force to a reified discourse object, which the gesture construed as being thrown aside. However, here it is the implied proposition 'speaker/be a politician' that constitutes a force, while the gesture's lateral movement construes negation as an extended barrier that blocks that force. By negating the proposition linguistically and simultaneously locating the gesture in a space away from the interactional axis, the speaker achieves a construal operation in which the negated object is not only 'distanced' from both speaker and addressee but also blocked from view. In moving the Vertical Palms outwards slowly, the speaker either 'moulds' a vertical surface (like a wall) or the hands actually 'embody' and become understood as such a wall. This is coherent with studies that construe negation metaphorically as when 'a referent is outside the conceptualizer's visual field' (Kryshtaliuk 2012: 101). The metaphor this is based on is Negating is Blocking From Sight: what is negated is not visible.

    The Vertical Palm gesture with lateral movement supports descriptions in cognitive linguistics of negative construal as distance between the cognising

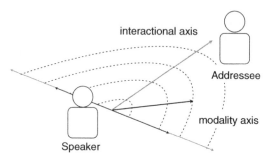

Figure 4.15 Lateral movement or placement achieves 'distancing' along a modality axis

subject and some proposition, thought or idea (Chilton 2006, 2014; Langacker 1991b). It could be argued that cognitive distance motivates the lateral movement of the VP-Lateral, with which speakers appear to enact throwing aside as they utter linguistic negation. Locating the barrier instantiated by the VP gesture at a tangent from the interaction axis also suggests a discourse referent is being positioned 'off to one side', that is, distanced from both speaker and addressee. In addition to an interactional axis, we can also posit a modality axis structuring gesture space (Figure 4.15).

The modality axis could essentially be evoked in any direction away from the primary interaction axis. However, the examples so far suggest it is prominently along a lateral axis from the speaker's central gesture space to a peripheral space, or along a diagonal axis running away from the interaction axis.

4.2.3   Wiping Away, Removing, and Pushing

A third variant of Vertical Palm gestures occurs when speakers raise the Vertical Palm and then oscillate it (VP-Oscillate). Vertical Palm gestures can be performed with repeated lateral movements, that is, the Vertical Palm formational core is embedded in an oscillatory movement. The Vertical Palm with no movement reproduces blocking (VP-Ø), and the Vertical Palm with lateral movement reproduces throwing aside (VP-lateral). Oscillating the Vertical Palm amounts to 'erasing' or 'rubbing out'. With VP Oscillate gestures, the palm of the hand applies pressure to and 'erases' or 'rubs out' matter from the construed surface it contacts. The salient semiotic mode of representation is acting. Additionally, examples of the VP-Oscillate in my corpus were performed either with one hand or both hands. Single-handed variants were all performed towards the addressee, while both-handed variants were performed at the speaker's own body.

Linguistically, the Vertical Palm Oscillate gesture is integrated with utterances where linguistic negation serves to apologise, to refuse offers or suggestions, and to negate implied propositions. In each case, performing the gesture construes the negation as the speaker's desire to remove something forcefully from the discourse. Conceptually, the salient image schema combines both BLOCKAGE and REMOVAL. The gesture may be located along the interactional axis towards the addressee to indicate the origin of a force, however the oscillatory movement serves to propel imagined discourse referents along a modality axis from that location.

The extract in Example 39 occurs during an informal discussion between the participants and the cameraman about safety in their city, which took place once they had finished playing the board game. As an example of not feeling safe, the cameraman has recounted how one night he was the victim of attempted robbery at knife point just outside his house. This story surprises one of the other speakers, C, who feels relatively safe, although he concedes 'like you might get a few guys, a few guys might harass you' (line 1). Immediately after saying this he tentatively evaluates his own experience as 'gentle harassment' (line 1). But before he finishes the word 'harassment', he interrupts himself in order to clarify he is not now referring to the cameraman's experience. The clarification begins with an apology as C says 'sorry, what you had wasn't gentle harassment', which he then asserts, 'it was awful' (line 2). He performs a Vertical Palm gesture with oscillation towards his addressee as he negates 'gentle harassment'. This is sequenced with a Palm Presenting gesture or 'PP' (Kendon 2004) with 'it was awful' (Figure 4.16).

Example 39 K_C ds 02.55 not gentle harassment
1 C like you might get a few guys, a few guys might harass you (.) gentle har-
          +++++++++++++++++++++++++++
2   sorry what you had wasn't gentle harassment (.) it was awful
       |~~~~********************************/**********_.|
                     [1]   [2]
3 S   yeh
4 C   but in general what we said like before guys at the victoire going like 'oi oi'
5   this kind of stuff
6 S   yeh
7 C   but in general i would . . .

[1] Vertical Palm – oscillate, [2] Palm Presenting.

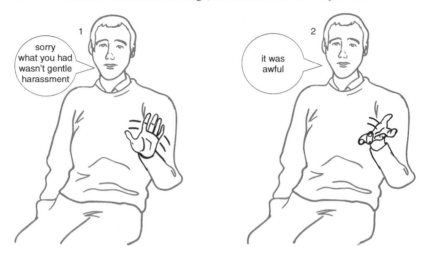

Figure 4.16 The speaker apologises to the cameraman and negates
a potentially offensive comment

This example indicates at least two sources of force motivating the gesture
form. One is the addressee's potential objection, which motivates the location
of the gesture along the interactional axis. As the source of a possible objection
to the term 'gentle harassment', the gesture is oriented towards the addressee.
The second source of force is the reification of an unwanted discourse object,
which motivates the repeated lateral movement that enacts erasing the said
object. As a term that risks understating the cameraman's experience, 'gentle
harassment' is reified by the speaker and erased by the oscillation of his Vertical
Palm gesture.

This example also illustrates how gestures may be sequenced (see Chapter 5),
and their sequencing here further supports our interpretation of the various
conceptual structures. The Palm Presenting gesture that follows the Vertical
Palm gesture is a recurrent gesture that has been established as performing the
function of presentation (Kendon 2004; Müller 2004). By integrating this gesture
with the expression 'it was awful', the speaker 'presents' a more suitable term to
his addressee than the one he has just erased (with meta-linguistic negation).
The addressee's 'yeh' can be interpreted as an acceptance of the apology and an
acknowledgement of 'awful' as an appropriate term.

In the next example of this gesture variant, the speaker is exemplifying the
faultless hospitality that he reportedly received in Australia (cf. Example 36).
To that end, he recounts a time when he was visibly uncomfortable under the
hot sun, at which point a complete stranger offered him a bottle of water to

drink. In response to this act of kindness, the speaker first tells how he 'wanted to give him something' (line 4), meaning he wanted to offer the stranger some money as a token of appreciation (with this expression the speaker enacts taking money out from his pocket and offering it [1]). However, he then reports how this offer was met with an immediate rejection: '"no" he said'. The speaker integrates a VP+Oscillate gesture to this reported rejection ([2], Figure 4.17).

Example 40 X_D 05.28 no, he said
1 X   and that day was very very hot (.) and it was erm (.) i was sweating
2   and this guy came with a bottle of water
3   and said would you like to have some water because you know (.)
                                                    +++++++++++++
4   i said oh thank you i wanted to give him something (.) NO he said
          |~~~~~~***************/~~~~********_.|
                      [1]   [2]
5   which was very nice of him you know
6 D   yeh yeh
[1] Enacts taking money from pocket to give, [2] Oscillates Vertical Palm.

Figure 4.17 Speaker reports that an offer was negated, both verbally and gesturally

In this example, the speaker seems to be re-enacting the scene both verbally and gesturally. In saying 'no' and performing a Vertical Palm Oscillate gesture, the speaker could be suggesting that the Australian man had reified the financial offer as an object, the negation of which conceptually constituted an erasure of the object. For the Australian, the offer was a force of which the current speaker was the origin, and the gesture he performed acted forcefully upon that offer reified as a discourse object.

    In Example 40, a Vertical Palm Oscillate gesture is performed in relation to a discourse object that has only been implied by the discourse. The general conversation topic is 'a job you'd like to have'. The speaker is recounting his time with the American Security Forces and says 'I went to Kuwait' (line 3), which surprises his addressee who interjects 'Really?' (line 4). Possibly playing to this surprise, the speaker proceeds to elaborate and reports he was 'driving round in Hummers' and 'running round with guns' (line 5). He depicts these activities with referential gestures, both of which begin in advance of the verbal reference. First he uses curved hands to mould the trajectory of a hummer vehicle over dunes [1], then he enacts holding a rifle in a 'tactical carry' position [2]. This elaboration is followed by a one-second pause (line 6). Presumably aware of a plausible concern that his addressee might have recovered from the discourse at this point, the speaker then says 'No I didn't have to shoot anybody' (line 7). He integrates a VP-Oscillate gesture to this utterance – both hands are used and the gesture is located in a neutral area of gesture space (i.e. there is no visible effort to extend towards his addressee). He also shakes his head for the duration of his gesture stroke (Figure 4.18).

Example 40 K_C gm1 28.19 Didn't shoot anybody
1 K   so i was with the security forces
2   running round in the desert.
3   i went to Kuwait
4 C   really?
5 K   yeh so (.) driving in hummers and was just running round with guns
        /‿‿‿‿***************/-.-.-.-.-.-****.-|
                    [1]   [2]
6   (. . .)
            +++++++++++++++++++++++++++
7   NO i didn't have to shoot anybody (. . ..)hm
        |‿‿‿‿*******************-.-.-.-.-|
                    [3]
8 C   you were in the, it was in the . . . hm . . .

[1] Moulds dunes (being driven over), [2] Enacts holding rifle [3] 2VP oscillate

Figure 4.18 Speaker negates undesirable implication and oscillates his Vertical Palms

The mention of 'security forces', 'Kuwait', 'Hummers' and most importantly 'guns', along with their vivid gestural enactments, appear for the speaker to evoke the implication that he had to shoot somebody. Regardless of what the addressee was actually thinking at this point, this implication can be seen as one force, while the speaker's negation and gesture constitute another force which is applied to not only block the first force but to remove it from the realm of possibility.

The last example of the VP-Oscillate gesture is integrated to a pause in speech and serves to refuse a suggestion. Within the context of discussing 'a sport you enjoy', one speaker T has said she likes 'anything with moving my body' (line 1). However she adds the exception that she's 'not into boxing though' because, as she says, 'I don't like getting my nose punched' (lines 2–3). In conjunction with this utterance the addressee B jokingly suggests 'You should try it!' with enthusiastic intonation (line 4). T replies immediately with a two-hand Vertical Palm gesture with oscillation movement and a head shake (line 5; [1]). As the addressee begins laughing (line 6), T follows up with a specific reason for her rejection, namely that her nose has 'been broken already it doesn't need it' (line 7). With this follow-up utterance, she performs a series of gestures associated with negation: a repeated Horizontal Palm gesture [2], followed by a gesture in which the palms are both down and making sweeping movements together through space [3]. Finally she tags another Vertical Palm gesture with oscillation movement during a pause onto the end of her utterance [4]. She performs all these gestures while shaking her head (Figure 4.19).

Example 41 B_T gm 23.08 not into boxing
1 T   i like anything with erm moving my body
2   i'm not into boxing though (.) i don't i don't (.) like getting my nose
       3 punched
4 B   you should try it!
           +++++
5 T   (. . .)
       |~*****.-|
          [1]
6 B   hahaha
              +++++++++++++++++++++++++++++++++++++++   ++++++
7 T   Like (.) it's been broken already (.) it doesn't need it   (. . .)
       |~~~***/*********/~~~******/~~*************.-| |~*****.-|
          [2]   [3]   [4]

[1] 2VP-Oscillate and head shake, [2] Horizontal Palm gesture, [3] Double palms down sweeping gesture, [4] 2VP-Oscillate

Figure 4.19 VP-Oscillate gesture serves to refuse a suggestion

In this example, the speaker's use of gesture construes her addressee's suggestion to try boxing as an unwanted object, which she performs a series of Vertical Palm gestures, first to erase or rub out, then to sweep away out of the gesture space. In doing so, she illustrates how recurrent gesture forms may also be creatively manipulated so as to increase the performativity of the actions which they reproduce.

When speakers oscillate their Vertical Palm gesture, they indicate an interplay of forces that further illustrate dynamic conceptual structure related to negation. The Vertical Palm gesture with oscillation construes objections, offers, implications, and suggestions coming from their addressees as forces that are further construed as reified objects, to which negation may apply a counterforce. The form of the VP-Oscillate suggests that in these cases the counterforce from negation is construed as erasing or rubbing out. Like the VP gesture with no movement, the VP gesture with oscillation is an interactive gesture whose location is determined to some extent by the interaction axis between speaker and hearer – one-handed variants may be located towards the addressee. However, unlike the VP-Ø but like the VP-Lateral, the VP-Oscillate involves lateral movement as part of the stroke which allows the speaker's desire to 'distance' an unwanted discourse object along a modality axis moving laterally or diagonally away from the speaker's body. This suggests the modality axis may also be located at points along the interaction axis and transformed to wherever the gesture form is located (Figure 4.20).

These construal operations associated with negation, including distancing along a modality axis, are dynamic and flexible. In our last example, a speaker produces a Vertical Palm gesture with two hands in a context where he is weakening an assertion. The example is taken from the same discussion as Example 34, where a conversational pair are discussing gender equality in France and one of the speakers tentatively claims to

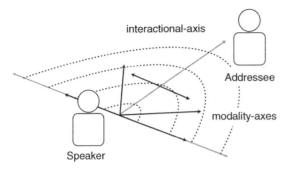

interactional-axis

Addressee

modality-axes

Speaker

Figure 4.20 A 'distancing' operation may be located at different points along the interactional axis and in different locations of gesture space

be witness to gender inequality in France. The speaker K has already attempted to weaken this claim with various hedges and the discourse marker 'I don't know', which he previously integrated with a Vertical Palm gesture raised in space (cf. Example 34). To further weaken his claim, he now states 'I don't say it', meaning that he does not actually accuse people of gender inequality in everyday life, he only observes and takes note of it. As he says this 'I don't' the hands are raised in a Vertical Palm position, but with the word 'say' he elongates the vowel (transcribed as 'sa:::y') and moves one of his vertical palms outwards on a trajectory away from the interaction axis (Figure 4.21).

Example 42 K_C gm3 03.19 I don't say it
1 K but still i kind of get this little sense of like you still
2   it's that i'm the man (.) the man's the boss
3 C yeah i suppose they like to keep that idea don't they
4 K yeh (.) i mean i i i don't know but
            /~~~~~*************** -.|
                     [1]
5 C bit of a power struggle then i suppose
6
7 K and i don't i don't sa:::y it i just watch it
            |~~~~~*********** .-|
                     [2]
8   It's kinda the impression that I'm getting so

[1] Speaker raises both palms open and vertical in front of chest (see Example 34, Figure 4.9), [2] raises Vertical Palms to a hold, then right hand moves outwards (pushing).

Figure 4.21 Vertical Palm with sagittal movement enacts pushing

The speaker's claim or observation that gender is unequal in France constitutes the force vector to which he applies the blockage enacted by the Vertical Palm gesture. By moving one of the palms along the sagittal axis at a diagonal angle to the interactional axis, he then construes his negation as a pushing away of the unwanted discourse referent – this supports the view that the force is coming from the discourse referent itself rather than a potential criticism from the addressee. The salient image schemas here are first of all BLOCKAGE followed by DIVERSION. The sequencing of the Vertical Palm with no movement to one with a movement away from the speaker embodies the logic of image schematic construals of negation.

4.3   Discussion

Speaking is a construal operation in which conceptualisation is tailored for linguistic expression (Langacker 1987). Several examples of the Vertical Palm gesture associated with negation illustrate how speakers also use gesture to construe negation in terms of spatial relationships and forceful interactions, based on a set of underlying actions that the gesture reproduced. The actions include blocking, protecting, throwing aside, erasing, and pushing. How these actions connect explicitly to the linguistic negation is accounted for through common image schematic structures involving FORCE, DISTANCE, and BLOCK-AGE (Chilton 2014; Johnson 1987). This relationship between form, underlying action, and image schema is summarised in Table 4.1.

In construing negation as blockage, force, and distance, the class of Vertical Palm gestures suggest common cognitive processes driving speech and gesture.

Table 4.1 *Proposed derivations, modes, and schemas for three main VP variants*

VP variant	Underlying action	Mode of representation	Image schema
1. VP+Zero	Stopping/blocking	The hand acts	BLOCKAGE
a. VP+Zero+Spe.	– Blocking speaker	The hand acts	BLOCKAGE
b. VP+Zero+Add.	– Blocking addressee	The hand acts	BLOCKAGE
c. VP+Zero+Upper GS	– Protecting/Holding back	The hand acts	BLOCKAGE
d. VP+Sagittal	– Pushing	The hand acts	REMOVAL
2. VP+Lateral	Throwing aside	The hand acts	REMOVAL
	Screening from view	The hand moulds/ embodies	BLOCKAGE
3. VP+Oscillate	Erasing/Rubbing out	The hand acts	REMOVAL

Construal operations appear dynamically in gesture but the embodied routines they rely on to construe are also cognitively entrenched (Langacker 1987). Sensory-motor embodiment and cognitive entrenchment are therefore key to understanding the relationship between grammar and gesture.

In addition to supporting cognitive accounts of linguistic negation, the analysis has thrown light on the interaction between operations in conceptual space and real-time dynamics of the face-to-face interactive space. Speakers locate their Vertical Palm gestures in relation to an interaction axis between speaker and hearer, which may reflect the speaker's conceptualistion of the origin of a discursive force. Locations away from the interaction axis may be motivated by the conceptual distance that negation characteristically evokes.

5 Gesture Sequences
Wrist as Hinge for Shifts in Discourse

You can't study 'no' without studying 'yes.'

—Herb Clark

5.1 Introduction

Gestures are rarely performed singularly with individual utterances in isolation. The impulse to gesture often culminates in a 'burst' of gestures, that is, a sudden stream of gestural forms, multiple in number, sometimes overlaid and seemingly inextricable the one from the other. Within these bursts, various patterns have been identified and referred to as kinesic contexts, ensembles, and gestural sequences (Calbris 2011: 32–3). This chapter identifies and describes a specific type of gestural sequence involving gestures associated with negation. To understand the form and function of such sequences, we must now venture beyond the linguistic organisation and conceptual import of gestures at the utterance-level to explore their role in the structure and organisation of discourse.

In terms of kinesic organisation, the gesture sequence to be described here occurs when a speaker organises two or more clearly identifiable gestural forms in succession and performs this sequence within the bounds of a single movement excursion, known since Kendon (2004) as the gesture unit (Figure 5.1). The gestural forms in our sequences include vertical or horizontal manifestations of the Open Hand Prone gesture in coordination with other recurrent gestures, especially the Palm Up Open Hand or 'Palm Presenting' gesture (Müller 2004; Kendon 2004). As part of this organisational unit, the first gesture is preceded by a preparation phase, and a retraction phase follows the second gesture, although sometimes the sequence may itself be embedded in a broader, more complex kinesic context (examples of this are saved for Chapter 6). Within the sequences to be considered here, each gesture has its own stroke and the transition between the two gestures involves a smooth rotation of the wrist from prone to supine (or vice versa), usually involving only a short preparation phase into the second gesture.

Figure 5.1 Gesture sequence: gesture unit composed of two gesture phrases

A series of examples will show that gesture sequences occur over utterances that ensue as part of a single rhetorical move, speech act, or argument, usually within the confines of a single turn at talk. Within the move, act, or argument structure, the connection between the gestures – achieved kinesically by a rotation of the wrists – reflect 'shifts' at the level of discourse. To briefly offer an example, a speaker describing a game of Frisbee in the park says 'first time we'd played Frisbee, having a great time'. He performs a Palm Presenting gesture with 'first time we'd played Frisbee', then rotates the wrists and performs a Horizontal Palm gesture with 'having a great time'. As will be developed later, to understand how these two linguistic segments relate and to understand why the speaker orders them in this way at that point in the broader discourse, the form, meaning, and function of the co-occurring gesture sequence must be taken into account. Open Hand Prone and Open Hand Supine gestures have previously been separated for analysis (e.g. Kendon 2004), but they often occur in a sequence. As part of our endeavour to understand how gestures associated with negation work, we must therefore also address how they function together with the Palm Presenting gesture in such sequences. To understand one form, we must also understand its relation to another – as suggested by Herb Clark's advice concerning verbal 'yes' and 'no'.

Gesture sequences like this are abundant in everyday conversations, but they have not figured prominently in the previous literature on gesture studies. The potential for conventionalised sequences and combinations of hand movements has often been viewed as a property of sign languages, while spontaneous gesturing that accompanies speech reportedly shows 'no potential for syntactic combination with other gestures' (McNeill 2005: 7). Yet gesture sequences show how speakers combine gesture to organise meaning sequentially and hierarchically for face-to-face communication (cf. Fricke 2013). Recall that '[g]estures often constitute re-enactments of basic mundane actions, grounding the gestures' communicative actions in real world actions' (Bressem et al. 2013: 1106). When a speaker sequences two or more gestures together, the sequence constitutes a series of actions that he or she deems coherent to deploy *together*, one after the other, or as part of a two-step procedure. Since recurrent gestures tend to operate on the level of discourse or function pragmatically (Kendon 2004; Ladewig 2014b), gesture sequences can constitute a series of such actions or procedures that the speaker applies in organising the utterances they accompany in view of the broader discourse. This procedure may suggest the speaker's construal of meaning as manual action (cf. Chapter 4), or may provide a gestural construction – a framework of manual actions through which verbal content can be organised and understood. In such a sequence, the rotation of the wrist is not only a mechanism needed to connect the two gestures but also an embodied equivalent to the shift in discourse. The differential experience of actions involving the palms prone (down) or supine (up) makes the contrast between them an integral part of this gesture-based construction.

This chapter takes our study of recurrent connections between verbal and gestural forms from the micro-level of individual utterances ('grammar–gesture neuxs') to the discourse level of cohesion. Clause-level phenomena such as the grammar of negation, its node, scope, and focus still provide an empirical basis to our analyses, but the function of gesture sequences relates to broader stretches of language and highlights how discourse considerations may shape a given gestural impulse. Gesture sequences emphasise the role of a particular stretch of language in relation to the broader discourse; they are part of the speaker's attempt to clarify his or her point. Gesture patterns are part of what it takes to organise speech coherently, to make logical arguments, and to tell interesting stories.

5.1.1   The Kinesic Context and Hand Transformations

In her work on kinesic contexts, Calbris (2011) documented gestural sequences as a regular feature of gesturing. Examples in *Elements of meaning in gesture* of sentences with two parts revealed different gestures coordinated with each part, and Calbris showed how 'gesture (.2) depends on gesture (.1)' (p. 32). In the sequences she observed, the second gesture could be seen as an elaboration of the first gesture. A Ring gesture, for example, could be performed with a first part of the sentence 'to represent "precision", "rigour"', then with a second part of the sentence the Ring gesture could undergo a 'transverse movement (representing "totality")' (p. 32). A further example showed a similar sequence starting with a 'frame configuration' gesture 'depicting a defined object' that was then 'displaced to the left ... then to the right ... recentred, opens' then 'opened again in a transverse symmetrical movement (representing "totality")' (ibid.). In both examples, Calbris (2011) demonstrated how a formational feature from the first gesture was conserved in the second gesture, creating semantic cohesion across the two gestures while maintaining concepts being applied in the co-occurring speech.

Reviewing the kinesic contexts of gestures associated with negation, a particular sequence involving two gestures recurs. One of the gestures is either a horizontal or vertical manifestation of an Open Hand Prone gesture, while the other is a variation on the gesture known as the 'Palm Up Open Hand'

(Müller 2004) or the 'Palm Presenting' gesture (Kendon 2004). Kendon (2004) described the Palm Presenting gesture in his study of Open Hand Supine gestures, which he contrasted with the gestures in the Open Hand Prone family studied here. Observing them separately, he found that '[i]n terms of context-of-use, the two families are quite different' (p. 248). Gestures in the Open Hand Prone family are 'used in contexts where something is being denied, negated, interrupted or stopped', while gestures in the Open Hand Supine family are used in seemingly opposite contexts 'where the speaker is offering, giving or showing something or requesting the reception of something' (p. 248). In my observations, gestures from these different families often occur *together*. When Open Hand Prone and Open Hand Supine gestures occur as a sequence, not only is a form feature shared (as observed in Calbris's treatment of gestural sequencing), but also there is an important transition that occurs between them. Specifically, the wrists rotate to enable a renewed orientation of the palms, and this mechanism often accompanies a reorientation or 'shift' in the discourse; for example, from presenting an idea to defending it; from posing a condition to signalling its consequence.

The transition that occurs between gestures in our sequence seems similar to what Kendon (2004) has referred to as 'hand transformations'. In his description of gestures in the 'precision grip' family, namely Grappolo gestures and Ring gestures (pp. 225–47), Kendon observed that variations on both those gestures involved 'hand transformations' into and out of their precision grip hand shapes. Kendon argued that such variations 'can be understood as ritualised forms of "precision grip" actions' (p. 283). These actions essentially relate to sequences of manipulation we may perform when holding, presenting, showing, squeezing, and releasing small objects. Applied to the co-occurring speech, the actions reflected different discursive aims that speakers were hoping their utterances could achieve. In the Grappolo-family for example, while 'the Closure-to-Grappolo is associated with topic-nomination, the Grappolo-to-Open is associated with the comment' (p. 234). Similarly for the Ring-family, Kendon distinguished a Ring-to-Open sequence that occurs when 'the speaker focuses on a specific feature of what he is talking about' (p. 242).

Kendon's transcriptions suggest these were not different gestures entering into a sequence but 'derivations' on one particular gesture achieved through 'different phases of stroke action' (p. 363). In the examples I will show, transformations between gestures from Palm Up and Palm Down variants involve the combination of two or more different gestures into a recurrent gesture sequence. Rather than the closing or opening of the hands observed for the Grappolo and Ring gestures, it is the reorientation of the palms produced by the rotation of the wrists in our sequences that is integral to understanding how the speakers are using gesture to organise discourse.

5.2   Gesture Sequences

5.2.1   *Palm Up to Horizontal Palm Gesture Sequence*

The examples of sequences involving the Palm Presenting gesture and the Horizontal Palm gesture (PP-to-ZP) suggest at least three uses of this pattern. First, the sequence may be used to present information through a topic–comment structure, whilst also indicating the role of the co-occurring utterance in relation to the discourse. Second, it functions as part of a conditional statement, where the first gesture accompanies the IF-clause and the second gesture accompanies the consequence. Third, the sequence occurs in absence of speech to express the meanings of the gestures in relation to a verbal context previously established. The referential content of the utterances we will consider is different in each case, but there are similarities in the way the information is organised and its role in the overall discourse. The gesture sequence is central to those similarities.

The first example illustrates how a speaker's use of the PP-to-ZP sequence reflects a topic–comment structure and relates the utterance it occurs with to an argument made previously in the discourse. As part of the board game they are playing, Paul has been asked by Andrew to describe his 'typical weekend'. Paul begins his answer by acknowledging this as an 'interesting question' and says that 'I can never truly establish a typical weekend because I never know what is going to change' (line 1), presenting himself as a person open to new experiences. Having determined his orientation towards the question, he now illustrates his standpoint by offering up an 'example' of what he did 'not the weekend just passed but the one before' (line 2). Describing his previous weekend, he says 'we went out and played Frisbee' (line 4). As if to make a side note, he then leans slightly towards his addressee and says 'It's the first time we'd played Frisbee, having a great time' (line 5). The transcript below shows how he accompanies 'first time we'd played Frisbee' with a two-handed Palm Presenting gesture [1], which transitions into a Horizontal Palm gesture as he says 'having a great time' [2]. He follows this utterance with the assertion that 'everybody loved it' (line 6), before being interrupted by a request about the park's whereabouts (line 7) (Figure 5.2).

Example 43 JB gm1 04.19 Having a great time (PP-to-ZP)
1 P   never truly establish a typical weekend because i never know what is going
       to change (. . .)
2   i might like for example last weekend not the weekend just passed but the
3   one before
4   we went out, perfect sunny day (.) we went out and played frisbee.
5   it's the first time we'd played FRIsbee . . . HAving a great time
       |~*************************/~~~~~~************** -.|
                [1]   [2]

6   everybody loved it
7   A   where did you play frisbee?
[1] Palm Presenting gesture, [2] Vertical/Horizontal Palms lateral gesture.

Figure 5.2 PP-to-ZP sequence to illustrate-then-defend a point he is making

Verbally, 'first time we played Frisbee' emphasises the novelty of the activity and can be considered a topic, while 'having a great time' comments on that topic by describing the experience positively. The occurrence of the Palm Presenting to Horizontal Palm gesture sequence indicates the speaker's pragmatic and rhetorical aims in the broader interaction. The PP's semantic theme of 'offering' indicates that 'first time we played Frisbee' is not just a state of affairs but an *example* of why the weekend was characteristically atypical. The ZP's semantic theme of 'interrupting' or 'stopping a line of action' then frames 'having a great time' not only as a qualification of the experience but also as a *defence of* or *justification for* such weekends, supported by the follow-up assertion 'everybody loved it'. Playing Frisbee for the first time could be annoying (e.g. if nobody knew how to play or if the park was unsuitable for the game). But in making the Horizontal Palm gesture whilst saying 'having a great time', the speaker is specific that it was not the case that trying something new led to any annoyance, frustration, or disappointment. Taken together, the utterances describe a state of affairs on a verbal level, but also illustrate and defend a broader argument on a gestural level. The PP-to-ZP gesture sequence reflects this discursive move of illustrating then defending. The gesture sequence emphasises the role of the utterance in the discourse, namely to defend his preference for atypical weekends. In other words, the gesture reminds us why he is telling us that he had a great time; the gesture sequence connects the current utterance back to the speaker's larger discursive argument.

The second example of this gesture sequence occurs within the boundary of an utterance and reflects the information structure of its different parts, namely, a topic–comment structure. Furthermore, the utterance is part of a story, and the performance of the gesture highlights the role of the co-occurring utterance in the overall structure of the narrative. The speakers in this example have been discussing the topic 'things you'd like to learn'. One speaker, T, mentions that she would like to learn languages, but interrupts her answer to tell a story related to her passion for language and communication. She starts the story with 'You know what was really cool? I was at Happy Hour over at St Paul's the other day, did I tell you this story?' ('St Paul's' was a popular bar in the city where this recording was made). The story that ensues lasts three minutes and centres around an encounter with three men at the bar. Building up her story, she explains that she 'found out all sorts of interesting things' about these men, including their jobs, where they lived, and their hobbies (lines 4–6). This may not seem news-worthy, until she then introduces a complicating action to her narrative (Labov and Waletzky 1967). She says 'and I found it all out using like symbols and sign language because they're all Deaf'. When she says 'they're all Deaf' she produces a Palm Presenting gesture. As can be seen in the transcription, T holds this gesture as her addressee B requests clarification seemingly in disbelief, 'all of them?'. As T repeats 'all of them' she reactivates the PP gesture with a beat, then executes a Horizontal Palm gesture in rapid succession with the element 'were Deaf' (Figure 5.3).

Example 44 BT gm 11.57 All of them were Deaf (PP-to-ZP)
```
1    T   you know what was really cool? i was at happy hour over at st paul the other day
2        did I tell you this story?
3        . . .  (narrative continues for 30 seconds)
4        and so i found out all sorts of interesting things about them (.) like the one
         guy was
5        from paris the other guy was from guyana the other guy like teaches at here
         and the
6        other one- you know
7        . . . (narrative continues for 20 seconds)
8        and i found it ALL out using like SYMbols and sign language
9        because they're all DEaf
             |~**************
                            ‾‾‾‾‾‾
                  [1]
10   A   all of them?
11   S   ALL of them (.) WEre deaf
             **********/~~~*********-.|
             ‾‾‾‾‾‾‾‾‾‾        ‾‾‾‾‾‾‾
               [2] beat            [3]
12       and er yeh i ended up seeing them again later (.) it was really it was just like
         i went
13       home feeling soo (.) cool about life
```
[1] Palm Presenting gesture, [2] beat of PP gesture, [3] Horizontal Palm gesture.

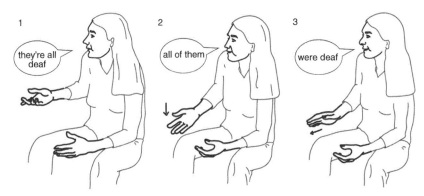

Figure 5.3 Example of PP-to-ZP sequence illustrating internal structure of utterance

The speaker performs a Palm Presenting to Horizontal Palm gesture sequence as she reveals the critical moment in her narrative, that is, 'All of them, were Deaf'. While the first PP serves to present this moment (and successfully invite the addressee to engage with it), the following PP-to-ZP serves to assert its validity. Note how the two instances of 'were Deaf' are accompanied across this stretch of utterance by different gestures, first a PP and then a ZP. This illustrates how a gesture sequence is influenced not only by the content of language it occurs with, but also by the speaker's communicative goals of the utterances she is using. While the PP is consistent with the goal of presenting the first 'were Deaf' as new information, the ZP with the second instance is consistent with her goal of asserting it. This assertive function of the ZP has previously been related to the expression of implicit negation (Kendon 2004) – in performing a ZP gesture with the positive expression 'all of them were Deaf', the speaker additionally expresses the implied negative that 'none of the men were hearing'.

A third example illustrates that the PP-to-ZP gesture sequence has a conventionalised meaning potentially with unit status, to the extent that given the appropriate verbal context, the pattern can be coherently produced and perceived in absence of any occurring speech. Jane and Amy (who are both English teachers) are discussing the board game they have been playing as a potential resource for the English as a Foreign Language classroom and evaluating whether it could facilitate oral interaction between students in an ESL class. Amy has voiced the concern that it could turn into a question–answer session and 'just go very quickly' (line 1). Jane has added that a potential problem could arise if students 'were young or just shy' (line 2). Amy now suggests one way to increase chances of interaction would be to 'add a question why? And add a few maybe extra questions somehow' (line 3). She now thinks about this for a second whilst looking at the board game. She then agrees with Jane's previous statement about shy students by saying 'Yeah that's true' (line 5) and proceeds to adopt the persona of a shy student. In line 6, she first enunciates an example of a topic from the board game by saying 'someone you'd like to meet', then she says 'oh I'd like to meet' and completes her utterance with a PP-to-ZP gesture sequence. When the gesture sequence is finished, her addressee acknowledges her embodied completion (Olsher 2004) with 'yeh that's true' (Figure 5.4).

Example 45 A_J ds 02.09 Shy student (PP-to-ZP)
1   A   it would just go very quickly wouldn't it
2   J   i suppose if they were young or just shy
3   A   or add a question why? and add a few maybe extra questions somehow
4   J   yeah
5   A   yeah that's true
6   someone you'd like to meet (.) oh I'd like to meet (...)
                                    |~***/***-.|
                                    [1]   [2]
7   J   yeh that's true

[1] Palms Presenting gesture, [2] Horizontal Palm gesture.

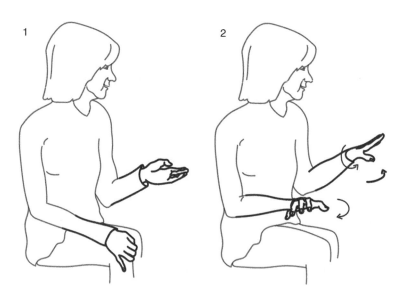

Figure 5.4 PP-to-ZP sequence to offer an answer then indicate end of turn

The speaker's gestural rendition of an imaginary shy student exemplifies the form, meaning, and function of the PP-to-ZP gesture sequence. The PP gesture serves to imitate a student *giving* or *offering up* a name in response to the question, either by suggesting that the student would perform such a gesture in conjunction with a short answer or by using the gesture to capture the idea that an answer would be offered. With the ZP gesture that follows, the speaker shows how the student would *only* give a name. There would be *no* elaboration or explanation, so that by offering a name the student would purposefully *halt* her line of communicative action (Kendon 2004), and thereby end her turn (thus thwarting any opportunities for interactive learning in the process). As with the PP, the ZP could also refer to an actual gesture that a student might perform to end his or her turn, or more abstractly to the idea that the turn would be ended. The addressee's utterance, 'yeh that's true', is not only a sign of agreement. It may also be a response to seeing her partner perform a turn ending ZP. The function of the ZP is applied to both contexts, the imaginary context that she is imitating and the interactive one she is involved in.

A fourth example illustrates a variation on the PP-to-ZP sequence, namely a reverse sequence in which the speaker performs a Horizontal Palm gesture first, closely followed by the Palm Presenting gesture. The example includes a conditional sentence with a negation in the IF-clause (the *protasis*), and the second clause expresses its consequence (the *apodosis*). The gesture sequence is analogous to this grammatical construction. One of the speakers has been discussing her propensity for sport and explaining that she runs 'on an average three to four days a week' (line 1). She then says 'If I don't run three days a week I'm like dead, like sad' (line 2). She coordinates a ZP-to-PP sequence with the utterance so that the ZP occurs with the node and scope of 'If I don't run three days' and the PP gesture presents its consequence 'I'm like dead, like sad' (Figure 5.5).

Example 46 BT gm 21.40 If I don't run (ZP-to-PP)
1 T   at least (...) like hm on an average three to four days a week
2   if i don't run three days I'm like dead (.) like sad
       |~*****************/~~~~~~**********-.|
              [1]   [2]

[1] Horizontal Palm gesture, [2] Palm Presenting gesture.

The order of the sequence is consistent with the organisation of the conditional construction. The Horizontal Palm connects to the sentential negative in the IF-clause and 'poses' the condition, while the Palm Presenting gesture accompanies and 'presents' the consequence. The rotation from palm down to palm up is the gestural equivalent of the discursive shift from IF to THEN, that is, from protasis to apodosis (interestingly from Greek *apodidonai* 'give back'; *Oxford Dictionary of English*).

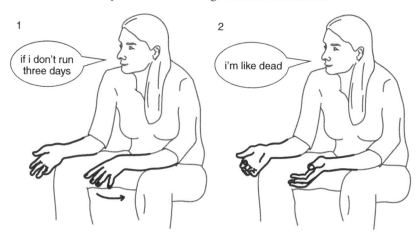

Figure 5.5 ZP-to-PP sequence with IF-THEN clause structure

Gesture sequences may accompany discourse structures on different scales and levels. The Palm Presenting to Horizontal Palm gesture sequence can be motivated by the relationship between the co-occurring utterance and an argument made earlier in the discourse (Example 43), or the structure of a broader narrative (Example 44). It can map onto the information structure within an utterance, in this case topic–comment (Example 43 and Example 44) or *protasis–apodosis* when reversed (Example 46). The PP-to-ZP has a conventionalised meaning to the extent that given the right verbal context it can be performed in absence of co-occurring speech, whereby its schematic meaning gets elaborated by the rich context (Example 45). In all cases, the shift in discourse is experienced multimodally with the change in orientation of the palm which results from the rotation of the wrist.

5.2.2   *Palm Presenting to Vertical Palm Sequence*

A related gesture sequence observed in the data comprises a Palm Presenting gesture (PP) and a Vertical Palm gesture (VP). The examples suggest that the semantic theme of the PP-to-VP sequence is similar to the PP-to-ZP sequence, the difference being the semantic themes of the Horizontal Palm and Vertical Palm gesture (Kendon 2004). While the PP indicates the speaker is introducing a new topic, the VP gesture interrupts that line of communicative action. The sequence can be said to provide a construction that allows the speaker to achieve this present-interrupt move, which is interpreted differently depending on the broader discourse context.

The first example shows how the PP-to-VP gesture sequence can accompany an argumentative move whereby the speaker offers an argument (PP) then supports it with a reason (VP). The example also offers insight to the role of gesture patterns in constructed dialogue, that is, multimodal reported speech (Debras 2015). The speaker is describing the competitive relationship she has with her sister, and in particular, the discomfort her elder sister felt when the speaker, as the younger sister, began to grow taller than her. The speaker describes how she stressed to her older sister that being taller also brought some disadvantages, such as larger feet. The speaker explains how her sister initially 'flipped out' when her younger sister (the speaker) 'overpassed her as far as shoe size' (line 1), which was an index for the more general scenario of the younger sister getting bigger than the older sister. The PP-to-VP gesture sequence occurs when the speaker then says 'well you're glad for it now, you don't have size tens' (line 3). With 'well you're glad for it now' she is performing a variant of the Palm Presenting gesture in upper gesture space [1], then with 'you don't have size tens' she tilts her head and rotates her wrist slightly so that her palm moves into a Vertical Palm formation [2] (Figure 5.6).

Example 47 BT ds 10.15 Size tens (PP-to-VP)
1 T   i remember when i overpassed her as far as shoe size, she FLIpped out.
2 B   really?
3 T   yeah and i was like well you're glad for it now (.) you don't have size tens
           |~~*******************/~******************-.|
                   [1]   [2]
[1] Palm Presenting gesture, [2] Palm Vertical gesture and head cock.

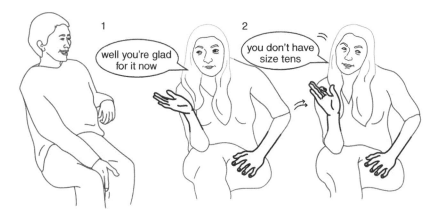

Figure 5.6 PP-to-VP sequence to offer argument then supporting evidence

In this example of a gesture sequence, the PP indicates that 'well you're glad for it now' is the presentation of an argument, while the VP indicates that 'you don't have size tens' is supporting evidence for that argument, which consequently should serve to halt the sister's complaining. On a linguistic level, the VP here connects to the negation 'don't', while on a discursive level, it applies a theme of stopping to the complaining of the younger sister in the hypothetical dialogue. This example additionally highlights the role of gesture sequences in reported speech, or constructed action. Analysing how people discuss 'political' topics, Debras (2015) has shown how speakers use subtle shifts in head positions, facial expressions, and gestures to indicate different elements of stance towards the speech they are reporting and the speakers they are embodying during constructed action. In our example, the speaker plausibly attempts a faithful re-enactment of her former self in interaction with her sister, and we can wonder whether she originally performed this gesture sequence too. Regardless of whether she did or not, the constructed action with her current utterance illustrates how the speaker managed to outsmart her sister at the end of the day, and the gesture sequence is part of the communicative repertoire for doing so.

In the next example, the PP and VP are reversed into a VP-to-PP gesture sequence. This presents the opportunity to further explore how their semantic themes interact, evaluate their connection to discourse cohesion, and refine our understanding of these sequences. The speakers are sharing their views on relationships and loyalty, in particular the impact that jealousy can have on a relationship. K adopts an absolutist stance and builds up to a rejection that suggests infidelity is unavoidable, and in doing so would absolve himself of any blame. But he is also presenting himself as someone who would not seek to control his partner or become jealous. Having said 'the girl's gonna do what she wants to do' (line 4) and 'eventually it's going to happen' (line 5), he leaps to a worst case scenario and hypothesises that 'If I had a girlfriend and she slept with someone else I'd go hhh you made your decision' (lines 7–8). With the IF-clause, he looks at his addressee and performs a Vertical Palm gesture with both hands raised high up in gesture space [1], then with the apodosis (THEN-clause) he tilts his head, breaks mutual gaze, and performs a Palm Presenting gesture [2]. The hands are still high up in space but now oriented away from the interactional axis (Figure 5.7).

Example 48 KC gm3 00.18 If I had a girlfriend (VP-to-PP)
1   C   in general I find guys a lot more (. . .) I suppose open about how they
2   feel about their girl
3   kind of they're almost romantic like this is my girlfriend you know
4   K   i'd say hey the girl's gonna do what she wants to do (.) whether
5   eventually it's gonna happen
6   if she wants to start talking to other people and

7   if i had a girlfriend and she SLEpt with someone else i'd go
|~**/

                [1] *beat*

8   hhh you made your decision
****************-.|

                [2]

9   C   mm

10 K   i'm not gonna cry about it but i'm not going to stay with you either

11   that's just my approach maybe it's not normal but

[1] Vertical Palm gesture, [2] Palm Presenting gesture.

Figure 5.7 VP-to-PP sequence with IF-THEN clause structure

The grammatical pattern is clear: the first clause expresses a condition (*the protasis*), and the second clause expresses its consequence (*the apodosis*). We have a hypothetical situation and its consequences. While the Vertical Palm embodies that condition, the Palm Presenting gesture asserts the validity of the main clause given the condition is met. The speaker is using the Vertical Palm gesture to show his belief that whether or not his partner cheated on him is a situation that he has no control over. The Palm Presenting gesture presents the following utterance as the logical conclusion – the unfaithful partner would have effectively ended the relationship.

The gesture sequences involving the VP gesture reflect the speaker's concern for the utterance to be cohesive with the broader argument at play in the stretch of discourse, the communicative aim, or the actual activity underway. On a more local scale, they map onto components inherent to the grammatical structures being used as part of those moves (notably, IF-THEN structures).

Kinesically, the essence of these sequences hinges on the rotation of the wrists and consequent reorientation of the palms. Two gestures in a sequence make up a conceptual whole in line with the rhetorical aim of the speaker, something made manifest in the rotation of the wrists.

5.2.3   Broader Sequences

Gesture sequences are not restricted to the pairing of two gestures. Nor are they restricted to only including recurrent gestures. So far we have considered sequences involving gestures associated with negation (ZP/VP) and the Palm Presenting gesture. Now we consider how other gesture forms can enter into a sequence-like relationship with gestures from the Open Hand Prone family. Examples indicate that the gesture sequence may include other gestures and reflect the organisation of larger stretches of discourse, indicative of broader interactive moves.

The first example illustrates a sequence of three gestures – in which the Palm Presenting to Horizontal Palm gesture sequence incorporates a referential gesture too. The participants of this discussion are sat on the veranda of a bar at a campsite in France. One of the participants is visiting his friend, who is fielding questions and offering background information about the campsite. When the visitor asks 'How many people live here?' (line 1), his friend responds 'a couple of hundred' and emphasises 'it's a big place' (line 2). Using 'but' to indicate a departure, this speaker then interjects some 'terrible news', namely, that 'next year 2008 is the last year of the camping' (line 3). The transcription below shows how he accompanies each stage of this announcement with a gesture, sequencing three gestures into one gesture unit. He uses a Palm Addressed gesture to offer 'the terrible news' to his interlocutor [1]. Then he uses an iconic metaphoric gesture to trace the schematic leap forward encoded in 'next year' [2]. Following this, he performs a Horizontal Palm gesture as he says it's 'the last year' [3] (Figure 5.8).

Example 49 D_B_3 00.20 Terrible news (PA-to-IND-to-ZP)
1 B how many people live here?
2 D in the camping? a couple of hundred (.) it's a big place but
3   the TERRible news (.) is that next year (.) 2008 (.) is the LAST year of the
       |~***********/~~~~~***************/~***************__-|
          [1]   [2]   [3]
4   camping (...) it's gone (.) yep already been sold to flipping developers
5   and they're gonna build ...
[1] Palm Addressed, [2] Deictic/Iconic, [3] Horizontal Palm (PDA).

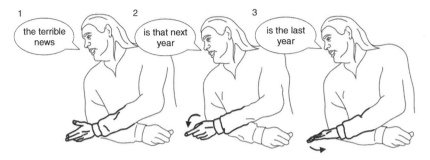

Figure 5.8 Palm Addressed–Iconic–Horizontal Palm pattern

Kendon (2004) observes that 'the Open Hand Supine may be directed toward another as if the hand is being placed to offer something, or to receive something' (p. 272). The first gesture in the pattern achieves this function as it brings the announcement of terrible news. In the second gesture, the index finger is iconic and metaphorically represents 'next year' as being a step 'further forward' in terms of the abstract space in front of him. The Horizontal Palm gesture then expresses 'the end' (Calbris 2011), which could imply the negative that no more years of the camping will be enjoyed (cf. Kendon 2002, 2004). The iconic gesture (which is also a conventionalised way to express a future time; Calbris 2011) is integrated to the sequence seamlessly. While the Palm Presenting gesture announces the news, the iconic gesture specifies it, then with a rotation of the wrist the Horizontal Palm finalises it – effectively indicating the end of an era on the campground. Gesture Sequences like PP-to-ZP may have slots where other gestures can be inserted to serve the structural cohesion, depending on specific informational content in the utterance.

All the previous examples of gesture sequences have been concerned with relatively short stretches of discourse, usually covering a few utterances at most and possibly a couple of turns. However, our last example suggests that gesture sequences composed of recurrent gestures may accompany a much larger stretch of discourse. An examination of the relations between the gesture sequences and the discourse in this context suggests similar functions, though on the much bigger scale of reflecting a particular argumentative strategy.

As part of a discussion about 'a job you'd like to have', the speaker K has been explaining his desire to pursue a career in politics. However, he is at pains to stress what kind of 'politics' he means. He has already said that in fact he does not like politics and gives the example of when he was in college not liking 'political music'. When he mentions 'political music', his addressee C requests clarification by repeating the phrase with rising intonation 'political music?'

(line 1). K responds by offering 'Rage Against The Machine' as an example and explaining 'I like the group but when they start talking about governments, revolutions, this, that' (line 2). With this enumeration of topics that the group's music addresses he performs a cascade of PP gestures [1/2/3/4]. After a short pause he then evaluates how he felt about this by saying 'it just didn't concern n' I was like that's just ... it's NONsense' (line 4). With the word 'nonsense', he performs a gesture from the Open Hand Prone family that we have not discussed yet – both hands oriented palms down 'swipe' downwards through the gesture space [2] – referred to elsewhere as the 'Throwing Away' gesture (Bressem and Müller, 2013a, 2013b; Bressem and Müller, 2014). In a somewhat contradictory but common rhetorical move, he then seeks to re-establish the characteristics he has dismissed. He positions them now as real-world concerns by first saying 'And you know what, the wars and this and that' (line 6), again performing a cascade of PPs [6/7/8], then finishing this argument with 'it is nonsense, but it's real, this is stuff that's happening' (line 7). Each of these final statements is accompanied with two-handed PP gestures [9/10/11] (Figure 5.9).

Example 50 K_C gm1 24.42 It's nonsense (PP-to-SWIPE-to-PP)
1 C   political music?
2 K   rage against the machine I like the group but (.) when they start talking about
3   governments revolutions this that (...) it just didn't concern
         |~*********/*********/***/***|
              [1]   [2]   [3] [4]
4   n' i was like that's just (...) it's NONsense.
                      |~*************-.|
                          [5]
6   and you know what (.) the wars and this and that
                      |~********/*****/*****-|
                          [6]   [7]   [8]
7   it is nonsense (.) but it's real (.) this is stuff that's happening
         |~**********/**************/********************-.-.|
              [9]   [10]   [11]

[1]–[4] Cascade of PPs, [5] OHPswipe ('Throwing away'), [6]–[8] Cascade of PPs, [9]–[11] lrPPs.

On the level of speech act structure, the first series of Palm Presenting gestures corresponds to the presentation of 'political' topics. The Palm Down gesture embodies the speech act of rejection as the speaker dismisses those features as 'nonsense'. The final cascade of PP gestures then serves to re-establish those features as real-world concerns, even if they may seem 'nonsense'. On the level of the discourse structure, this gestural sequence could therefore be described as achieving PRESENTATION – REJECTION – RE-ESTABLISHMENT.

Figure 5.9 PRESENTATION – REJECTION – RE-ESTABLISHMENT with a sequence of Palm Ups to Palm Down to Palm Ups

On a broader level of argumentation, recall the speaker deploys this pattern as a rhetorical move to justify a seeming contradiction in his previous discourse: he wishes to work in politics, even though he does not like politics. To achieve this, he opts to spell out his personal evolution from political apathy (former self in college) to acknowledgement (current self with mindful professional ambition). This evolution hinges on what is to be considered as 'nonsense'. 'Nonsense' in the first sense means topics that as a college student he felt unconcerned with, while 'nonsense' in the second sense means the needless wars and other man-made calamities that urgently need attention. With the first utterance of 'nonsense', he performs a Palm Down gesture that is coherent with his rejection of politics. The Palm Up with his second utterance of 'nonsense' shows his acceptance of the realities of nonsense and provides visual evidence for his growth. Although logically speaking, he contradicts himself by claiming that the nonsense he rejects is real, the juxtaposition of different gestures with the identical expression of 'nonsense' clarifies that he seeks to redefine what he means by that. In other words, he is demonstrating for the listener how he has refined his position on political matters, and the gesture pattern of PRESENTATION − REJECTION − RE-ESTABLISHMENT allows him to do that.

5.3   The Status of Gesture Sequences

Bursts of gesturing may be populated with forms from the Open Hand Prone gesture family that connect with the speaker's expression of negation in speech. These gestures may occur in their own gesture unit, succinctly orchestrated with the realisation of linguistic negation. But often the kinesic context of a gesture reveals more complexity than the individual gesture form under study. Speakers may perform a gesture immediately before or after a gesture in the Open Hand Prone family. 'Immediately' means the two gestures are part of the same gestural excursion or unit (Kendon 2004) − they involve a 'gestural sequence' (Calbris 2011: 32). This chapter examined how such sequences operate at the level of discourse cohesion.

Gesture sequences tend to occur within the confines of a gesture unit and appear to be part of the same linguistic and discursive move. The kinesic structures of these sequences are thus similar to the 'hand transformations' described by Kendon (2004). They appear to be specialised to map onto a co-occurring two-part structure at different levels of linguistic and discursive structure. On one level, each gesture in the sequence can be said to reflect the linguistic content or pragmatic aim of the utterance it occurs with. Examples show how they may map onto grammatical structures (e.g. protasis–apodosis or IF-THEN), information structures (topic–comment), speech act structures (e.g. present–reject), narrative structures (e.g. resolution and evaluation), and broader rhetorical strategies (e.g. argument–supporting evidence or concession-rebuttal).

The gesture sequences involve the coordination of fundamentally different gestures, most saliently in our examples are gestures from the Open Hand Prone family (Vertical Palms/Horizontal Palms/Throwing Away) with gestures from the Open Hand Supine family (Palm Presenting/Palm Addressed). But it is no coincidence that both families involve the Open Hand (Kendon 2004). The transition to or from the OHP gesture is central to these gesture sequences, since they mark a shift in the discourse, either a resolution, a conflict, a logical consequence, or other. If the key kinesic feature of hand transformations involving 'gestures of precision grip' is the transition into or out of the grip, the key feature of the sequences involving the Open Hand Prone gestures is the rotation of the wrists into or out of a palm down (from our perspective), which leads to a consequent reorientation of the palm that corresponds to a reorientation in the discourse.

To illustrate this key feature, many of the examples show the gesture sequence spreading across two clauses, both of which contain similar (if not identical) linguistic components but with different meanings and belonging to different (but related) communicative goals. The gesture carries the specific meaning for how the verbal content is to be understood. Salient instances include 'first time/great time' (Example 43), 'you're glad/you don't' (Example 47), 'next year/last year' (Example 49), and 'nonsense/nonsense' (Example 50). It is precisely the rotation of the wrist(s) and reorientation of the palm(s) at the boundary of the clauses that indicates the language now has a different meaning or function, despite having a similar form. It suggests that the organisation of the gesture sequence is planned not only to occur with specific linguistic segments, but also to be cohesive with broader discursive moves underpinning the discourse. The rotation should be seen as a conceptual process too: the gestural transformation invites a 'flipped' perspective on the meaning, literally and metaphorically. Gesture sequences may therefore be an important practice within 'speech handling' gestures (Streeck 2009).

A growing body of research examining gestures in spoken discourse has explored whether similar conventionalised connections between gesture and speech may have anything to contribute to the cognitive linguistic theory of construction grammar (Goldberg 1995). Several studies have found construction-like features in gesture, namely in the acquisition of speech–gesture ensembles among children, their initial inseparability then later flexibility (Andrén 2010, 2014), the routine connections of particular gestures to well-documented grammatical constructions (Zima 2014; Schoonjans 2018; Zima and Bergs 2017), and the stability of the form, meaning, and function of certain gestures in regard to the cognitive 'scenes' they systematically encode (Bressem and Müller 2017). Our examples of recurrent gesture sequences involving the Open Hand Prone gestures seem based on the fundamental distinction between the open hands turned up or down, and in particular, the rotation of the wrists needed to achieve the reorientation which results. We can borrow from the 'scene' developed by Bressem and Müller (2013) namely the 'AWAY ACTION SCHEME' (see also Bressem and Müller 2017). This is based on a conceptual blend whereby conceptual objects become physical objects and linguistic negation becomes physical, manual removal of those objects (Lapaire 2006a, 2006b). However, within a gesture sequence, we see how this one scene can be coordinated with other scenes with a certain degree of conceptual coherence. A scene of 'OFFERING' encoded by the Palm Presenting gesture for instance may precede or proceed the 'away action' scheme coherently; indeed, we saw how this was elaborated into an actual argumentative strategy that unfolded over the stretch of several utterances (Example 50). The conventional status of a recurrent gesture sequence may thus be similar to 'multimodal constructions', although gesture sequences may have the capacity to function at much larger scales of discourse than the constructions previously described. All symbolic structures reflect conceptualisation (Langacker 1987). So the sequences seem to afford their own kind of discursive frame, and this frame can be applied at different levels.

The sequences described here are not only conceptually cohesive but also discursively cohesive. Verbal cohesion is defined as 'how words relate to each other within the text, referring backwards or forwards to other words in the text' (Cutting 2008: 3). We saw how gestures could be arranged into sequences that illustrated the discursive relationship between the verbal segments of the utterances they accompanied. A number of examples also showed how gestures could be performed in relation to elements evoked sometimes several utterances earlier than their co-occurring verbal segment, effectively linking their current utterance back to an idea raised earlier in the discourse, or to a theme that was tying together the larger stretch of discourse as a whole, such as by exemplifying a point made earlier. The role of gesture in cohesion has previously been shown for gestures and propositional content on the level of neighbouring utterances (e.g. Chui 2009), as well as during collaborative discourse with the addressee(s) (Chui 2015). The category of recurrent gestures, in this case associated with negation, allows coherence to occur on a much broader discursive scale, such as over the stretch of several turns. As Cutting (2008) writes: 'Grammatical cohesion ... is what meshes the text together' (p. 8). Recurrent gesture sequences are part of this textual meshing.

6   Patterns of Gesturing

The Business of 'Horizontal Palming'

> A person's charm, a person's gestures, Foucault's gestures were aston-
> ishing … They were a bit like gestures of metal, of dry wood, strange
> gestures, fascinating gestures, very beautiful.   —Gilles Deleuze

6.1   Introduction

Specialists of gesture and multimodal communication rarely go on record
admiring the beauty of an individual's gestures as explicitly as Deleuze formulated his admiration for Foucault's gestures. To acknowledge the uniqueness
of a person's gestures or express a subjective opinion on them could jeopardise
the perceived empirical basis of one's analysis. But within the field of gesture
studies, specialisms have developed based around particular types of gestures,
usually culled from similar speech settings and analysed with a shared methodology. Studies of speakers narrating cartoons, giving directions, problem
solving, teaching, learning, story-telling, and debating all lead to descriptions
of different types of gestures, and ultimately, to accounts of different types of
gesturing. Like Deleuze, gesture researchers may also be more fascinated by
some gesturers than by others.

If you have found the gestures described in this book interesting so far, you
might share an appreciation for the conventional side of the impulse to gesture.
Gestures may exhibit recognisable forms and achieve routine functions, such as
the gestures associated with negation exemplified in previous chapters. Despite
the regularities observed so far, the examples here and in other research suggest
immense variation in how, when, and why people perform such gestures. For
example, one speaker in an informal business meeting performed a particular
recurrent gesture sixty times over the course of her 80-minute interaction. This
was the Horizontal Palm gesture, following Kendon's (2004) terminology (also
analysed in Chapter 2). No two of its occurrences were identical, and each was
embedded in a kinesic context differing in degree of complexity. To borrow
some adjectives from Deleuze, I find this particular person's use of the
Horizontal Palm gesture both 'strange' and 'fascinating', 'astonishing' and

'beautiful'. Her gestures too appear to contribute to her 'charm'. Translated into key concerns for gesture studies, her gestural behaviour in the meeting raises the issue of individual difference, interactive genres, and stylistic variation in gesturing.

This chapter continues to view the impulse to gesture with speech as a communicating body's response to the interaction between its cognitive-linguistic system and a face-to-face communication setting. Focusing now on the setting for communication, we explore how recurrency in a speaker's impulse to gesture over the course of an interaction may reveal a 'pattern of gesturing'. Taking a pattern related to the Horizontal Palming gesture as our starting point, we examine the relationship between the speaker and her communicative aims within the wider professional and social context for interaction.

6.1.1   From Recurrent Gestures to Recurrent Gesturing

Studying a recurrent gesture such as the Horizontal Palm has traditionally meant studying a 'stable form-meaning unit [that] recurs in *different* contexts of use over *different* speakers in a particular speech community' (Ladewig 2014b: 1559–60; emphasis added). The emphasis I added on 'different' reflects the common methodological procedure for identifying such a gesture and establishing it as recurrent: researchers search multiple data sets with several speakers to collect and compare instances of a particular gesture form in use (cf. Kendon 2004: 226; Ladewig 2014b).

But recurrent gestures may also be performed recurrently by an individual speaker in a particular interactive context. Müller's (2004) classic study of the Palm Up Open Hand gesture was based on approximately seventy instances of the gesture during a 12-minute stretch of spontaneous conversation. Lempert (2011) studied the repeated performance of one gesture by one speaker over several similar contexts, namely the Ring gesture by Barack Obama during debates over the course of his 2008 presidential campaign. The repeated performance of Ring gestures has also been observed to occur frequently by particular types of speakers in a different context: professors and students often use the gesture repeatedly during oral presentations in academic contexts (Yerian 2016). Why are some gestures (sometimes) so recurrent? The repeated use of a particular gesture calls for research into an understudied dimension of gesturing, that is, individuals' propensity to gesture in recurrent ways in particular contexts.

To identify a pattern of gesturing, the ToGoG approach laid out in Bressem et al. (2013) advocates examining 'the use of gestures over larger time spans' and searching for 'the recurrent use of similar or same gestural form features over the course of a discourse' (p. 1114). McNeill (2005) has argued that recurrences over a stretch of discourse relate to discourse themes and referred to them as 'catchments'. The logic of catchments is that 'discourse themes produce gestures with recurring features; these recurrences give rise to the catchment ... thus the catchment offers clues to the cohesive linkages in the text with which it co-occurs' (McNeill 2005: 117). Müller and Tag (2010) relate recurrent features in gesture to the presence of a metaphor underpinning the discourse in spontaneous conversation. The reappearance of features of gestures that encode aspects of the metaphor serves to highlight or foreground its salience at strategic points in the interaction, populating the flow of gesturing with what they called 'multimodal salience structures' (p. 765). Lemmens (2016) observed individual differences in recurrence of form features in gesture when speakers were describing spatial scenes, such as speakers who repeatedly used 'oscillatory' forms or 'swaying' forms. He argued that such 'idiogests' may 'imply and maintain a certain perspective (semantic or pragmatic) on the scene described' (p. 37). Bressem et al. (2013) offered a different perspective relating to pragmatics when they observed that recurrent features across a stretch of gesturing may reflect discourse structure and organisation when they result in 'the successive use of pragmatic gestures' (p. 1114). The repeated performance of a pragmatic gesture associated with negation, namely the Horizontal Palm gesture, is at the heart of the pattern of gesturing to be studied here.

In the current chapter, the form, organisation, and conceptual import of gestures associated with negation established so far provides an empirical basis to examine how one speaker uses the Horizontal Palm gesture recurrently over the course of an informal business meeting. We take the 80-minute meeting as an analytical unit and examine one speaker's repeated use of the Horizontal Palm gesture over the course of the interaction. The chapter invites us to view recurrency not only as a product that leads to 'recurrent gestures', but also as a dynamic process that results in 'recurrent gesturing'. We explore the process of recurrency at work within a given interaction and how it sheds light on the relation between the speaker, her communicative aims, and the discourse context or interactive 'genre'.

6.1.2   Data and Context

In the previous interactions we have studied, the communicative aim of the speakers has been to have the conversation itself, often stimulated by a board game called 'get to know one another'. To pursue a particular pattern of gesturing, this chapter presents a study of one speaker's repeated use of the Horizontal Palm gesture over the course of an informal business meeting she had in a coffee shop in France. The aim of the meeting was to prepare for an upcoming visit to France's largest salmon factory, where the speaker and her addressee (myself) were employed on a project in organisational communication. Some background to this context is necessary to understand the nature of the data.

In summer 2009, I proposed a project to the management of a fish factory in France to use gesture studies as a way of understanding communication along their production lines. As part of the project, I spent two months in the factory and developed a communication system involving lights and conventionalised gestures for workers to experiment with along one of the production lines (Harrison 2013). Six months after leaving the factory, the manager invited me back to conduct one week's further work on implementing the system and training the workers to use it. The speaker we will study, M, held an undergraduate degree in Communication and Information Studies from a university in Paris and had also received relevant training in a Masters she had started elsewhere. Hoping she could assist me during the revisit, I invited her to collaborate on the project and, with her permission, filmed our first meeting for future research.

In *The language of business meetings*, Handford (2010) identified three pieces of information necessary to contextualise a business meeting. These are (i) the relationship between the speakers, (ii) the meeting purpose, and (iii) the meeting topic (pp. 8–15). I have stated that M and I were primarily friends, thus 'peers', but my previous work on the project and invitation to M to assist me also reflects a 'manager–subordinate' dimension to our relationship. M's own description of her role in this project on her Linkedin page reads 'consultant in internal communications' thus introducing an additional expert–novice dimension to our relationship: M as communications expert, me as novice. In terms of the purpose of the meeting, Holmes and Stubbe's (2003) category of 'planning, or prospective, meetings' typically involve 'forward-oriented' activities similar to those we engaged in, such as 'assigning tasks, requesting permission or action, strategizing, making decisions' (p. 64). Following descriptions proposed by Handford (2010: 14–15), the topic of our meeting mixes 'strategy' (overall objectives of the project and bigger picture) with 'procedure' (ways to achieve those objectives through short-term goals and work tasks at the factory).

While some researchers may feel uncomfortable analysing data in which they appear, my presence and active participation in the meeting under study is a crucial form of ethnographic data I will draw on during the analysis. My prolonged and in-depth experience of the speaker, the context of our meeting, and the project we are discussing, along with a retrospective interview I conducted with M (see Chapter 8), offer a valid form of triangulation to leverage findings in such qualitative data analysis (Dörnyei 2007).

6.1.3   Capturing the Complexity of the Horizontal Palm

Capturing the complexity of the Horizontal Palm gesture means identifying its diverse form variations and kinesic contexts. According to Calbris (2011): 'The kinesic context encompasses preceding and simultaneously occurring gestures' (p. 33). In keeping with the main methodology for this book, we adopted a 'form-based' view on co-speech gestures (Müller et al. 2013a) and accordingly employed Bressem et al.'s (2013) linguistic annotation system of gestures to analyse our data. This method of gesture analysis requires three general stages of coding: (i) annotation of gestures, (ii) annotation of speech, and (iii) annotation of gestures in relation to speech (and discourse).

Applied to our 80-minute interaction, this method was used in ELAN first to identify and describe all potential instances of the Horizontal Palm recurrent gesture (or 'ZP' following Kendon 2004) performed by M. Inclusion criteria for potential instances of ZP gestures were derived from the definitions provided in previous accounts of the gesture primarily in French (Calbris 1990, 2003, 2005, 2011), but also in Italian (Kendon 2004), English (Harrison 2009b, 2010, 2014a; Kendon 2004) and German (Bressem and Müller 2014a, 2014b). This body of research into the gesture converges on several salient features that appear to constitute its 'formational core' (Ladewig 2014b), namely, an open handshape, the palm oriented downwards, and lateral movement of the hand(s) across the body during the stroke. However, variation among descriptions of individual instances of the gesture abound in examples in the literature. Bearing this variation in mind, an analytical tier in the ELAN template was created for 'Horizontal Palm gestures' to code gesture strokes characterised by an open hand, palm down, and horizontal movement, allowing for variation and potential influence from adjacent gestures. This initially yielded sixty potential Horizontal Palm strokes.

Each Palm Down stroke was then coded for the phrase structure of the surrounding gesture unit (working with distinctions introduced by Kendon 2004: 111–13). This stage of descriptive work established that the sixty strokes were embedded in thirty gesture units containing over 200 gesture phrases. Having coded the kinesic context for each Horizontal Palm stroke, the sound was then switched on to code the gesture's relation to speech in a tier created immediately above the gesture unit. Within each gesture unit, I selected each gesture phrase, played the selection, and transcribed the associated speech. For gesture phrases that contained a Palm Down stroke, I attended to the organisation of speech in relation to the internal phase structure of the particular gesture phrase (e.g. preparation, holds, and stroke). This process helped discover temporal associations between the Palm Down gesture strokes, the surrounding gesture phrases, and the corresponding verbal units (along with their salient lexical and grammatical structures).

The final step involved analysing the semantic and pragmatic contributions of the Horizontal Palm gestures to the utterances they accompanied. The semantics of the Horizontal Palm gesture have previously been described by Kendon (2004) and Calbris (2011). While Kendon (2004) identified that the gesture involves a 'general semantic theme' of 'halting, interrupting, or indicating the interruption of a line of action' (p. 281), Calbris (2011) presented 'a sample giving the various contextual meanings of this gesture' and identified 'the range of notions that it can represent' (p. 178). Since Calbris's (2011) studies were based on the gesture in French, the notions she found provided an ideal starting point to consider each of my own examples. Classically, these notions include, for example, *quantity, totality, directness*, and *negation* (Calbris 1990, 2003, 2005). The pragmatic contributions of the gesture could be observed by considering the local discursive context-of-use, and bearing in mind those speech acts/functions identified by Kendon (2004: 255–62). Furthermore, I followed Bressem et al.'s (2013) recommendation to regard each gesture 'with respect to their positioning within turns, their dynamic use over time, their relation with the verbal speech act, and their pragmatic function' (p. 1112). An Excel file was used to add various qualitative notes in columns associated with each instance of stroke.

Capturing the complexity of the Horizontal Palm gesture thus involved coding on a series of levels and in itself constituted a form of micro-analysis of Horizontal Palm gesturing. The next section presents this micro-analysis as the empirical pre-requisite to then consider the speaker's pattern of gesturing in relation to the business meeting context and her communicative aims therein.

6.2   A Micro-Analysis of Horizontal Palm Gesturing

The Horizontal Palm gesture has a flexible formational core. How the speaker articulates a particular instance of Horizontal Palm gesture stroke may vary along any form parameter. Previous research on form variations in recurrent gestures has been able to identify systematic correlations between a change in form and a corresponding context of use (e.g. Ladewig 2014a; Müller 2004; Bressem et al. 2015). But variations in our data set could not be tied down to a particular discursive context. Instead, our examples showed how variations in the gesture form of Horizontal Palms exhibited a range of influences, including kinesic influences (through co-articulation with other gestures in the kinesic context), semantic influences (primarily from co-occurring speech, but also from the meaning of a particular sequence of gestures), and stylistic influences (when the variation in form parameter mirrors a departure in tone or other expressive character in the speech). In each case, a critical mass of other features characteristic of the gesture persist to render the gesture identifiable as a Horizontal Palm.

Table 6.1 *Handshape variations of the Horizontal Palm gesture*

Parameter	Variations
Handshape	Spreading of fingers (adducted to spread, tight or loose); protrusion of the thumb (both upwards and downwards from the flat hand configuration); inclusion of a 'ring' articulation (tips of thumb and index in contact); handshape composed of only index and middle finger; handshape composed of only index finger, etc.
Orientation	Palm could be 'completely down' (i.e. parallel to the ground), but also marked as 'lateral' (i.e. facing to the side) and 'towards body' (i.e. perpendicular); orientation of palm may transform internally during the stroke
Movement	(a) Of the palm through space: horizontally, diagonally, and sagittally. For example, two instances were observed to be 'completely horizontal', while others were marked as 'diagonal down movements' (b) In terms of different degrees and locations of accentuation: different phases of the gesture phrase could be accentuated, including the pre-stroke and the stroke phase; furthermore, when coding a series of Horizontal Palm gesture strokes, a comment was noted that the first stroke was accentuated, while in a different series, the second stroke appeared to be accentuated (c) In terms of internal configuration: it was observed that in some instances the configuration of the hand could undergo a subtle modification or transformation during the stroke. In one case this modification involved the shape of the hand, while in a different case it involved the rotation of the wrist. In both cases, commentary suggested this was related to prior or subsequent gestures in part of a sequence (co-articulation)
Location	Only one instance was marked in terms of location, more precisely as 'upper'

6.2.1   A Flexible Formational Core

No two instances of Horizontal Palm stroke in the corpus are articulated in precisely the same way. The range of variations observed for each of the main form parameters is presented in Table 6.1.

Table 6.1 provides an overview of the variation in formational features that the Horizontal Palm gesture may exhibit. In addition to the four form parameters, other observations of variation in the articulation of Horizontal Palm gesture strokes, as noted in the Excel file, included handedness (whether one or two hands were used), size of stroke (e.g. 'minimal' and 'large') and clarity of articulation (e.g. 'crisp'). Salient examples of these form variations will now be illustrated through a study of the kinesic contexts of the Horizontal Palm gestures.

6.2.2   Complexity of Kinesic Contexts

Kinesic contexts of the Horizontal Palm gesture may instantiate different degrees of complexity, defined as the type of gesture phrase structure the

Table 6.2   *Complexity of gesture units (GU) containing a Horizontal Palm (ZP)*
stroke

Characteristic	Occurrences
1. GU consists of single ZP stroke (simple)	4
2. GU consists of a series of ZP strokes (simple)	3
3. a) GU is complex including a single ZP stroke	6 (10)
b) GU is complex including an apparent pattern (single stroke)	4
4. GU is complex with a single series of ZPs	8
5. GU is complex with multiple ZPs throughout, single and/or series	2
Total:	27

stroke is surrounded by. The sixty Horizontal Palm gesture strokes in our data were part of twenty-seven gesture units, which in total contained over 200 gesture phrases. These contexts ranged in degrees of complexity and influenced the types of variation found in individual gesture form features. The different categories of complexity and relative distribution of occurrences is summarised in Table 6.2.

To exemplify and analyse this complexity, we will proceed from least kinesically complex gesture units ('simple', e.g., when a gesture unit contains only one stroke) to more kinesically complex gesture units ('complex', e.g., when a gesture unit contains several gesture phrases and multiple strokes).

(1) Gesture unit is simple, consists of a single ZP stroke
A single Horizontal Palm gesture stroke can constitute an entire gesture unit, meaning that the sole reason for the gestural excursion was to perform a Horizontal Palm gesture stroke (four instances). The bulk of previous literature on the Horizontal Palm gesture has been devoted to occurrences that exhibit this basic level of complexity, as evidenced by examples in previous work (such as Calbris 2011; Kendon 2004; Harrison 2010, 2014a; Bressem and Müller 2013).

An example from the introductory phase of the meeting illustrates this category. S is explaining his vision for the outcome of the project. By introducing a new communication tool, he hopes to create a factory that 'communicates different to before' and that 'becomes a pleasant factory where people are happy to come to work' (lines 1–2). After a short pause, he looks up towards M and snorts with laughter, plausibly acknowledging that his description is somewhat unrealistic for the difficult work environment of a fish factory. As he begins to continue '*et err*' ('and er'), M bursts out laughing, points at S [1], and shakes her head while cautioning '*faut pas que tu fasses ça quand tu leur dis*' ('you can't be doing that when you tell them'; line 3). She then says '*Parce que là tu perds complètement de la crédibilité*' ('Because there you will lose completely [your] credibility'; line 4). With this last utterance she performs a gesture unit consisting of a Horizontal Palm with a single stroke (left hand), which she coordinates with the adverb '*complètement*' ('completely'). The hand is flat and the movement is diagonal-lateral-downward [2] (Figure 6.1).

Example 51 GU6 Perds complètement de la crédibilité
    and the factory communicates different to before (.) it's ... that it becomes a
    pleasant
1 S et l'usine ne communique plus comme avant (.) c'est.. que ça devient une
    pleasant factory where people are happy to come to work ... Hahah ... And
    err ...
2   usine agréable où on est content de venir travailler .... Hahah ... Et err ...
    hahah you can't be doing that when you tell them
3 M hahah faut pas que tu fasses ça quand tu leur dis (.)
    |~~~~~~~~~~***********************-.-.-.-.|
                    [1]
    because there you will lose completely [your] credibility
4   parce que là, tu perds complètement de la crédibilité
    |~******-.-.-.-.|
        [2]
    [1] Raised index towards addressee, [2] Horizontal Palm gesture.

faut pas que tu fasses ça quand   tu perds complètement de la
tu leur dis   crédibilité
you can't be doing that when   *you will completely lose*
you tell them   *credibility*

Figure 6.1 Gesture unit consists of single Horizontal Palm stroke

Consistent with examples in Calbris (2011), the Horizontal Palm gesture here emphasises both the *totality* of credibility that S risks losing and the *direct* nature in which he would lose it. At the level of speech act, the utterance not only interrupts S but also constitutes a warning. It is as if M uses a Horizontal Palm gesture to stress to S the negative consequence of not taking that warning on board. However, the diagonality of the palm orientation and movement trajectory combine with the location of the gesture 'off to the side' to weaken the strength of her warning. M's laughter, facial expression, and loose handshape further suggest that the warning is a jovial one.

Humour like this is often used to hedge speech acts in a workplace context (Holmes and Stubbe 2003).

(2) GU is simple, consists of a series of ZP strokes

A gesture unit may consist entirely of a series of Horizontal Palm gesture strokes (three instances). An example of this level of complexity occurs in the main body of the meeting, during a stretch of interaction where S and M are discussing the level of insistence needed to establish communication as a priority on the agenda at the factory during the week of their visit. S describes the requirement he perceives for the workers to understand '*qu'on communique au maximum*' ('we communicate to the maximum'; line 1). He then starts to explain what concrete actions this will necessitate during the week and begins an utterance with '*Donc pendant la semaine il faut qu'on*' ('So during the week we need to'; line 3). N interrupts him and latches on to his grammatical structure, completing the utterance by saying '*qu'on soit chiant, qu'on se répète, qu'on soit des mamies qui radotent*' ('[we need] to be annoying, to repeat ourselves, to be like grannies who drone on'; line 4). With her utterance, she performs a gesture unit composed entirely of a series of Horizontal Palm gesture strokes. Each stroke is timed to occur with the different actions she is stressing, and in the pause immediately after her utterance, she markedly averts eye gaze from the addressee and looks off to the side with an expression on her face that I interpret as suggesting '*I'm being crafty*' (Figure 6.2). At this point, note how S acknowledges M's contribution positively and ratifies it '*oui ha tu peux dire ça aussi*' ('yes ha you can say that too'), the initial laughter possibly a sign that he finds her analogy to old women amusing. But he also then offers his own reformulation '*qu'on va les embêter cette semaine (.)*' ('that we are going to be annoying them this week (.)'), explicitly including the caveat '*mais de manière gentille*' ('but in a friendly way') (Figure 6.2).

Example 52 GU19 Des mamies qui radotent
    they must understand that we communicate to the maximum
1 S il faut que eux ils comprennent qu'on communique au maximum.
    there you go
2 M voilà
    so during the week we need to
3 S donc pendant la semaine il faut [qu-]
    to be annoying, to repeat ourselves, to be like grannies who drone on
4 M [qu]'on soit chiant (.) qu'on se répète (.) qu'on soit des mamies qui radotent (.)
    |~*****~~~~***********~~~~****~*****~~*******_.-|
        [1]   [2]   [3] [4]   [5] [6]
    yes haha you can say that too that we are going to be annoying them this week (.)
5 S oui (.) haha tu peux dire ça aussi (.) qu'on va les embêter cette semaine (.)
    but in a friendly way
6   mais de manière gentille

[1–5] Strokes of a Horizontal Palm gesture, [6] 'I'm being crafty' facial expression.

Qu' on soit chiant, qu'on se répète, qu' on soit des mamies qui radotent
To be annoying, to repeat ourselves, to be like grannies who drone on

Figure 6.2 Example of simple kinesic context: series of ZP strokes constitutes gesture unit

This instance of the gesture is performed with both hands. Because the elbows are resting on the table, the laterality of movement stems from rotations of the wrists. The clarity of articulation and extent of movement of the gesture increase with each repetition, resulting in a final form held briefly where the thumb protrudes vertically from a handshape that is 'flapped' – the flap occurring at the main (metacarpal) knuckles. Semantically, the gesture expresses both the *laying out* of a sequence of events as well as the *fixed* and *frank* nature of that process (cf. Calbris 2011). In doing so, it iconically embodies the repetitive approach that M is advocating in speech, translating on the level of pragmatics into a demonstration, indeed a rehearsal, of the level of intensity she envisages that S potentially had in mind. In line with this, the increase in articulation of the Horizontal Palm gesture strokes appears to be the consequence of the utterance culminating to completion. The pattern of accentuation within the gesture unit matches the one being expressed in speech to culminate in a crescendo of multimodal resources. With her utterance, the speaker both describes the approach to adopt and illustrates that approach – the repetition of the Horizontal Palm strokes is a central part of that illustration. The 'I'm being crafty' facial expression is characterised by a 'side-eye' glance that adds the speaker's critical stance to the approach she is advocating. Response by S must be considered at least a partial ratification of that approach, in addition to a way in which he attempts to maintain some control of the discourse (cf. Holmes and Stubbe 2003: 73).

(3) GU is complex and includes a single ZP stroke

A single Horizontal Palm stroke may occur embedded in a series of other gestures, meaning the gesture unit is composed of multiple gesture phrases, one of which contains a single Horizontal Palm gesture (ten instances, and therefore the most common category in the current data set).

To illustrate this category, consider M's use of the Horizontal Palm gesture in the following example at the start of a gesture unit that contains three gestures, one of which is an emblem. The participants of the meeting have been discussing how they will introduce themselves to the workers and what details they will give about their motivation for the project. M is illustrating what she thinks to be good practice by pretending to address the workers with an utterance that describes her role in the factory in a way that will not be met with resistance. Performing a Horizontal Palm with '*pas*' ('not'), M proposes that '*Le mieux c'est surtout on est pas venu là pour vous faire chier*' ('the best [thing to say] is that we didn't come here to annoy you'). In this instance of her Horizontal Palm [1], her index finger and thumb are joined in a 'ring' formation, a variation influenced by the topicalisation structure of her utterance (Harrison and Larrivée 2015). She holds this gesture with the linguistic material following '*pas*', then embeds it in a vertical beat [2] as she says '*On est là pour*' ('we came to') and maintains another hold for '*améliorer la situation*' ('improve the situation'). M finishes her utterance by saying '*en toute convivialité il y a pas souci*' ('in all conviviality there's no need to worry'). With this last phrase, which is produced to a sing-song melody, she swings both hands upwards to a position at either side of her head, the palms facing her addressee, and sways her torso from side to side [3] (Figure 6.3).

Example 53 GU2 En toute convivialité
   the best is that we didn't come here to annoy you
1 le mieux c'est surtout on est pas venu là pour vous faire chier
         |⁓⁓*************************/
                    [1]
   we came to improve the situation
2 on est là pour améliorer la situation
     ⁓⁓************************/
         [2]
   in all conviviality there's no need to worry
3 (.) en toute convivialité il y a pas souci
     ⁓⁓****************************-.-.|
           [3]
[1] Horizontal Palm with ring formation, [2] vertical beat of ring, [3] 'Faire le guignol' emblem.

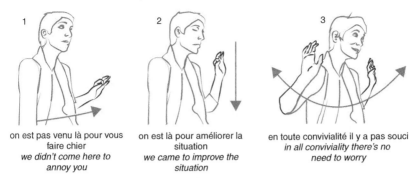

| on est pas venu là pour vous faire chier | on est là pour améliorer la situation | en toute convivialité il y a pas souci |
| *we didn't come here to annoy you* | *we came to improve the situation* | *in all conviviality there's no need to worry* |

Figure 6.3 Complex kinesic context: single ZP stroke among other GPs constitutes GU

This example illustrates how different linguistic structures in addition to nega-tion can influence the form of the Horizontal Palm – in this case a topicalising structure that leads to a ring handshape. It also illustrates how other gestures may be related to the Horizontal Palm within a particular gesture unit. While the Horizontal Palm is part of rejecting an assumption that the speaker believes the workers may hold (that the project will '*annoy*' them), the 'vertical beat' of the ring handshape establishes the reason for the visit ('*improving the situa-tion*'). The gesture occurring with the end of this sequence is what could be a French emblem glossed as '*faire le guignol*' (to play the clown/fool). Combined with her melodic tone of voice, the speaker is conveying that she thinks the workers in the factory will respond better if she appears as non-threatening as possible, as a clown would to a child. This last gesture is therefore no longer part of what she intends to say to the workers, but rather her own critical reflection on how she intends to say it, and potentially on the gestures she intends to use when saying it, which included the Horizontal Palm.

In (3b), as a sub instance of the previous category, the gesture unit may be complex and include a single Horizontal Palm stroke in apparent combination with another gesture. Four instances in the data appeared to be part of a two-stroke combination, what we earlier termed a gesture sequence (cf. Chapter 5).

(4) GU is complex with a single series of PD strokes
The gesture unit may be composed of several gesture phrases, a series within which involves Horizontal Palm gesture strokes (eight instances). To exemplify this category, we will consider a gesture unit comprising six gesture strokes, four of which are variations of Horizontal Palm gestures. In Example 54 the pair are discussing what they will need to explain to impress on the workers the importance of communication. In the discourse immediately prior to this example, S has described to M that in some contexts people have naturally

developed a codified system of gestures similar to the ones the current project aims to implement at the fish factory, and he gives an example of workers on the stock exchange (presumably thinking of the description in Morris 2002). As we join the transcript, M picks up on this previous research as a potential way to make an important point to the employees, who she reasons might be able to identify with, that is, to draw similarities between the stock exchange workers and their managers (lines 1–2). After S acknowledges this analogy (line 3), M elaborates how she could convey this to the workers by explaining that '*même des gars comme ça ils ont besoin de gestes pour mieux s'en sortir sinon (.) mauvaise-mauv- communication pas de rendement ... nul zéro*' ('Even guys like that they need gesture to better get by otherwise, ba- bad communication, no performance, rubbish, zero'; lines 5–6). The gesture unit that accompanies this entire stretch of utterance illustrates the fourth level of kinesic complexity. M performs a thumb point off to the side as she references the managers [1], which she beats as she emphasises how those managers would also need to gesture to communicate effectively [2]. Without retracting the gesture, she then performs a series of four Horizontal Palm strokes as she lists the negative consequences to not using gesture. Each stroke coordinates with a particular negative consequence and exhibits a micro-variation in form [3–6]. Immediately after M's utterance, S acknowledges 'oui' ('yes') (Figure 6.4).

Example 54 GU8 Même des gars comme ça
  it would be good to tell them about the stock-exchange
1 M ce serait bien de leur en parler de la bourse
  because the stock-exchange it's the kind of guys like their managers
2   parce que la bourse c'est le genre de mec comme leurs managers.
  yes
3 S oui
  we will need to explain that
4 M il va falloir leur expliquer que
  even guys like that they need gesture to better get by
5   même des gars comme ça ils ont besoin de gestes pour mieux s'en sortir
  |~~~*****~~~~~~~~~~*******************************
      [1]   [2]
  otherwise, ba- bad communication, no performance, rubbish, zero.
6   sinon (.) mauvaise-mauv- communication pas de rendement (.) nul zéro
  ~~~~*****~~~~~~~~~~~~~~~~~~******~~~~~~~***~~~***-|
      [3]   [4]   [5]   [6]
  yes
7 S [oui]
  [1] Thumb point off to side, [2] beat of thumb point, [3] Horizontal Palm gesture, [4] ZP with staccato stroke, [5] ZP with slow/arced movement, [6] ZP with ring hand shape.

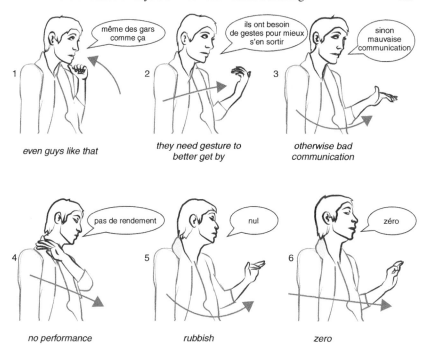

Figure 6.4 Complex kinesic context: series of ZP strokes among other GPs constitutes GU

While the first two gestures in the unit are part of establishing the scenario of people using gesture to communicate effectively, the series of Horizontal Palm gestures refer to the consequences of ignoring such a scenario. Each stroke in the series is performed saliently in central gesture space, but the formational features differ in terms of handshape and movement pattern. The opening stroke is the largest and potentially captures the *negation-refusal* inherent in the uttered theme 'bad communication', as well as the widespread negative effects of such communication in the factory. The staccato stroke that follows connects to the specificity of the example being given and plausibly serves to express the rejection of 'performance' (hence the ricochet movement it includes). The somewhat slower and more arced movement of the third stroke captures her sweeping characterisation of poor communication as '*nul*' ('rubbish'). The final stroke is not only performed on a downward diagonal trajectory, but also incorporates a Ring handshape (tips of index and thumb are in contact). Overall, the first three flapped handshapes are related to *negation-refusal* and, in particular, to the negative value judgements that M expresses towards poor communication. The Ring variation reflects the gestural translation of 'zero', specifying a quantifiable result of poor communication. Throughout the gesture unit, sustained horizontality of the gesture maintains themes such as *certainty* and *totality* across all instances of the strokes performed here (Calbris 2011). These forms and semantic relations culminate in an utterance with which, pragmatically, M demonstrates relevant knowledge of communication theory (i.e. that 'communication affects everybody'). An element of constructed action suggests that M may also be demonstrating if not rehearsing how she could warn, and possibly even intimidate, the employees she envisages working with. Evoking scenarios and rehearsing lines of communicative action begins to emerge in these examples as an important communicative aim of the speaker.

(5) GU is complex with multiple ZP strokes throughout, single and/or series

In this final category of kinesic complexity, Horizontal Palm gesture strokes were observed to occur in both single and repeated manifestations, embedded in different locations within a gesture unit consisting of numerous other gestures (two instances). A gesture unit that illustrates such complexity occurs towards the end of the main body of the meeting. The unit accompanies a 20-second stretch of discourse that M uses to lay out two different options for imparting the responsibility of the project on the workers. This particular gesture unit contains nineteen Gesture Phrases, three of which are characterised by individual Horizontal Palm gesture strokes. In other words, M's hands are continuously in motion during her stretch of discourse, this gestural flow occasionally punctuated by a Horizontal Palm gesture.

M is seeking to clarify with S whether the plan is to tell the workers that the system is being trialled to evaluate its suitability or that it is being implemented to be used as of now on. The gesture unit accompanies several utterances but all three instances of her Horizontal Palm gesture occur as she is explaining how she would address the workers in the case of the first scenario. The first instance occurs at the very beginning of the gesture unit as she starts her constructed address by saying '*On essaie un programme cette semaine c'est détendu*' ('We are testing a program this week there's no pressure'; line 2). In an apparent gesture sequence, she performs a Palm Presenting gesture as she introduces this utterance with '*On essaie*' ('we are testing') [1], holding this gesture in a partial retraction until saying '*c'est détendu*' ('there's no pressure'), with which she performs a Horizontal Palm gesture characterised by a diagonal-downward movement [2]. She then performs a cascade of Palm Up gestures as she indicates what will nevertheless need to be done despite there being no pressure [3], such as making an effort for the week (line 3), then evaluating whether or not the new system is efficient (line 4). She continues by evoking a sub-scenario in which the system is indeed efficient and the workers will continue with it on their own (line 6). But she raises an important condition to this case. Again using a gesture sequence [4], she performs a Palm Up gesture as she stipulates (i) '*mais dans ce cas-là*' ('But in that case') then another diagonal-downward Horizontal Palm gesture as she cautions (ii) '*il faut pas compter*' ('you can't count'), followed by a thumb point off to the side with (iii) '*sur la hiérarchie*' ('on the hierarchy'). The third and final instance of Horizontal Palm gesture in this unit occurs immediately afterwards, as she explains '*pour s'occuper de ça parce qu'ils auront pas le temps pour le moment*' ('to attend to it because they won't have the time for the moment') [5]. With 'to attend to it' she transforms the previous thumb point into a downwards stabbing motion of a flapped open-hand oriented palm down (i), produces a Palm Presenting gesture with 'because they' (ii), then rotates the wrist with 'won't have the time for the moment' into a Horizontal Palm gesture, a variant in which the palm is lateral at its end point (iii). She ends this segment on the first scenario by giving the start date of the hypothetical project, saying '*ils commenceront en janvier 2011*' ('they will begin in January 2011') and producing a large looping gesture coherent with the temporal span being evoked [6i–iii].

Continuing to gesture in various ways, M ends this stretch of discourse by evoking the second scenario in which the system is implemented with immediate effect. In line 9, she uses a Palm Presenting gesture with beats as she introduces the alternative with 'or', specifies 'if this is the case', then introduces the scenario that 'we start the project now' [7]. She then warns about the heavy time investment that it would require (line 10). Performing another beat of the Palm Presenting gesture, she says '*mais alors là*' ('but well then') and concludes '*ça implique un investissement important*' ('it involves a heavy investment'). With the first part of this conclusion she sweeps an open palm oriented laterally from left to right to back again [8], then beats a Palm Up gesture [9i] as she stresses the investment needed will be 'important', before finally retracting her gesture and ending the gesture unit [9ii]. S takes a turn at this point beginning with an acknowledgement 'oui' ('yes', line 11). All salient gestures are illustrated in Figure 6.5 following the transcript below, with the instances of Horizontal Palm gesture highlighted with a bold frame.

Example 55 GU28 time C'est détendu
　　　　if we tell them we are starting a program they will have to follow up or if we tell them
1　M　si on leur dit on commence un programme il va falloir suivre ou si on leur dit
　　　　we are testing a program this week there's no pressure
2　　　　on essaie un programme cette semaine c'est détendu
　　　　|~***-./~~~*******
　　　　　　　　　　[1]　　　　　　　　　　　　　[2]
　　　　you just have to try this for one week make the effort

3   il faut juste que vous fassiez passer ça cette semaine que vous fassiez l'effort
    /∼∼∼∼*******/**********************************/*******************
           [3i]   [3ii]   [3iii]
    then   if we see that it is going to be efficient
4   après si on voit que ça va être efficace
    /****/*********-.-.-.-.-.-.-.-.-.-.-.-.-.-
    [3iv]   [3v]
    either you can start to get going by yourselves
5   soit vous pouvez commencer à le lancer vous-même
    /**
                [3vi]
    but in that case you can't count   on the hierarchy
6   mais dans ce cas-là (.) il faut pas compter sur la hiérarchie pour
    *****/∼∼∼∼*******/∼∼∼∼***********/∼*************
         [4i]   [4ii]   [4iii]
    to attend to it Because they won't have the time for the moment
7   s'occuper de ça parce qu'ils auront pas le temps pour le moment
    /∼***********/∼∼∼∼*****/********************
      [5i]   [5ii]   [5iii]
    they will begin in 2011
8   ils commenceront en janvier 2011
    ****
           [6i,ii,iii]
    or   if it is the case   we start the project now
9   (.) ou est-ce que dans ce cas-là on commence le projet maintenant
    /∼∼**
            [7]   *beat*
    but well then it involves a heavy investment
10   mais alors là ça implique un investissement important
    ********/∼******************/∼∼********-.-.|
    beat   [8]   [9i] [9ii]
    ah yes   ah no we must . . .
11 S   ah oui ah non il faut que . . .

[1] Palm Presenting gesture, [2] Horizontal Palm gesture with diagonal-downward movement, [3] Palm Presenting gestures, [4i] Palm Presenting gesture, [4ii] Horizontal Palm gesture with diagonal-downward movement, [4iii] Thumb point off to side, [5i] Downward stabbing of flapped hand, [5ii] Palm Presenting gesture, [5iii] Horizontal Palm gesture from palm up to palm lateral orientation, [6i,ii,iii] Large looping gesture, [7] Palm Presenting gesture with beats, [8] Palm oriented laterally sweeps left to right, [9i] Palm Presenting gesture, [9ii] Retraction

M's Horizontal Palm gesture in this example occurs repeatedly over 20 seconds of discourse within a gesture unit with several different form variations in terms of movement characteristics, orientation of the palm, and kinesic embedding. Furthermore, the instances of Horizontal Palm gesture are sequenced with multiple gesture forms that have equally multiple meanings and functions.

Figure 6.5 GU is complex with multiple single strokes of PD throughout

Salient among these is the Palm Presenting gesture. As we observed in Chapter 5, the Palm Presenting and Horizontal Palm gestures may be coordinated into a recurrent sequence in which the rotation of the wrists reflects a flipped perspective being taken in the co-occurring discourse ('PP-to-ZP'). Gesture sequences [1–2], [4i–4iii], and [5] constitute additional examples in support of this.

To summarise, the Horizontal Palm gesture can be individually produced, part of a series of Horizontal Palm gestures, or integrated with various other gestures. The complexity of its context affects the precise form of the Horizontal Palm stroke. The position of the individual gesture stroke within its series or broader gesture unit also affects its form, for example, if an increased intensity of expression effected a greater articulation of form. Gestures other than the Horizontal Palm produced in sequence with the Horizontal Palm could also affect its formational features, including referential gestures and other recurrent gestures, especially for transitions into and out of the Palm Presenting gesture. The ability to combine with other gestures and to be embedded in kinesic contexts of varying degrees of complexity emerges as a central characteristic of the Horizontal Palm gesture.

6.3   The Business of Horizontal Palming

The recurrence of a particular linguistic feature across a stretch of interaction is key to understanding the nature of the meeting and the goals of its participants (Handford 2010). Holmes and Stubbe (2003) studied eighty meetings from nine different companies as a crucial component of workplace communication and identified a number of linguistic and discursive resources that participants deployed in meetings to manage interaction, navigate the agenda, and appeal to each other's face needs. Handford (2010) analysed sixty business meetings from twenty-six different companies and found 'there are linguistic items and features that play a critical interpretive role in terms of the understanding and development of the meeting context' (p. 40). If the Horizontal Palm gesture qualifies as a 'critical item' in our data, then its relation to communicative aims in the wider social context may shed light on the genesis for the pattern that characterises the speaker's impulse to gesture. Establishing a relation between a pattern of gesturing and the business meeting context could also have wider implications for the role of gesture in discourse as social practice or big 'D' discourses (Gee 2014), including issues of style, identity, and genre.

To identify 'critical items' within a business meeting context, Handford (2010) found that 'language items and features can be classified as potentially of interest if: (i) they are frequent, (ii) they are statistically significant, (iii) they are stylistically salient or culturally key, (iv) they have been shown to be important in other, related studies' (p. 40). In our data, the average recurrence of the

Horizontal Palm gesture every two minutes during the interaction suggests it is a frequent item in this context. Cultural salience of recurrent gestures is often highlighted in the literature generally (Ladewig 2014b; Bressem and Müller 2014b), and the Horizontal Palm gesture has been described as a key gesture for French speakers specifically (Calbris 1990, 2003, 2005, 2011). The landmark studies by Calbris alone establish the importance of the gesture for French speakers, but observations of the crucial role played by gestures associated with negation in early French language acquisition support this importance (Beaupoil-Hourdel et al. 2015; Morgenstern et al. 2016).

Given the potential criticality of the Horizontal Palm gesture in our data, our micro-analysis provides both the meaning of the gesture in relation to its local linguistic and discursive context and an empirical basis to now consider its relation to broader practices in relation to the business meeting context.

6.3.1   From Gesture in Discourse to Practice

The specific meanings of a critical item in context contribute to how speakers accomplish various practices within the genre of a business meeting, including discursive, professional, and social practices (Handford 2010). While some practices are observable in the lexico-grammatical features of text, other practices 'can be explained in terms of the social identities and the community of the speakers, their relationship with the other participants, and the goals they are navigating' (Handford 2010: 66). This relationship between textual features, discourse, and various kinds of practice can be extended multimodally to provide a framework to explore the recurrence of Horizontal Palm gesturing in our spoken language data.

Drawing on Bhatia's (2004) work on practice and genre (cf. Swales 1990), Handford (2010) defines 'practices' as: 'shared, sanctioned, recurring, constraining and enabling communicative conventions' (p. 32). He explains: 'These conventions are socially ratified within the specific unfolding context by the powerful participants and the tacit agreement and involvement of the less powerful participants, and are acquired over time through membership of a particular community' (ibid.). Practices thus occur at different levels varying in proximity to the linguistic features of a text, on the one hand, and to the widening social context on the other. Discursive practices, for instance, are 'located in the text' (Handford 2010: 63), meaning they 'signify recurrent patterns of linguistic behaviour that are decipherable in transcripts of business meetings' (p. 66). Recurrent linguistic features observable in the data contribute to interactional moves at a discourse level that are relevant, if not expected, within a particular genre (Swales 1990). In the case of a business meeting, relevant discursive moves may include opening, summarising, checking or emphasising shared understanding, and bringing a topic to a close (p. 77).

Figure 6.6 From text to social practice (following Handford 2010: 67)

Professional practices are the forms of knowledge, expertise, and activities relevant to the specific context that speakers may demonstrate or 'activate' by performing their discursive moves. Activating professional practices amounts to activating 'knowledge necessary for effective participation' in that context (p. 64), which for a business meeting could include knowledge of the company in which the meeting takes place or of the business operations being discussed as part of the agenda (Handford 2010). Professional practices must be inferred from the text, but identifying them amounts to acknowledging that 'meetings have various implicit goals which also relate to the organisation's business' (Holmes and Stubbe 2003: 62). Social practices 'work at a more general level' (p. 63). They appear to allow categorisations of the array of professional practices as a broader coherent form of practice, such as what could be called 'classroom teaching, conducting medical consultations and management practices' (p. 63), the last of which would be a relevant category for the current data.

Concretely then, a speaker may use a critical item to accomplish certain discursive moves, which in turn allow them to illustrate particular forms of knowledge or expertise relevant to their context. Doing so helps establish the speaker's membership of a particular community of practice in which they can legitimately participate in a form of social practice, such as a meeting between business professionals. Figure 6.6 captures Handford's (2010) bridge from text to practice, where the double-ended arrows reflect the bi-directional influences of the different layers of practice (cf. Bhatia 2004).

Positing the Horizontal Palm gesture as a 'textual realisation' of a critical item, three broader segments will be studied to evaluate its role in the different forms of professional and social practice observable in the meeting data. The segments have been taken roughly ten minutes apart over the main body of the meeting. They each illustrate how a core element of organisational communication is being discussed, illustrated, negotiated, and agreed on, and they allow us to consider the role of the speaker's Horizontal Palm gesture in indexing those elements of professional practice. The Horizontal Palm gesture displays communicative acts that achieve discourse functions with which the speaker demonstrates professional knowledge relevant to the context; namely, (1) breaking down hierarchies, (2) managing interpersonal relations, and (3) monitoring follow-up of the project. Based on the analyses, we then discuss whether the Horizontal Palm gesture could be considered a sort of 'key-gesture' – a gestural equivalent of a keyword – in the business meeting context.

6.3.2   Practice 1: Breaking Down Hierarchies

Over the course of the business meeting in our data, breaking down hierarchies and emphasising teamwork emerges as central to M's agenda regarding her role on the project. A specific segment of discourse occurs approximately half way through the meeting that illustrates her commitment to this classic principle of effective organisational management (Jones 1994). In this segment, M lays out a plan to convince the line operators to invest themselves in the project of trialling a new communication system. Part of this plan is exposed through a series of discursive moves; namely, demystifying the superiority of the managers and placing all staff on a level footing (lines 1–3), warning about the universal negative impacts of poor communication (lines 4–5), dispelling a potential misconception that line operators are uneducated and thereby increasing the perception of the workers' self-worth (lines 7–9), and finally, establishing that communication affects all staff in an organisation regardless of position in the hierarchy (line 10–12). On a linguistic level, these discursive moves are achieved with utterances saliently structured by grammatical elements such as maximal scope adverbs (*all, everyone*) and negative markers (*no, nothing*). Consistent with our micro-analysis of M's Horizontal Palm gesturing, she synchronises strokes of the Horizontal Palm gesture with several of such elements, as indicated in bold in the transcript. The original French and English translation are presented separately to facilitate reading.

Example 56 GU8_GU9_GU10 Tous au même niveau (38.40)

1	M	ce serait bien de leur en parler de la bourse
2		parce que la bourse c'est le genre de mec comme leurs managers
3		il va falloir leur expliquer que
4		même des gars comme ça ils ont besoin de gestes pour mieux s'en sortir
5		**sinon (.) mauvaise-mauv- communication pas de rendement (.) nul zéro**
6	S	oui
7	M	donc c'est pas tellement que dans des usines c'est ceux qui ont des idées qui [sont]
8	S	[oui]
9	M	entre guillemet plus intellectuels ou que vous non
10		**vous êtes on est tous au même niveau la dessus**

11 S   oui
12 M   **la communication elle touche tout le monde (3)**
13 S   même toi (.) arrête de parler
14 M   hahahah
15 S   ça c'est la mauvaise communication ça

      (English translation)
1   M   *it would be good to tell them about the stock-exchange*
2   *because the stock exchange it's the kind of guys like their managers*
3   *we're going to have to explain that*
4   *even guys like that they need gesture to better get by*
5   ***otherwise (.) bad ba- communication no performance (.) nothing zero.***
6   S   *yes*
7   M   *so it's not so much that in factories it's those who have the top jobs who are*
8   S   *yes*
9   M   *so-called more intellectual and you no*
10   ***you are we are all on the same level in that respect***
11 S   *yes*
12 M   ***communication it affects everyone***
13 S   *even you, stop talking*
14 M   *hahahah*
15 S   *that's bad communication that.*

The speaker's Horizontal Palm gesturing over the course of this segment contributes to the speech acts with which she lays out her plan. While the first series of strokes emphasise her rejection that managers higher up the hierarchy are unaffected by such menial concerns as communication, the second and third instances emphasise her assertions about the universal effects of communication. Together, these discursive moves reflect her commitment to an important practice in the management profession, namely the need to break down perceived hierarchies and encourage teamwork. In addition to emphasising speech acts that 'orient' towards this aspect of professional practice, the repeated performance of the Horizontal Palm gesture over this stretch potentially increases the perlocutionary force of her utterances by enhancing the persuasiveness of her discourse and, in turn, establishing the authority of her expertise. Indeed, if M's addressee responds humorously to her plan by pretending to reprimand a worker for 'bad communication', it is perhaps because of the perceived severity of M's discourse.

Note how the speaker uses role shift ('you' and 'we') to show how she will communicate her plan. By rehearsing how she would actually address the workers, she demonstrates the communication skills needed to execute her plan. Stylistic variation in the form of her Horizontal Palm gesture with her final utterance '*la communication elle touche tout le monde*' ('communication it affects everyone') suggests that she is fully aware of the meta-communicative strategy she is deploying. Figure 6.7 illustrates how during the performance of her Horizontal Palm, M diverts eye-gaze from her addressee, uses a stylised preparation in order to slingshot her Horizontal Palm gesture across the gesture space, then smirks once the gesture is complete. Though the whole gesture unit occurs within a two-second time frame, at least three distinct phases can be identified to the preparation of the gesture. Reproducing this as Example 57, as she says 'la communication' she raises her hand from a rest position on the table to a Palm Up position in her central left gesture space [1]. With '*elle touche*' ('it affects'), she raises her hand into upper gesture space and rotates the wrist so that the palm is now facing outwards in a precision grip configuration [2]. This appears to be the starting point for the stroke, because as she says '*tout le monde*' ('everyone'), she momentarily lowers her hand back down before cocking it across her body [3] and finally produces the lateral movement characteristic of the Horizontal Palm [4] – all in one 'slingshot' movement. During a post-stroke hold, she then produces a facial expression in which she diverts eye-gaze even further from her addressee and smirks [5] (Figure 6.7).

Example 57 N_S GU10 Communication affects everyone
communication it affects everyone.
M la communication elle touche tout le monde (. . .)
|〜〜〜〜〜〜***********-.-.-.-.-|
[1]   [2]   [3–4]   [5]
[1] Preparation phase 1 (palm up position), [2] preparation phase 2 (vertical precision grip position), [3] stroke phase 1 (downwards then across body one way), [4] stroke phase 2 (slingshot back across the body).

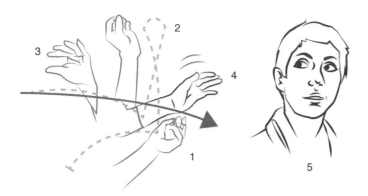

Figure 6.7 Stylistic variation of the Horizontal Palm; Facial expression

This meta-awareness indicates a form of 'stylistic wiggle room' (Coupland 2007) in the gesture. Specifically, M is playing with the kinesics of the Horizontal Palm gesture by manipulating its preparation and stroke phases. She is critically evaluating her role in the project and, to some extent, distancing her current self from the persona she believes she will need to adopt when motivating the factory workers. The facial expression and gaze pattern during the gesture are similarly central to this moment of style. By breaking mutual gaze at the start of the gesture, M invites her addressee to view its performance as a demonstration. During the post-stroke hold, she diverts gaze further by slightly rotating her head and producing a glance off into the distance, possibly giving some 'side eye' to the workers she is pretending to address. Furthermore, M accompanies this facial expression with a smirk, as if to acknowledge that her addressee might be watching, indeed, appreciating her multimodal utterance. On a broader level, this could be one way that M shows to her addressee that she is rehearsing her intervention and provides the opportunity for her co-worker to align with or challenge the plan she is advocating.

6.3.3   Practice 2: Managing Interpersonal Relations

A second segment from the business meeting illustrates how M exhibits further expertise relevant to her role in this context. A number of examples discussed previously have highlighted M's awareness of the need to be both friendly and firm when dealing with workers at the factory. In the stretch of discourse analysed here, she explicitly describes positive and negative aspects to managing interpersonal relations as an apparently salient aspect of her consultancy. This explanation occurs in response to S reporting previous experience with workers joking around on the shop floor (line 1). M demonstrates her expertise on this issue by juxtaposing different styles of management (lines 6–7), rejecting a common misconception about a strict approach to management (lines 11–12), concluding that a balance of styles is necessary (line 14), and warning of negative consequences to adopting a misinformed approach (line 16). Her Horizontal Palm gesture strokes occur with the positive and negative evaluations that form the basis of the management styles she is juxtaposing.

Example 58 GU13_GU14 Mauvais plan (53.00)
1   S   mais il y avait eu pas mal de blagues sur le cul et tout ça avant (inaud.)
2   M   euh bien il faut que tu te concentres
3   S   bien j'essaie de juste faire: (. . .)
4   M   non mais ça éventuellement ça va si tu veux juste il faut qu'on reste crédible
        quoi
5   S   oui
6   M   donc même si on blague avec eux **ce qui est vraiment positif** ils vont
        comprendre

7		que de temps en temps on recentre sur le souci de [(inaud.)] et tout ça
8	S	[voilà]
9	M	(inaud.)
10	S	oui
11	M	je dis pas qu'il faut qu'on soit autoritaire (inaud.)
12		**sinon c'est mort c'est mauvais mauvais plan**
13	S	oui
14	M	mais er il faut qu'on soit à la fois sympa mais à la fois pro quoi
15	S	oui
16	M	sinon ils ne vont pas nous écouter

(English translation)
1	S	*there were quite a few foul jokes before (inaud.)*
2	M	*huh well you need to stay focused*
3	S	*well I just try to: (...)*
4	M	*no but that in the end is fine actually just we need to remain credible right*
5	S	*yes*
6	M	*so even if we joke with them **which is really positive** they will understand*
7		*that from time to time we refocus on the question of [(inaud.)] and so on*
8	S	*[Exactly]*
9	M	*(inaud.)*
10	S	*yes*
11	M	*i'm not saying we have to be authoritarian (inaud.)*
12		***if so it's dead it's a bad bad plan***
13	S	*yes*
14	M	*but er we need to be both nice but also pro right*
15	S	*yes*
16	M	*otherwise they aren't going to listen to us*

The semantic contribution of the speaker's Horizontal Palm gestures throughout this segment is consistent with findings both from the earlier micro-analysis and from previous research. Kendon (2004) observed that Horizontal Palm gestures may occur in contexts where speakers are making 'universal statements' whether positive or expressed with negative markers (pp. 258–9). For Calbris (2011), the semantics of *quantity* and *totality* may extend metaphorically to value judgements of superlativity and perfection respectively. M's Horizontal Palm gestures contribute semantically to her assertions throughout the segment: the first stroke occurs when she asserts that, on the one hand, some level of informality is actually 'really positive' (line 6), while a second instance of Horizontal Palm gesturing occurs when she asserts that, on the other hand, being authoritarian would be 'dead, bad, bad plan' (line 12). Discursively, the first instance contributes to the speaker making a side-point, potentially establishing that point as common ground; while the second instance contributes to a speech act with which she is dissuading and warning. Given the salience of gesture in performing these discursive moves, the pattern of gesturing arguably plays a part in the speaker clarifying her understanding of the appropriate styles needed to manage interpersonal relations. As with the previous example, this could also be a means for M and her addressee to establish common ground concerning best practice and align their approaches.

6.3.4   Practice 3: Monitoring Follow-Up

Towards the end of the meeting, M's verbal and gestural strategies demonstrate another form of managerial expertise relevant to the context. Her repeated performance of the Horizontal Palm gesture in this last extract is integrated to discursive moves that establish the exit strategy she envisages for the project. Over the course of several utterances, M expounds her vision for maintaining contact with the factory to monitor their performance once the project has finished. To do this, M first establishes an appropriate time frame for receiving feedback (line 1), then role shifts to report speech from a hypothetical manager who would have been identified and placed in charge of providing such feedback (line 2). In the utterances that follow, she shifts back and forth between the manager's perspective and her own perspective. This strategy establishes M's awareness of how a manager at that level would communicate, such as frankly (line 2), honestly (line 3), and exactly (line 7), whilst at the same time suggesting how she and S could react in response, such as by giving tips (line 8) and sharing insights from communication theory (line 9). Her Horizontal Palm gesturing over the course of these different moves appears to be part of displaying the professional knowledge they achieve.

Example 59   GU_26 Ils nous disent exactement
1   M   eventuellement leur demander qu'une fois par mois il y a
2   un des managers qu'il nous envoie un truc pour nous dire **voila comment s'est évolué**
3   bon là **j'ai un peu perdu** qu'il soit **vraiment net** quoi
4   puisque là [s'il y a un problème]
5   S   [réunion téléphonique tous les mois]
6   M   soit téléphonique soit autre chose euh je sais pas mais toujours êtes-il
7   qu'ils nous disent **exactement** ou ça en est (inaud.)
8   puisque nous on peut **dire des dirigés** au niveau de la comm

(English translation)
1   M   *at a push (we) could ask them that **one time per month** there are*
2   *managers who send us something to say **look this is how things** evolved*
3   *well **i lost a little** that he's really honest you know*
4   *so **that [if** there's a problem]*
5   S   *[telephone meeting every month]*
6   M   *either telephone or other i don't know but in any case*
7   *that they tell us **exactly** where it's up to (inaud.)*
8   *so that we could **give tips** about comm because maybe*

Salient notions expressed by Horizontal Palm gestures in this example include *flatness* and *directness*, both literal and figurative (Calbris 2011). When speaking from the perspective of the manager, the gestures first connect to the regularity, systematicity, and transparency of the communication she expects. When speaking from the perspective of herself and her addressee, the gestures connect to the immediacy and subsequence of missives they would give in response. As a result of expressing these notions, M illustrates competence in both developing and implementing a realistic exit strategy and in communicating such a strategy. Indeed, the regular occurrence of Horizontal Palm gestures could index her ability to deliver such missives effectively. Finally, note how M negotiates S's somewhat unrealistic proposal to request a monthly telephone meeting with the factory management by playing down the importance of the medium of such communications. This is further support that such segments of discourse allow the participants of the meeting to rehearse their upcoming intervention and align their approach, and Horizontal Palming plays a key role in that process.

6.3.5 The Horizontal Palm Gesture – A 'Key-Gesture' in Business Discourse?

Three segments have illustrated the effect that repeatedly performing Horizontal Palm gestures could have on the speaker's discourse. The particular semantic themes of the gesture are integral to discourse moves that limit, specify, and restrict, but also that maximise, include, and assert. Within the context of the business meeting, performing these moves constitutes aspects of M's expertise, such as breaking down hierarchies and encouraging teamwork, managing interpersonal relations, and monitoring a project after completion. Together, such professional practices provide insight onto this interaction as to what broader social functions the meeting allowed the participants to achieve.

As a form of social practice, the meeting provided an opportunity for the participants to rehearse the roles they were going to adopt, with an emphasis on the importance of *clearly* defined roles. Second, over the course of the meeting, the participants established that the factory is a potentially hostile condition and agreed upon the type of approach they would need to take, in this case, an *assertive* and *authoritative* one. Third, this meeting allowed the leader and the assistant to *establish common ground* on several levels, ranging from terminology specific to the project, to the goals of the intervention, to the approach they were to adopt. The meeting thus served the function of allowing the participants to *align* their approach, that is, to get 'on the same page'. Beyond discussing the details of the factory intervention, the meeting also allowed the participants to appraise each other as colleagues. While M had the opportunity to demonstrate her competence relevant to the project, S could verify his assumption that M

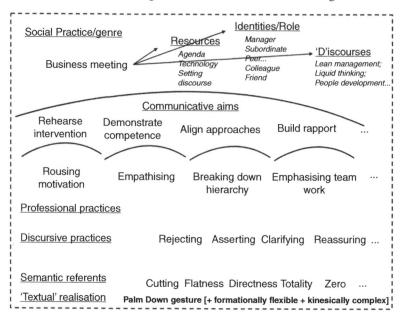

Figure 6.8 The Horizontal Palm gesture: from textual realisation to social practice

would be ideal for the job. The frequent use of humour in the segments suggests the participants were also building and maintaining their social relationship as friends.

The connection between these widening layers of structure and the Horizontal Palm gesture is illustrated in Figure 6.8, where the role of a repeated Horizontal Palm gesture may be visualised either from the top down or bottom up.

The absence of one-to-one correspondences between semantic referents and discursive practices on the one hand and between discursive practices and professional practice on the other hand reflect the flexibility and complexity of the Horizontal Palm gesture, as may vary for any particular speaker. The dashed line around the figure respects that genres and social practices do not occur independently of any particular speakers or context: they may be co-constructed, negotiated, contested, and flaunted. Furthermore, the figure could be said to capture a snapshot of this speaker's gesturing, which could be considered as one interaction within a chain of interactions relevant for understanding her gesturing. In Figure 6.9, for example, we see the speaker two months later in the factory face-to-face with the workers she was rehearsing to address. The communications

Figure 6.9 Intertextuality: the Horizontal Palm in practice

sheet that M is holding in her left hand documents the protocol for the new system that our project established – essentially more work for these managers without a guarantee of the improved process that M is hoping to get across. Her performance of the Horizontal Palm gesture offers an intertextual connection to the pattern of gesturing observed during the meeting two months earlier.

The Horizontal Palm gesture is specialised to express particular semantic referents (Calbris 2011), or a more general 'semantic theme' (Kendon 2004). When coordinated with speech this gesture can achieve an array of discourse functions (cf. Calbris 2011; Kendon 2004). However, how it may be used to demonstrate various professional practices is unique to the current speaker's communicative aim in the business meeting data. In this context, the Horizontal Palm has emerged as a 'keyword' or rather 'key gesture'. Streeck (2009) suggests that a person may have a 'signature gesture' over the course of a particular interaction, and this may offer analysts 'a clue to his core conflict or concern' (p. 156).

Differences in keywords and key gestures stem from differences in the nature of verbal and gestural modalities. Key gestures can occur with a stretch of speech. They can be held over segments of talk. They are specialised to occur in complex kinesic contexts (or 'clusters'), and their precise form or 'textual realisation' can vary because of kinesic, semantic, and stylistic influences. Corpus linguistic analyses of business meeting data may reveal other such key gestures if based on multimodal data.

6.4   Towards a Gestural Genre

Why, then, are recurrent gestures (sometimes) so recurrent across a stretch of discourse? Recurrency in gesture form may stem from recurrency of discourse themes or 'catchments' (McNeill 2005), including both concrete themes and metaphoric ones (Parrill 2007; Müller and Tag 2010). A sustained way of gesturing can reflect a speaker's overall semantic and pragmatic perspective on a scene he or she is describing (Lemmens 2016). But recurrency may also stem from broader discourse functions. Recall that a speaker's perceived 'sharpness' during the 2008 presidential debates in North America was in part due to his repeated performance of the Ring gesture (Lempert 2011). The current data suggests that M's perceived assertiveness, authority, and competence in the context of an informal business meeting is in part due to her repeated performance of the Horizontal Palm gesture, which emerged as a key gesture in that context.

Tracking the use of the Ring gesture by Obama across his 2008 election campaign revealed 'pathways of semiotic motivation that run from cospeech gesture to candidate persona' (Lempert 2011: 242). In Lempert's (2011) study, the Ring gesture could be performed to *mirror* a focus operation achieved linguistically in a co-occurring utterance (phase 1) and it could *achieve* that focus operation when applied to linguistic material in the co-occurring utterance (phase 2). When it was performed as a beat to accompany a range of points being made, the gesture could indicate that *focused speakership* was an attribute of the speaker (phase 3). Repetition of the recurrent gesture over the course of the presidential debates thus became a 'pragmatic resource for performativity' (Lempert 2011). Obama was able to leverage his perceived sharp speakership as a positive aspect of his identity – an aspect of his identity relevant to debating skills specifically, and to political discourse more generally.

In the context of the business meeting, M's performance of the Horizontal Palm gesture could emphasise or reflect various speech acts, such as rejections and assertions (phase 1). When performed alongside other speech acts, it could imply that those utterances were nevertheless assertions (phase 2). When repeated over a longer stretch of discourse such as the entire meeting, the gesture form allowed a particular speaker attribute to emerge, namely a speaker who was capable of being assertive, commanding, categorical, and even authoritative. These are highly relevant to the context of the business meeting, in which the speaker was able to demonstrate her competence for the project. Repetition of the Horizontal Palm gesture may thus be such a 'pragmatic resource for performativity' in a given context. And that performativity will be genre-specific and contribute to the speaker's overall communicative aims.

Swales (1990) has argued that genres 'comprise a system for accomplishing social purposes by verbal means' (p. 40). The pattern of gesturing studied here suggests that gestural means are also a resource with which speakers accomplish their social purposes relevant to the genre. As Handford (2010) notes: professional practice is 'knowledge necessary for effective participation' (p. 64). To operate in a genre is therefore to know the tricks of the trade. Our analysis demonstrates the speaker has abundant knowledge about her profession. Her frequent deployment of the Horizontal Palm gesture was part of demonstrating that knowledge. The recurrency of Horizontal Palming in this context is thus suggestive of what we could tentatively term a gestural genre.

To evaluate such a concept, other recurrent gestures described in the literature could be explored for any genre-specific behaviours, including 'Palm Up Open Hands', 'Cyclics', 'Brushing offs', etc. We now understand the discursive functions of these gestures, but we are yet to explore how a speaker may use those discursive functions within a particular context to 'orient towards' certain forms of expertise or 'professional practices'. However, note that such functions would be a property of the relation between the speaker and her communicative aims in the context, rather than of the gesture form itself. Demonstrating professional practice relevant to the business meeting context is not a function inherent to the Horizontal Palm, but a property of how the speaker is using the gesture form. In a conversational context, such repeated Horizontal Palming may exhibit some similar properties to the current study (such as an assertive, authoritative style), but it would not be orienting to the professional practices it helped our speaker demonstrate in the context of a business meeting (such as 'breaking down hierarchies'). Having insider knowledge of the genesis of the interaction, relationship between the speakers, and details of the project they were discussing emerged as central to understanding the nature of the pattern of gesturing in the specific interaction.

Studies of recurrent gestures are common but studies of the individual speakers who use them are lacking. Yet the importance of identifying patterns of gesturing goes well beyond understanding how an individual uses gesture. Although one speaker's use of gesture may catch our attention, its uniqueness must be understood in relation to the wider sociolinguistic context that it stands out from or can be contrasted with. As Brookes (2014) has found in group communication among male youths in urban South Africa, which aspects of gesture are systematically enhanced and foregrounded in one context reflect the fact that 'environmental, social, cultural and historical factors' are always at play in the deployment of particular patterns of gesturing (p. 66). On the one hand, group-specific patterns of gesturing served to distinguish different sociocultural groups and social divisions, while, on the other hand, such patterns provided a baseline to be skilfully extended, manipulated, and innovated by more entertaining, popular, and ultimately powerful members of the group. Patterns of gesturing may therefore reflect 'the need to display who one is' (Brookes 2014: 72), be it a group leader, an eager conversationalist, a professor, a student, or in the case of the current data, a competent manager in organisational communication.

Finally, Deleuze marvelled that 'Foucault's gestures were astonishingly sharp and elegant' (cited in Dosse 2010). In the pattern of gesturing studied in this chapter, the Horizontal Palm contributed to a person's apparent competence, authority, and accuracy in their manner of speaking. The speaker was capable through gesturing to show enthusiasm and passion, as was relevant given the purpose of the business meeting in which she was participating. Perhaps Deleuze was not alone in having identified a particularly interesting gesturer in his data after all.

Appendix

Table 6.3 *Horizontal Palm semantic coding scheme (collated from Calbris 1990, 2011)*

Referent	Specification
Quantity	
	As a value judgement: Superlative
Totality	
	Completion
	As a value judgement, Perfection
Directness	
	On the temporal level
	On the logical level: Consequence, Determinism, Obligation, Certainty (direct logical consequence)
	On the value judgement level: Frankness
Cutting	
	Total
	Definitive
Negation–Refusal	
	Categorical: certain, absolute
The end	
	Fixed
	Total
	Clear-cut
	Certainty
Flatness	
	A surface, literally and figuratively
	A second surface covers the first, literally and figuratively
	To lay something out flat, literally and figuratively
	A level, literally and figuratively
	Making something level, that is, equality in one domain or another

7 Wiping Away

Embodied Interaction in Speech and Sign

> Grammatical concepts are not bound to one specific modality. They are truly embodied in our everyday forms of language use and interaction.
>
> —Cornelia Müller

7.1 Introduction

What does it mean for a grammatical concept to be *truly* embodied? Cornelia Müller's use of the adverb *truly* was not to add sincerity or drama to her claim about grammar. It was a call for a paradigm shift in our understanding of the relation between language, minds, and bodies. Cognitive linguists taught us that grammar is shaped by the body (Heine 1997; Lakoff 1987; Lakoff and Johnson 1980, 1999). But grammar is also brought into being by the body in interaction. This chapter documents how a movement of the body through interaction becomes a conventionalised sign that has a specific grammatical function.

Focusing on negation, previous chapters have established the centrality of gesture to expressing grammatical concepts in interaction. Speakers express negation by swiping the open palm turned down laterally through space or raising their palms vertically in front of the chest. These gestures undeniably offer a 'window onto the mind' (McNeill 1992) and a 'backdoor to cognition' (Sweetser 2007). They reflect how people construe thought through schemas and mappings (cf. Chapter 4), and provide us a tool 'to reveal' how people think (Parrill et al. 2013). Windows and doors, however, trap cognition inside the speaker's head and risk reducing gestures to a diagnostic on 'what takes place *within* individuals' (McNeill 2016: 47; original emphasis). A truly embodied approach to language and gesture views cognition instead as thinking 'beyond-the-skull' (Wilson and Foglia 2017).

Speakers do not gesture to 'reflect' anything. They gesture to embody, embed, enact, and distribute cognition in action and interaction with others (Hutchins 1995; Williams 2013; Cuffari and Jensen 2014; Jensen and Cuffari 2014). To analyse how physical actions in interaction are transformed into

159

abstractions and may become linguistic signs, this chapter puts face-to-face conversations like those studied so far within more complex ecological contexts of situated activity (Goodwin 2000). In lifeguarding a beach or cleaning an apartment, for example, people mobilise their hands for physical action but continue to gesture when they speak. We examine the continuity between action and gesture through a case study of 'wiping away': the everyday action of using the open palm to remove or eliminate something from a surface, such as unwanted marks and stains.

In such contexts, the distinction between physical actions and gestures is not always possible. Real-world actions such as wiping away may vary in level of communicative explicitness and representational complexity (Andrén 2014), and may thereby constitute critical moments in the interaction not unlike gestures. Furthermore, action and gesture may interact with language in a way that produces full-blown linguistic signs. This is demonstrated by examining the wiping away action in signed language interaction, where it is the basis both for signs that function similarly to interactive and pragmatic gestures in spoken language and for signs that operate as a grammatical marker for negation.

The transformations from physical action to abstract linguistic markers documented in this chapter account for the impulse to gesture with grammatical concepts in everyday spoken discourse. They situate the origin of gestures associated with negation not only as conceptual content in the minds of speakers, but also at the intersection of language, minds, and bodies in interaction with their environment. Before examining examples of wiping away in interaction, different opinions on the relation between action and gesture are relevant and a primer on signed language is needed.

7.1.1   Gestural Action and Practical Action

A truly embodied view of cognition must acknowledge the link between gesture and everyday practical action (such as wiping away). But to do so is to take a stance on the origin and nature of gestures. On the one hand, gestures *are* a form of everyday action – one that we engage in whenever we speak. But on the other hand, prominent differences between gestures and everyday actions abound. A question that currently captures these tensions is: do gestures derive from everyday practical actions?

A negative answer to this question views gesture as distinct from practical action. McNeill (2016: 38–53), for example, distinguishes between 'action–actions' and 'gesture–actions'. Action–actions are phylogenetically and ontogenetically 'old'. They constitute goals that relate to a world that is 'external' to the speaker, that is, to 'real world goals'. However, gesture–actions differ because they are 'new' – they co-evolved with language and exhibit hallmarks of human intellect. The goal of gesture–actions is to orchestrate speech and relates to inner psycholinguistic processes, such as inseparable units of imagery and language called 'growth points' (cf. McNeill 2005, 2012, 2016). Unlike action–actions, gesture–actions occur largely involuntarily. Support for this view is found typically in descriptions of how gestures 'reveal', 'shed light on', and 'reflect' cognition (e.g. Parrill et al. 2013).

Observations of gestures in human behaviour from a range of settings question this rigid distinction between gesture and practical action. When people grab and place objects as they speak, Andrén (2014) observed how such actions can exhibit gesture-like coordination with speech, including co-expressivity and gesture phrase structure (p. 169). Andrén also exemplified how a person's speech may 'add a dimension of pretence' to an otherwise purely physical action and thereby imbue physical action with symbolism more typical of gesture (p. 167). A person's gestures may require elements in the physical surround as an integral part of their semiotic structure (p. 170), what Goodwin calls 'environmentally-coupled gestures' (Goodwin 2007, 2000). Instead of viewing actions and gestures as distinct entities, Andrén (2014: 171) laid out continua between action and gesture based on levels of communicative explicitness and representation (i.e. symbolic) complexity.

A positive answer to the question of whether or not gestures derive from everyday practical actions situates gesture as one form of kinesic expression among others (Kendon 2004). Gesture is viewed as a form of practice (Streeck 2009), often based on the re-enactment of everyday practical actions (Morris 2002; Calbris 1990; Streeck 2009; Müller 2004; Müller et al. 2014). As the claim goes, 'gestures often constitute re-enactments of basic mundane actions, grounding the gestures' communicative actions in real world actions' (Bressem et al. 2013: 1106). Evidence for this view includes similarities in form and function between gestures and physical actions. Etymology of various speech acts with which people perform such gestures has also been proposed as evidence, such as for negative speech acts (Lapaire 2006a) and verbs of speaking (Streeck 2009: 199–201). Actions related to 'wiping away' in particular have been proposed for the basis of a number of gestures associated with negation (Calbris 2011; Kendon 2004; Harrison 2009b; cf. Chapter 4).

7.1.2   Gestures and Signs in Interaction

Sign language is said to offer 'a visual treat' (Quinto-Pozos 2007), not least because it involves, as Taub (2001) has noted, 'an integration of visual imagery with linguistic structure on a scale that no spoken language can equal' (p. i). Because gesture and embodied actions play a major role in that integration (Liddell 2003; Quinto-Pozos 2007; McCleary and Viotti 2010; Johnston 2013), examining how signers use an action like 'wiping away' provides an original feature on which the impulse to gesture and sign may compare.

This comparison is not based on the 'myth' that 'signed languages are nothing more than forms of pantomime and gesture' (Johnston and Schembri 2007: 14). Ever since being subject to rigorous linguistic analysis from the 1960s onwards (Stokoe 1960), we know that sign languages exhibit similar linguistic complexity to spoken languages, with levels of structure akin to phonology, morphology, lexis, and syntax (Klima and Bellugi 1979). This is why each Deaf community has a distinct sign language replete with socio-linguistic varieties, dialects, and accents (Neidle et al. 2000: 7–8). Despite this diversity, properties of the gestural medium facilitate contact varieties of sign, and sign lingua francas emerge more readily than for spoken languages (Johnston and Schembri 2007). Some of these properties are shared by gestures of spoken languages, such as iconicity, the use of space, and embodied actions. One lab study of sign language acquisition, for example, found that spoken language users were equipped with 'gestural skills' they could transfer to the task of learning sign (Taub et al. 2008). However, given the differences between how gestures and signs are articulated, researchers have also observed that gestures can be a 'source of error' when people learn to sign (Chen-Pichler 2011). In a real classroom, sign language learners were observed trying to perform signs inaccurately because they were simultaneously using aspects of gesture to request feedback from their teacher (Harrison 2013).

These studies indicate that clearly separating gesture and sign is a problem-atic way to address the issue, both for a theory of language and gesture (Kendon 2008; Johnston 2013) and for a better understanding of what signing involves. This problem is relevant to the current chapter, because the action of wiping away at the origin of gestures associated with negation is also apparent in sign.

Traces of the 'wiping away' action are manifest as linguistic signs in various sign languages related to the expression of negation (Zeshan 2004). The website www.spreadthesign.com aims 'to share sign languages from different countries via the internet', and a search for 'no' provides video clips of signers from China, Ukraine, India, and Estonia performing a sign very similar to the action of wiping away and the Vertical Palm oscillate gesture. In French Sign Language, furthermore, a number of signs exhibit more general similarities to gestures associated with negation in speech. JAMAIS ('never') and NON ('no') involve swift movements of the hand or fingers away from the body, integrated with specific handshapes that reflect initialisation from a finger-spelled alpha-bet (respectively 'J' and 'N'). A number of signs with positive meanings such as VOULOIR ('want'), CONNAITRE ('know'), and AIMER ('like') may be negated by embedding the sign in a rotation and downwards or away movement, as has been observed in American Sign Language too (Liskova 2012). Beyond these aspects of signs, certain signs exhibit similar forms and functions to recurrent gestures, such as the Palm Presenting gesture glossed as 'well' in ASL (Hoza

2008). The sign for MAIS ('but') in French Sign Language is the same form as the Vertical Palm gesture observed with negation in spoken languages – the open hand is raised vertically in the gesture space with the palm orienting away from the body (cf. Chapter 4).

7.2   Wiping Away the World

The first example offered by my dictionary of the verb *to wipe* is 'he wiped down the kitchen wall' (*Oxford Dictionary of English*). This is preceded by the definition to 'clean or dry (something) by rubbing with a cloth, a piece of paper, or one's hand'. The addition of an adverbial 'to wipe *away*' emphasises the end result of removing, eliminating, and deleting some unwanted object or substance, such as dirt or water. This action of wiping away can be seen when people interact with their environment, such as when drawing in the sand or cleaning an apartment.

7.2.1   More or Less Gesture-Like Phenomena

A lifeguard on a beach in France explains to his colleagues how to find south without a compass. As part of his instruction, he repeatedly draws then wipes away diagrams in the sand immediately in front of where he is seated – a common resource for creating meaning in interaction when sand is available (see Green 2014). Over the five-minute interaction he makes three attempts to explain the direction-finding system (Williams and Harrison 2014), while also using shifts in eye-gaze and body orientation to monitor bathers in the swim-zone (Harrison and Williams 2017). During these three attempts, he uses the palm of an open hand to wipe away aspects of his diagram four times. At a glance, these could seem separate to the concerns of a book about gesture. But slowing the video down and scrutinising them individually reveals what Andrén (2014) proposed as 'a range of more or less gesture-like phenomena' (p. 171). The wiping away actions in the following examples are closely coordinated with speech and may indicate a shift in the discourse, maintain discursive cohesion, and communicate that an interactive sequence has finished.

In the first instance, the speaker's wiping away action indicates the end of one discourse segment and the start of another. This instance arises after his first demonstration, as he now begins to introduce a complicating factor – the need to take into account Daylight Saving Time in winter. Crouched over his original diagram, the lifeguard (L) introduces this distinction by saying '*tu vois avec quand ça tourne*' ('you see when it [the time] changes'; line 1), then starts to develop an example based on a specific time '*tu vois le soir quand il est*' ('you see in the evening when it is'; lines 1–2). He now hesitates and looks down, pauses in speech and uses his left hand to wipe away his diagram [1]. He then prepares to draw a new diagram with his right hand and resumes his speech '*je sais pas er*' ('I don't know er'). As he draws a new diagram, he repeats his previous utterance and now adds the time '*tu vois le soir quand il est dix-neuf heures*' ('you see in the evening when it is 1900'; line 3 [2]) (Figure 7.1). His colleague, a Rookie (R) responds 'yes' (line 4).

Example 60 BLT 01:17 Tu vois le soir

        you see with when it changes (.) you see in the evening
1   L   tu vois avec quand ça tourne (.) tu vois le soir

     when it is er:::::::   *i don't know*
2   quand il est er:::::::::::   (1.2)   je sais pas er
        |~~~~***************_-_-_|
              [1] |~~~~~~

    you see in the evening when it is 1900 hours
3   tu vois le soir quand il est::: quand il est dix-neuf heures
       ************************_-_-_|
          [2]

     yes
4   R   oui

[1] WIPING AWAY (lh-open hand prone), [2] draws circle of clockface (rh-index).

    when it is   ...   *when it is 19h*

Figure 7.1 Wiping away ends one segment and opens another

Is this wiping away purely practical, void of communicative effect? The speaker's wiping away of his diagram potentially communicates the end of a segment of his explanation, and more specifically, the need for a new diagram to explain the following segment. This information is not explicitly formulated by the instructor's speech, but could arguably be part of the addressee's ongoing interpretation. The wiping away action is an essential stage in the development of the lifeguard's discourse.

The next instance occurs with the segment of speech immediately after the one above. Now, the speaker uses a wiping away action to remove a specific inscription from his diagram, and this is coordinated with a meta-linguistic negation that achieves exactly the same function in the verbal modality, albeit more abstractly. In line 5, the speaker adds a '19' to his diagram to reference the position of a watch hand in the evening [1], saying '*t'as dix-neuf ici*' ('you've got 19 here'). However, he immediately realises that an analogue watch face would have a number seven not a nineteen, so he says 't'as pas dix neuf' ('*you've not got nineteen*') and wipes away the figure from the sand [2]. He then says '*t'as sept ici*' ('you've got seven here') and inscribes a seven into the space he has just wiped away [3] (Figure 7.2). In response to this inscription, the lifeguard operating the camera (C) requests justification for the location of the inscription (line 7).

Example 61 BLT 01:27 t'as pas dix-neuf
     you've got nineteen here
5 L (1) t'as dix-neuf ici (.)
     |~~~~***********_.
          [1]
     you've not got nineteen you've:: you've not got nineteen you've seven here
6   t'as pas dix-neuf t'as:::: t'as pas dix neuf t'as sept ici [(1)]
     ~~~~~~~********************~~~~~*****_.|
          [2]   [3]
7 C [pourquoi t'as sept là] pourquoi là
     why've you got seven there why there

[1] Adds 19 to apex of diagram (rh-index), [2] wipes away 19 (rh-open hand prone lateral palm), dusts off sand from palm with fingers (rh), [3] adds 7 to apex of diagram.

Figure 7.2 The wiping away corresponds to meta-linguistic negation

The first example of wiping away reflected organisation at the level of discourse, while this example of wiping away is inseparable from the speaker's negation of his own verbal material at the level of utterance. It is the physical parallel to the meta-linguistic negation structuring speech (Pullum 2012).

While the manual action wipes away '19' in the sand, the meta-linguistic negation negates the 'nineteen' in speech ('you've not got nineteen'; see Chapter 3 for examples of similar meta-linguistic negations). This 'co-expressivity' between the action and the speech suggests that wiping away in this instance is at least on a par with speech and gesture in terms of communicative effect. The speaker *does* negation coherently in both speech and action.

The next instance of wiping away occurs some 20 seconds later. It occurs as the lifeguard wipes away a number from the diagram, like the last example, however, now only to immediately reinstate the *same* number. This instance therefore does not appear to serve any practical action in relation to the ongoing development of the diagram. But because this wiping away occurs after a reorganisation of the interaction – a shift in the speaker and addressee's 'embodied participation framework' (Goodwin 2007) – it could instead reflect the speaker's intention (or indeed be a strategy) to refocus attention onto the instruction after such a shift. In line 19, the lifeguard begins an utterance as the cameraman is shifting his position from one side of the lifeguard to the other (in order to re-establish a sustained orientation to the swimzone; see Harrison and Williams 2017). To accommodate this shift, the lifeguard interrupts his speech, pauses while the cameraman moves round him (i.e. 'freezes'; Depperman 2014: 263), then completes his utterance and tags the comprehension check 't'es ok?' ('you're ok?') onto the end of his utterance. After the cameraman responds 'yes' (line 20), the Lifeguard begins *'le soir quand il est quand il est dix-neuf heures (1) t'as le sept ici'* ('in the evening when it's when it's 1900 hours (1) you've got seven here'). In the first pause after 'soir' he rubs out the '7' on the diagram [1], then in the second pause after 'heures' he replaces it ([2], Figure 7.3).

Example 62 BLT 01.58 le soir
      your little hand it is::::: it's in line with the seven you're ok?
19   L   ta petite aiguille elle est::::: (1) elle est au niveau du sept t'es ok?
      yes
20 C   oui
21   (1)
    |~~~~
      in the evening when it's when it's 1900 hours (1) you've seven here
21   L le soir (.) quand il est quand il est dix-neuf heures (1) t'as le sept ici
    ~~~~******_.-.-.-.-..-.-.-.-.-.-.-.-|
        [1] |~~~~~~~~~~~~~~~~~~~~~~~~~~~******_.-./
                                    [2]

[1] Rubs out '7' (lh-open hand prone), [2] prepares and inscribes 7 in same place (rh-index).

(from previous example)   *in the evening...*   *you've got seven here*

Figure 7.3 Rubs out '7' inscribed earlier, only to immediately replace it

Because the '7' was already on the diagram, wiping it away only to immediately reinstate it potentially served functions additional to any practical action. Given the hitch in interaction it followed, this instance of wiping away could be a way to restate the topic and refocus the interaction back on the diagram – as is often done verbally after 'a perturbation . . . has occurred' (Mondada 2014: 49). Wiping away could be serving this lifeguard as a pedagogical resource too.

Wiping away in the next example happens as the lifeguard wraps up this particular demonstration. This instance of wiping away is much longer than other instances and lacks a clear end point. These additional or 'marked' kinesic properties of the action suggest the possibility that wiping away here serves functions additional to those relating to the practical action (Andrén 2014). The wiping away is prolonged over a stretch of discourse in which the lifeguard offers a number of accounts (Heritage 1984), so the question arises as to how the action remains cohesive with the ongoing discourse. In line 30, the lifeguard concludes his demonstration of how to find compass direction with only a wristwatch by saying 'the bisector of the two, points towards south'. After his addressee confirms 'well yes yes' (line 31), the lifeguard proceeds to offer a first account, namely, 'whatever time it is in fact it works' (line 32). His addressee again acknowledges 'ah yes' (line 33), then breaks mutual gaze with the lifeguard by reorienting back to the swimzone (line 34). During a three-second pause that follows, the lifeguard now wipes away his diagram (line 35). He then utters two more accounts: one that he hasn't been very clear in his explanations, and two that nevertheless what he has done should be sufficient (line 36). With these accounts, he is still wiping away his diagram though with decreasing exertion (as indicated by the symbols -.*-.*-.*-.*-.*-.*-.*-).

Example 63 BLT 02:35 Ça fonctionne
>   *the bisector of the two points towards south*
30   L   la bisectrice des deux (.) va vers le sud
>   *well yes yes*
31   R   ben oui oui
>   *whatever time it is in fact it works*

32   L   quelque soit l'heure qu'il est en faite ça fonctionne
                                   |~*********-.-.|
                                        [1]

ah yes
33   R   ah oui
34   (R turns gaze back to swimzone)
35   L   (3)
         |~***********
                [2]
well I haven't been very very:: clear in my explanations but that's about it
36   alors j'ai pas été tres tres:: clair dans mes explications mais en gros c'est ça
         *-.-.|

[1] Circular tracing gesture towards diagram (rh), [2] prolonged rubbing away of diagram (lh-open hand prone).

Maintaining the action is practically unnecessary, but it helps maintain cohesion in his discourse. In prolonging the action of wiping away while offering accounts, the lifeguard's ongoing wiping action ties those accounts specifically to the diagram, indicating the part of his explanation to which his disclaimers apply. In this impromptu teaching situation on a beach, there is no practical import to wiping away the diagram in the sand. His wiping away action in this example communicates the end of the role of the diagram in the demonstration.

Our final instance of wiping away occurred before all the above instances, but deserves its treatment here at the end. This instance is undeniably a gesture, so it is useful to consider in how it is similar and different to the instances analysed so far. At the outset of his first explanation, the lifeguard is adding the first set of 'hands' to his clock diagram. As he adds the small hand he says '*t'as la petite aiguille (.) là*' ('you've got the small hand (.) here', line 1) whilst producing a 'clock hand' gesture immediately above the diagram [1]. He then indicates there is no need for the hour hand by saying 'ta grande tu t'en branles' ('your big one don't give a toss about', line 2). As he says this he performs a variant of the Horizontal Palm gesture. With 'ta grande' ('your big one'), he is preparing the gesture by moving his hand to a position across the diagram and orienting the palm downwards [2]. With 'tu t'en branles' ('don't give a toss about'), he abruptly moves his hand laterally over the diagram and rotates his wrist as if to 'swipe away' the imaginary unwanted hour hand [3], then immediately returning to a hold of the previous 'clock hand' gesture [4] (Figure 7.4).

Example 64 00.54 ta grande tu t'en branles
     you've got the small hand (.) here and then
1   L   t'as la petite aiguille (.) là et puis
        /~*******
             [1]

your big one you don't give a toss about
2   ta grande tu t'en branles
          ~~~~~~~******/~***
         [2]   [3]

you imagine a second hand at fourteen-hundred hours
3   t'imagines une seconde aiguille vers quatorze heures
      ***_.-.|
     beat   [4]   *beat*

[1] 'Clock hand' gesture (open hand lateral above diagram), [2] Horizontal Palm gesture above and across the diagram, [3] return to 'clock hand' gesture (plus subsequent beats).

the small hand here   then the big one   you don't give a toss   you imagine...

Figure 7.4 Open Hand Prone gesture coupled to diagram. '*La petite aiguille là et puis*', '*La grande tu t'en branles*', '*T'imagines...*'

The examples of a lifeguard wiping away diagrams in the sand as part of a demonstration indicate that actions and gestures coalesce in situated activity. In addition to achieving the practical function of erasing the diagram (or parts of it), each instance of wiping away can be interpreted as communicating information about the ongoing discourse or paralleling specific functions at the utterance level occurring in speech. Not only does the action remove or modify the diagram, but it can also indicate the end of an interactive sequence, the refocusing on the instruction activity, and the relation between what is being said and the role of the diagram in the overall activity. Beyond these functions, the wiping away of a specific part of the diagram may be co-expressive with a meta-linguistic negation in speech, in which case we have an 'environmentally coupled' gesture (Goodwin 2007). In the last example, the same form as the environmentally coupled gesture was produced above the diagram, where it was no longer coupled to the material surround but 'inflected' by it (Kendon 2004). Now the action was similar to a recurrent gesture for expressing negation, such as those we have studied throughout this book.

Drawing diagrams in the sand as part of a demonstration is a highly symbolic activity – the lifeguard used a patch of sand as a material anchor for conceptualisation (Liddell 2003; Hutchins 2005; Williams 2008). Within this context, we have shown how even a seemingly physical action (or 'action action'; McNeill 2016) such as 'rub surface' can communicate information relevant to the ongoing interpretation of discourse. Wiping away in the sand may remove something unwanted, which may include symbolic structures etched in the sand as a diagram. The wiping away action can be co-expressive with speech and constitute an environmentally coupled gesture, or a similar gesture may be detached from the diagram but performed above it (i.e. inflected by it).

7.2.2   Doing Wiping Away

The action of wiping away may also occur as part of more mundane activities, such as cleaning stains off a wall. This second context takes us from the sands of southwest France to the thirty-second floor of a concrete tower in urban China. A home-owner inspects the workmanship of the designer tiles her builders have just cemented to a six-metre-square wall in her future living room and notices a problem. The alcohol spirit they have used to remove instructions written in marker pen on the tiles has left white patches, damaging the artwork. As she tries using a cloth to wipe away the white patches in vain, one of the builders responsible for the tiles emerges from the kitchen.

The interactive sequence that follows provides several examples of wiping away that further illustrate the inseparability of this action from language and gesture, using interaction in Mandarin Chinese as a case study, and shifting from wiping away in the horizontal plane to the vertical plane. According to the builder, the white patches are part of the mural's design. But the home-owner who spent weeks choosing it knows they are not. She invites the builder to look closer as she continues her wiping away actions. It is within this 'embodied participation framework' (Goodwin 2000, 2007) that her continued (and observably futile) wiping away action becomes explicitly communicative (Andrén 2014). The communicative aspects of actions at this point are inseparable from those of her speech and gesture. She is not only wiping a wall. She is now *doing* wiping a wall. This formulation of 'to *do* [an action]' is borrowed from ethnomethedology and highlights that actions done in the presence of others are often organised in ways that draw attention to aspects of their being done (see on *doing* 'being ordinary' by Sacks 1985). When done by the home-owner, the action of wiping away allows her to accomplish several discursive and interactive functions, which are fundamentally connected to 不 'bù' and 没有 'méi yǒu', the two 'major' negative markers in Chinese (Xiao and McEnery 2008). As we will see throughout the interaction, these markers also systematically couple with gestures from the Open Hand Prone family.

In the first clip, for example, the home-owner (called Y) uses the wiping away action to draw the builder's attention to the problem and allocate blame, without doing so directly. This sequence begins as the builder approaches the wall where Y is wiping and points to an unrelated region where a hole for a television brace has been drilled and says 'Nòng hǎo dōu zhè yàng de' ('*This is what it is like when finished*'; line 2). Y delays a response to this comment and instead begins to orient to a problem with the wall 'děng yī xià shī fu wǒ jué de zhè gè . . . tā nèi ge . . . ' ('*wait a second builder, I think this . . . it's . . .*'; line 3; 'shī fu' is a form of address for workmen in China). Y does not complete her utterances verbally, but rather coordinates her pauses with shifting glances to different parts of the wall. She appears to be scanning the wall for its white patches – thereby establishing a focus for the interaction that ensues. She then points to a specific white patch and, holding this action, says 'ná zhè kuài cā bú diào le hái shì zěn me húi shì?' ('so this one can't be wiped off or something?') then shifts her gaze to the builder (line 4, [1]), the sustained gesture hold and the shift in eye-gaze working to solicit a response (Stivers and Rossano 2010).

During turns 5 to 10, the builder requests clarification (not shown), then tentatively claims 'nà bái de néng cā diào ba' ('I think that white stuff can be wiped off'; line 11; Chinese particle 吧'ba' has a hedge value, translated in this instance by 'I think'). In response, Y reaches high up to the spot she just pointed to with the cloth, on her tiptoes preparing to wipe, then says 'zhè gè bái de bú shì wǒ de' ('this white patch isn't mine', meaning, isn't my responsibility; line 12) and coordinates this utterance with firmly wiping the white patch several times with her cloth [2], then inspecting the part of cloth that she rubbed on the tile [3]. She now says 'bú shì zhè gè cí zhuān shàng miàn de' ('It is not on top of this tile'; line 13). The builder utters 'a' (啊) that suggests he requests clarification (line 14) and Y responds by repeating her utterance but adding 'na' (a discourse marker functioning here as 'look'). With the first part of her utterance 'bú shì cí zhuān shàng miàn de' ('it's not on top of this tile'), she identifies another white patch in a different location and performs a second instance of wiping away [4]. With 'na' ('look'), she pauses, retracts her hands from the wall, then prepares another wiping action, which she coordinates with a two-second pause in speech as the builder leans in to have a closer look [5]. The builder now responds by going to the wall and rubbing his own finger on the spot that Y has been wiping [6], claiming the white patch is part of the tile design, saying 'shén me bái de, zhè gè bái de jiù shì yuán lái cí zhuān jiù shì zhè gè yán sè ba' ('what white stuff, the white stuff is the original colour of this tile'; line 16). Y then stresses 'méi yǒu' ('no it's not') and continues 'zhè kuài bái de bú shì de' ('this white stuff isn't'; line 17) and explicitly wipes the part where the builder's finger just was [7] (Figure 7.5).

Example 65 YCW 00.46 Interactive sequence 1

1 Y (wiping wall)
      this is what it is like when finished
2 B nòng hǎo dōu zhè yàng de
      wait a second builder i think this ... it's ...
3 Y děng yī xià shī fu wǒ jué de zhè gè (.) tā nèi ge (.)
      so this one can't be wiped off or something? (shifts gaze to builder)
4   ná zhè kuài cā bú diào le hái shì zěn me húi shì (.)
      |~*************************************
                        [1]
(...)
      i think that white stuff can be wiped off
11 B nà bái de néng cā diào ba
      this white stuff is not my doing
12 Y (.)   zhè gè bái de bú shì wǒ de (.)
      |~~~***********/*********-.-.|
            [2]   [3]
      it's not on top of this tile
13 Y bú shì zhè gè cí zhuān shàng miàn de
14 B a
      huh
      it's not on top of this tile, look (2) (inaud.)
15 Y bú shì cí zhuān shàng miàn de na (2) (inaud.)
      |~~~~~~~~~~~~~~*********~~~~~*******-.|
                    [4]   [5]
      what white stuff, the white stuff is the original colour of this tile
16 B shén me bái de zhègè báide jiù shì yuán lái cí zhuān jiù shì zhè gè yán sè ba
      |~~~~~~~~~~~~~~~~~~~**********************-.|
                                        [6]
      no it's not, this white stuff isn't
17 Y méi yǒu zhè kuài bái bú shì de
      |~************************-.|
           [7]

[1] Y mobilises response in relation to the white patch [2] Y wipes away on wall (figure), [3] looks at cloth, [4] wipes away on wall, [5] repeats wiping away, [6] Builder approaches wall and wipes patch with finger, [7] Y wipes away same patch with cloth.

In this example, Y initially uses deictic expressions, gestures, and eye-gaze to draw the builder into an embodied participation framework in which she can raise an issue with the mysterious white patches on the wall. As the builder begins to suggest the patches are part of the mural's design, Y uses the wiping away action as a resource to present evidence to the contrary. This requires coordinating wiping away with speech and bodily conduct in a way that makes the action (and its unsatisfactory result) visible to the builder, such as by sequencing a wiping away with a look at the cloth, as if triangulating evidence

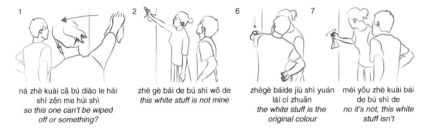

ná zhè kuài cā bú diào le hái shì zěn me húi shì
so this one can't be wiped off or something?

zhè gè bái de bú shì wǒ de
this white stuff is not mine

zhègè báide jiù shì yuán lái cí zhuān
the white stuff is the original colour

méi yǒu zhè kuài bái de bú shì de
no it's not, this white stuff isn't

Figure 7.5 Orienting to the wall, identifying stain, wiping away, demonstrating

of the problem. Moreover, the discourse marker 'na' ('look') followed by a pause during which the action is performed is used to explicitly integrate the action to the flow of discourse and orient attention to the action being performed. Instances of the action become *exemplars* of the action (Andrén 2014), and Y's wiping away gradually becomes a demonstration.

In the next interactive sequence, the builder uses a different part of the wall to claim the patches are part of the original design, and Y rejects these claims by reorganising the interaction to focus on a more visibly problematic patch, then coupling linguistic negation with instances of wiping away to show it is a stain. Y has begun wiping away at one patch, when the builder leans into the wall, points to a different patch [1], and says 'zhè gè shì zhè zhǒng yán sè' ('*this really belongs to a particular colour*'; line 1). Y tries to rub off the new patch but presumably realises it is correctly part of the design (line 2). The builder then laughs and steps back from the wall saying 'haha nǐ zhè gè dōu yí yàng yán sè' ('*haha these patches all have this same colour*'; line 3) effectively absolving himself from responsibility and disengaging from the participation framework. But during his utterance, Y locates another white patch that, for her, is clearly not part of the design. Immediately after the builder's turn, she says 'bú shì nǐ kàn zhè kuai' ('*no, you see this one*'; line 4) and points to the new patch on the wall [2]. The builder requests clarification 'huh?' and moves near the wall (line 5). Once the builder is back near the wall, Y continues pointing at the patch and explains that previously the number '11' was written in that patch (line 6), coupling the pointing gesture with the wall to also inscribe '11' in the space [3]. Now that the builder is in mutual gaze with Y, she holds the pointing gesture [4] and says 'nǐ kàn bái sè de dui ba' ('you see it's white, isn't it?'; line 7). She now begins another wiping away [5], continuing this as she tentatively negates 'zhè cā bú diào ma hái shì zěn me yàng' ('it can't be wiped off or something?'; line 8). She then steps back to the builder's position and now without any hedging, stresses that 'shì zhēn cā bú diào le' ('really can't be wiped off'; line 9) (Figure 7.6).

Example 66 YCW 01.43 Interactive sequence 2
This really belongs to a particular colour

1　B　zhè gè shì zhè zhǒng yán sè
　　　|~~***************-.-.|
　　　　　　　　　[1]
2　　　(Y tries wiping)
　　　haha these patches all have this same colour
3　　　haha nǐ zhè gè dōu yí yàng yán sè
　　　no, you see this one
4　Y　bú shì nǐ kàn zhè kuai
　　　|~~~~************
　　　　　　　　[2]
　　　huh? (moves nearer to the wall)
5　B　a
　　　no (.) look, this has been written 11, and (.)
6　Y　bú shì(.) nǐ kàn kàn, zhè lǐ yǒu shí yī xiě de rán hòu (.)
　　　***/
　　　　　　　　　　[3]
　　　you see it's white, isn't it?
7　　　nǐ kàn bái sè de duì ba
　　　*****************
　　　　　　[4]
　　　　　　　it can't be wiped off or something
8　　　(1)　　　zhè cā bú diào ma hái shì zěn me yàng
　　　/~**-.-.|
　　　　　　　　[5]
　　　(it) really can't be wiped off
9　　　shì zhēn cā bú diào le (walks back to builder's position)

[1] Builder approaches wall and wipes a white spot with finger, [2] Y points to different patch on wall, [3] continues pointing and inscribes '11', [4] maintains point and shifts gaze to addressee, [5] begins wiping.

Figure 7.6 Claim, counter-claim, demonstration (speech elaborates the action)

In this segment, the builder presents counter-evidence for Y's complaint that her designer tiles have been stained. However, Y was determined to convince the builder and used speech, bodily orientation, and eye-gaze to reorganise the interaction so that a different patch of tile could become the focus of attention. In this new participation framework, the linguistic negation 'cā bú diào' ('can't wipe off') can be seen to 'elaborate' (Hutchins and Nomura 2011) the action of wiping away by transforming it from a simple action to an illustration of 'something not being able to be wiped off', thereby constituting a visible rejection of the builder's claim.

Following this interactive sequence, the builder returned to the kitchen. As Y was still in the vicinity of the wall, the cameraman (myself) took the opportunity to ask her what she had been doing. As part of her response, she produced a series of utterances that further illustrated the inseparability of the wiping away action from aspects of linguistic negation. Specifically, we will see how a gesture can represent the action of wiping away iconically, but also how this gesture can be 'inflected' by the wall (Kendon 2004). Then, the action of wiping away may be reproduced in a gesture that connects to her verbal expression negating the possibility of wiping the wall. Finally, the gesture is performed as a negative response to whether or not the wall was able to be wiped. The figures for this specific series of examples are collected together after the last example (Figure 7.7).

In the first example, when I asked Y what she had been doing (line 1), she replied she had been wiping the wall (line 2) and performed an iconic gesture of wiping in conjunction with the verb 'wipe' (Figure 7.7a).

Example 67 YCW 11:04 I just wiped it
    what were you just doing here?
1　S　nǐ gāng cái yǒu zuò shén me zhè lǐ?
    i have just wiped
2　Y　wǒ gāng yǒu cā a
    |~~~~~~~~~~***-.-.|
         [1]

[1] handshape and movement suggest enacting wiping (rh).

Several turns later, Y is explaining how the cleaning alcohol that the builders used could have caused the stains (lines 1–2). As she then says 'suǒ yǐ tā qù lǐ miàn yǐ hòu xiàn zài bù kě yǐ xǐ' ('so, since it has infiltrated inside, now it can't be washed'; line 4), she produces a series of gestures. She first uses her left hand to touch the wall then produce a Palm Presenting gesture with 'since it has infiltrated' [2/3]. This transitions into a double-handed Palm Presenting gesture with 'inside, now' [4]. Then the gesture iconic of wiping away, that is similar to her previous one, is performed with 'it can't be washed' [5]. In this instance, however, she orients her gesture iconic of wiping away to the wall (Figure 7.7b).

Example 68 11.25 now can't clean it

> *because it has been a long time, it infiltrated inside, and because this is a new*

1 Y yīn wèi shí jiān jiǔ le rán hòu tā qù lǐ miàn le yīn wéi zhè gè shì yī gè xīn de

> *thing*

2   dōng xi

3 S hmhm

> *so, since it has infiltrated inside, now it can't be washed*

4 Y suǒ yǐ tā qù lǐ miàn yǐ hòu xiàn zài bù kě yǐ xǐ

|~~~~~~~~~~*****/**~~~*******/~~*****-.-|

[2] [3]   [4]   [5]

[2] Touches wall (lh), [3] Palm Presenting gesture (lh), [4] Palm Presenting gesture (lr-hands), [5] Open Hand Prone VP/iconic wiping away.

Following immediately on from this utterance, Y proceeds to explain the damaging effect that the alcohol has had on the wall (lines 5–6). She explains how the tile has now 'whitened … a little' (line 7). In the pause between 'whitened' and 'a little' she produces the wiping away gesture now in contact or 'coupled' with the wall (Figure 7.7c).

Example 69 11.35 white stuff a little bit

> *so use alcohol to wash. . . so use alcohol to wash, but alcohol will make*

5 Y nà yòng jiǔ jīng xǐ (.) rán hòu yòng jiǔ jīng xǐ jiǔ jīng de dōng xi kě yǐ bǎ

> *this kind of thing worse*

6   zhè gè dōng xi biàn de bù hǎo

> *so now the tile is whitened   a little*

7   suǒ yǐ xiàn zài jiù shì yī gè bái sè de (.) yī diǎn diǎn

|~~~~~~~******-.-.-.|

[6]

[6] OPHP VP / wiping away.

Finally, as the conversation comes to an end, I ask Y if she was able to remove any of the stains on the wall (line 1). To this she responds 'No méi yǒu méi yǒu méi yǒu' ('No nothing nothing nothing'), and with the first 'nothing', performs a Vertical Palm gesture with lateral movement associated with negation in her gesture space (Figure 7.7d).

Example 70 12.15 No nothing nothing

> *when you are wiping, is there anything now*

1 S nǐ cā de shí hou xiàn zài yǒu méi yǒu dōng xi

> *NO nothing nothing nothing*

2 Y NO méi yǒu méi yǒu méi yǒu

|~******-.-|

[7]

[7] OHPVP-lateral.

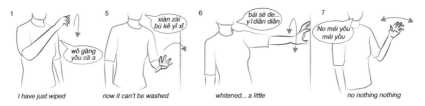

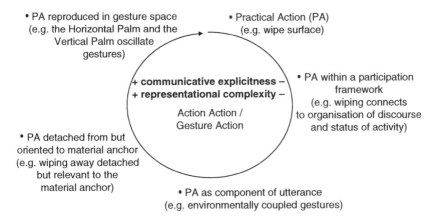

Figure 7.7 Gestures iconic of, oriented to, coupled with, and abstracted from wiping away

Figure 7.8 From Action–Action to Gesture–Action

The wiping away action may be enacted to illustrate an action being described in speech (iconic gesture). This iconic gesture may be inflected towards the wall, or produced in contact with the wall (environmentally coupled gesture). Finally, it may be used as a marker of negation, specifically to construe a negative speech act as an action of removal (cf. Chapter 4).

Based on examples of 'wiping away' in two contexts of situated activity, Figure 7.8 uses a circular arrow to diagram the continual progression away from 'action–action' (with no communicative intent) towards 'gesture–action' (with no practical, material effect). The diagram presents a series of different actions that, reading in clockwise order, increase with levels of communicative explicitness and representational complexity (Andrén 2014).

The diagram starts with the apparent 'Practical Action' (PA) of a hand interacting on the world, such as wiping a surface clean. Then, within an embodied participation framework (Goodwin 2000), a practical action may become part of the ongoing organisation and interpretation of discourse. In the French data, instances of wiping away could signal the end of an interactive sequence or the refocusing on a particular activity. In the Chinese interaction, the framework could be organised so that instances of 'wiping away' became demonstrations of the action. The practical action can furthermore become integrated to composite utterances such as 'environmentally coupled gestures' (Goodwin 2007). Wiping away on the diagram in the sand, for example, became an environmentally coupled gesture as part of a meta-linguistic negation in the lifeguard's speech. Similarly, wiping away on the wall for the Chinese home-owner became an integral deictic and iconic component of the negative speech acts she was producing verbally – reinforcing their illocutionary force. The next step occurs when the practical action becomes detached from its material anchor but remains oriented to or inflected by it, such as when the 'wiping away' action was performed above the sand diagram or towards the wall as the speakers verbally described exclusions and negations relevant to the material anchor. Finally, the practical action may be reproduced in gesture space as a recurrent gesture with a semantic theme and pragmatic function consistent with the original practical action, such as the home-owner's use of the gesture in negative response to a question following the activity. Diagrammed in this way, the aim is to visualise how practical and communicative actions intertwine and become progressively blended during situated interaction.

7.3   Gesture and Sign in Interaction

The form of the gesture we have associated with wiping away – Vertical Palm(s) oriented away from the body with oscillation movement – also appears in repertoires of linguistic signs for negation in various signed languages (Zeshan 2004; also as documented on www.spreadthesign.com). In the language we will consider though, French Sign Language, the Vertical Palms with oscillation is not formally recognised as a sign for negation (such as in online dictionaries like www.sematos.eu, www.pisourd.ch, www.lsfplus.fr or www.lsfdico-injsmetz.fr). Nevertheless, it occurs frequently in signed language interaction with functions that range from gestural and interactive to linguistic and grammatical. Through our study of wiping away in spoken language interaction, we showed the continuity between practical real-world actions (wiping away) and more abstract gestural symbols (specifically ZP and VP gestures associated with negation, coupled with, inflected to, or removed from the material surround). Observing the Vertical Palm oscillate form now in the context of a signed language class illustrates a subsequent step in the symbolisation process. In signed language, similar forms (based on practical actions) not only exhibit interactive and gestural functions shared with spoken language gestures, but can also operate as grammatical markers equivalent to verbal sentential negators like 'not'. Taking this process into account further helps understand Müller's view that grammatical concepts, such as negation, are embodied.

7.3.1 Interactive Functions of Gestures in Signing

Before addressing the linguistic functions of forms associated with 'wiping away' in sign language, an interactive usage of the Vertical Palm form will be illustrated in Example 71. This function is identical to those described elsewhere in discussions of gesture in spoken language (e.g. Licoppe and Tuncer 2014: 187). In this example, the teacher (who is Deaf) has asked her class of intermediate-level students to offer an example of a sentence based on the exercise sheet they have been working with. In [1] the teacher can be seen with the Palms Up and looking at all students with the aim of soliciting an example. The student to the teacher's left offers an answer. The teacher can then be seen interacting with this student, again using Palm Up gestures to solicit her answer [2]. During this interaction, two students sitting opposite the teacher continue to discuss in sign language (as evidenced by regular flashes of hands into the camera shot). This becomes distracting for the teacher who now uses the Vertical Palm to manage the interaction. In an interactive usage of this form, she orients her left Vertical Palm towards the student she is working with and her right Vertical Palm towards the pair of students having a discussion next to the camera [3]. As she extends her Vertical Palms in this way, she shifts head and gaze orientation to the pair of students and with a seemingly annoyed facial expression (knitted eyebrows) verbalises 'attend attend attend' ('*wait, wait, wait*'). She follows this with another sign addressed to the pair in which the open, flat hands move randomly around each other to represent 'noise' or 'distraction' in the visual modality [4]. The teacher then returns gaze to the student she was working with and invites her to continue by extending a flat hand turned down towards her and beckoning downwards [5] (Figure 7.9).

In their study of multiactivity, Licoppe and Tuncer (2014) have described a similar function in spoken language interaction when 'a talking participant raises his hand with his palm facing outwards while he attends to a contingent event, thereby signifying his orientation to putting on hold the ongoing interactional exchange' (p. 187). The teacher in our example uses her left hand in Vertical Palm formation to put the active student's signing exchange on hold, whilst using the right hand to momentarily deal with an 'out of frame' activity (Goffman 1974: 201), that is, to interrupt the students who are disrupting her ongoing pedagogical exchange with the other student. I imagine this function of the Vertical Palm in classroom management may resonate with those readers who are teachers – hearing or Deaf.

Example 71 SLC 49.50 Putting on hold

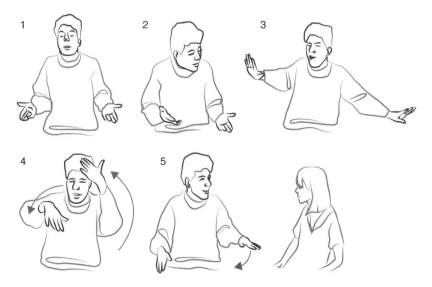

Figure 7.9 Interactive function of the Vertical Palm in sign interaction

7.3.2   Linguistic Functions of Gestures in Signing

The second instance of Vertical Palm in signing is not only interactive but also has an additional linguistic dimension. When the teacher uses a Vertical Palm Oscillate form to reject a statement proposed by one of the students, it constitutes a negative response signal and can be said to operate on the linguistic material being proposed by the student. In Example 72, this rejection occurs when the teacher is inviting students to contribute examples to an ongoing discussion by pointing around the group [1]. One particular student (who is unfortunately out of the camera shot), signs an utterance that the teacher attends to then immediately rejects. Addressing the student, the teacher first produces a double-handed Vertical Palm form with oscillation [2]. This is similar to previous instances of the form we observed in spoken language interaction; for example when a speaker refuses a suggestion by her addressee (cf. Chapter 4, Example 41), except the arms are extended towards the student and at face level. Following this rejection, which I have glossed as 'no, no, no', the teacher proceeds to enact taking an idea from her head and throwing it away [3a/b]. This is done with the conventional handshapes and movement patterns for linguistically picking up and displacing objects that we often find used conventionally in sign languages, and as such could be a 'partly-lexicalised sign' (Johnston 2013). In the context of the rejection, I have glossed this as 'get rid of that idea', or to capture a metaphoric aspect, 'remove that idea from your head'. Following this sign, the teacher addresses another one-hand version of the Vertical Palm Oscillate gesture to the same student, now with clear lateral movement across the body before the final oscillation [4] (Figure 7.10).

Example 72 SLC 28.35 remove idea from head
1 POINT
2 (student offers answer)
3 VP-OSCILLATE – 'remove idea from head throw' – VP-LATERAL/OSCILLATE

Figure 7.10 VP Oscillate for refusal followed by depiction of throwing

This is a highly gestural sequence of signing, since there is not one sign that can be identified from a lexical perspective. While the initial negative response signal is a performative use of the Vertical Palm Oscillate form, the 'get rid of that idea' sequence is a metaphoric elaboration on the theme of physical removal on which the original rejection is similarly based. By enacting the removal of an idea from her head, the signer specifies another embodied action associated with removing unwanted objects, in this case ideas from her head (metonymically standing for her addressee's head/mind). Furthermore, her inclusion of a horizontal movement into the final version of the Vertical Palm form also illustrates how signs may be gesturally flexible – they may be modified depending on the intended strength of illocutionary force. Given the strength of the rejection, it is unlikely that the student originally offered an answer but instead offered an excuse for not providing an answer (as would be common in the language-learning setting). Either way, the Vertical Palm form is produced in relation to that response and can be said to operate on it, that is, to reject it.

In addition to operating on linguistic material proposed by an addressee, the Vertical Palm form may operate linguistically within the confines of a signer's own utterance as a grammatical marker for negation. In the next example, a student has responded incorrectly to the teacher by offering an answer that was based on a previous task. The teacher now seeks to stress to the student the need to put the previous task to one side in order to focus on the new task. She first reminds the student of what the new task is – a revision of the work sheet they have in front of them in terms of facial expression, bodily action, movement and sign location (lines 1–2). She now mentions how this is different to the previous exercise that was based on emotions. After signing DIFFERENT and EMOTIONS, she depicts pushing aside in the space in front of her. She then likens the previous activity to performing signs separately as if they were written words by signing ECRIRE (writing) [1] SEPARER (separate) [2], following these two signs by pointing to her chest (MOI (me/I) [3]) then performing the VP Oscillate form (line 4; [4]). This entire last sequence is accompanied by a negative facial expression (brows knitted), as transcribed by over-lining the relevant signs and indicating the non-manual marker 'neg' (Figure 7.11).

Example 73 SLC 09.39 push idea to one side
    Why? – (directs attention to sheet) – revise each item on the list
1 POURQUOI – POINTS – REVISER-LA-LISTE
    What? – facial expression – body – movement – location – VP
2 QUOI – EXP.-VIS – CORPS – MOUVEMENT – LOCALISTION – VP
    Different – emotions – 'push to one side'
3 DIFFERENT – EMOTIONS – 'push to one side'
<u>   neg</u>
4 ECRIRE – SEPARER – MOI – **VP Oscillate**
    Write – separate – me – VP Oscillate

The meaning of the utterance in line 4 can be glossed as 'I don't like/want/do (signing in a way that is akin to) writing words down separately'. As I have

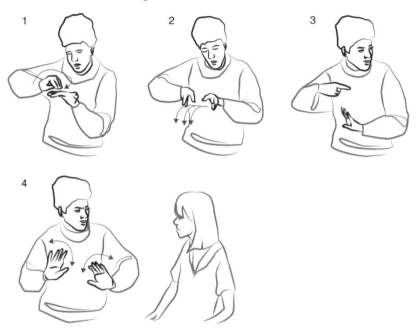

Figure 7.11 Vertical Palm negates the relation between subject and predicate

tried to indicate with this gloss, the function of the VP Oscillate form is to negate the relationship between the subject of the utterance (ME/I) and its predicate (WRITING SEPARATE). Alternatively, it is possible that the VP form might not be specifically negating the subject–predicate relation, but instead showing the speaker's disapproval of that type of signing. However, the co-extension of a non-manual marker for negation with the entire sequence suggests it is a negated statement (e.g. Neidle et al. 2000). In this case, the VP Oscillate form is functioning grammatically in a similar way to the verbal equivalent 'not'.

To illustrate a similar usage, the final example occurs when the teacher is commenting on a student's attempt at using constructed action to show how a plane might fly erratically in high winds. The teacher is drawing attention to a mistake the student has made in separating the sign for 'plane' from the movement of the hands that she produced afterwards to represent 'movement of the plane in the air'. The teacher first explains how facial expression and action need to be conflated and illustrates for the class how this would be done in the case of a plane flying in high winds. After her demonstration she produces a Palm Presenting gesture to the students as if to say 'voilà' (line 1). She then scans the rest of the group whilst signing COMPRIS ('understand'; line 2). After this comprehension check, she draws a contrast with her own correct performance by imitating the incorrect rendition previously provided by the student. To indicate she is about to sign incorrectly, she first signs PAS (not) – an extended index finger raised and oscillated laterally [1]. She then imitates the student performing first the sign for AVION (plane) [2] then, separately, the sign for MOUVEMENT [3]. Although she integrates the hand configurations of AVION into the sign for MOUVEMENT, she does not adopt the role shift and facial expressions that an accurate depiction would need. Having completed her imitation of the student's utterance, she now performs the sign for NUANCE [4], and follows this sign with the Vertical Palm oscillation gesture performed directly in front of the torso [5]. A negative facial expression is maintained over this entire sequence of signs, with strongest intensity with the initial negative particle 'NOT' and the final sequence 'NUANCE – VP Oscillate' (Figure 7.12).

Example 74 SLC 23.20 aeroplane in high winds correction
1 VOILA
2 COMPRIS

                                          neg
3 NOT – AVION – MOUVEMENT – NUANCE – **VP OSCILLATE**
4 SAME – PRO2

Figure 7.12 VP Oscillate as negative operator in LSF sign sequence

The teacher uses the conventional sign for 'not' first of all to negate the rendition of signing she is about to perform. Following that rendition, she performs the sign for 'nuance', which is not part of the clause previously negated by 'not', and uses the Vertical Palm Oscillate form to indicate that the feeling is wrong, undesirable, or negated. Overall, she is communicating the meaning: 'those are not the right signs (or way of signing), the nuance (of the signs) is not right'. In this instance of sign language, the same configuration of hands that we find in a spoken language gesture serves the grammatical function of negation. Oscillation of the Vertical Palms reverses the polarity of 'nuance' from positive to negative.

7.4   Discussion

This chapter aimed to situate gestures associated with negation in a broader framework for human activity by focusing on the everyday action of 'wiping away'. People engage in 'wiping away' when they rub the flat palms of the open hands against a surface to remove dirt, liquid, or other unwanted objects. The goal was to examine how this action related to gestures and linguistic signs when it occurred in interaction. We studied instances of wiping away in various social and professional contexts, where we found that people used speech and gesture to integrate wiping away actions to the communicative goals of their utterances. In these contexts, such physical actions form a natural bond with recurrent gestures and linguistic signs in interaction. Furthermore, examples from the sign language classroom demonstrate how forms similar to those we see in gesture not only exhibit similar pragmatic and interactive functions, but also acquire grammatical functions as linguistic structures in signing. Together, these observations further support linkages between grammar and gesture while establishing everyday embodied actions as central to their inseparability.

8 Impulse Theory
How, When, and Why We Gesture

8.1 Introduction

Readers at this point should not have been left puzzled or shocked by any of the gestures they have discovered whilst reading this book. The types of gestures that I have presented you with are so common in everyday language and interaction that experts agree to call them 'recurrent' (Kendon 2004; Ladewig 2014b; Müller et al. 2014). The settings that we have explored where people use these gestures should also be familiar – face-to-face conversations between people in various contexts for social and professional interaction. When you next talk to somebody, watch how he or she moves the hands when they speak. Before long you will see some of the gestures described in this book.

This chapter takes stock of our journey and sets out the Impulse Theory of gesture at the intersection of language, minds, and bodies. It takes two ideas developed throughout the book and strips them down to a basic theory – an answer to the question of how, when, and why we gesture. These ideas are that a) the impulse to gesture arises at the intersection between our cognitive-linguistic system and a face-to-face communication context, and that b) linguistic concepts, such as negation, shape and organise the impulse to gesture whenever people interact. This chapter draws on a number of sources to support Impulse Theory, situate it in relation to other theories, and extend it beyond the specific case of negation. But first, let's formulate exactly what the impulse to gesture is and lay out the conclusions of the book so far.

8.1.1 The Impulse to Gesture

The idea of an impulse to gesture was originally inspired by viewing wave forms created by a motion capture system that was computing the size, shape, and speed of a person's hand movements in real time as she gestured (Figure 8.1).

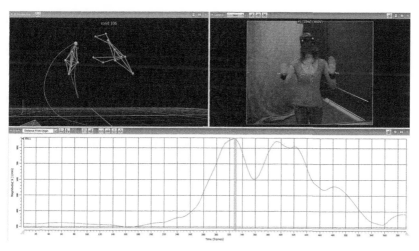

Figure 8.1 A gestural impulse as represented by motion capture technology

The physics definition of an impulse as 'a force acting briefly on a body and producing a finite change of momentum' is borne out by the motion capture screen shot (*Oxford Dictionary of English*). A person's actual body is acted on by some force, and the change of momentum produced is a gesture. So what determined, shaped, and organised the specific gestural impulse above? The answer in this case is obvious, because we had designed a gesture and asked a student in the lab to perform it for us precisely when we switched the machine on. The change of momentum was engineered by the design of our gesture and the impulse was triggered when we shouted the word 'now!'

Outside this experimental setting, things are not so simple. The impulse to gesture arises when our cognitive-linguistic systems and a face-to-face communication context intersect. As a way to examine this intersection, we focused on a universally attested linguistic phenomenon – negation. Studying gestures associated with negation, we have identified several fundamental constraints that determine, shape, and organise our impulse to gesture.

First of all, we identified **kinesic constraints** operating on the impulse to gesture (Chapter 2). Through a study of the recurrency of gesture forms associated with the expression of negation, we identified the grammar–gesture nexus – systematic and recurrent bindings of linguistic and gestural form at the level of utterance that produce regularity in speech and gesture whenever people negate. Within these nexus, Horizontal Palm gestures that express, mark, and enact negation exhibit conventionalised forms that reproduce everyday actions consistent with the linguistic and discourse functions of negation, including sweeping away, clearing aside, and cutting through.

Chapter 3 established how **linguistic constraints** from grammar in the utterance determine features of gesture organisation. Specifically, the grammar of negation imposes positional constraints on linguistic elements in the utterance, and these constraints yield sync points for gestures associated with negation. Sync points include negative particles and elements lying in the scope of negation, such as Negative Polarity Items and focused elements. The organisation of gesture in relation to these elements evidences a grammatical affiliation between gestures and speech, while illustrating the role of gesture phrase structure in organising the multimodal expression of a concept spread out across speech.

The conceptualisation of negation and negative speech acts leads to **conceptual constraints** on the form and function of the impulse to gesture (Chapter 4). When speakers gesture with negative expressions, their gestures often construe negation in terms of a particular action. These actions are consistent with the entrenched conceptual mappings, models, and schemas identified for verbal negation, which include construals of negation as *distance*, *force*, and *absence*. Similarly, variations in performance of the Vertical Palm gesture achieve construal on negation in spoken discourse as blocking, stopping, pushing, and throwing aside.

Chapter 5 reported **cohesive constraints** to account for the way speakers organise gestures into recurrent patterns, such as a Palm Presenting followed by a Horizontal Palm. The relation between semantic themes associated with those gestures and the centrality of the transition based on rotating the wrists was posited as a gesture construction specialised for indicating cohesive relations at the level of discourse; for example, in argumentation and narrative.

Taking an entire business meeting as an analytical unit, Chapter 6 argued that **coherence constraints** between the speaker, her communicative aims, and the genre of the business meeting could account for recurrency in form at the micro-level of gesture production. For that speaker, coherence was achieved by orienting towards broader discourses and demonstrating relevant professional practices. Professional practices were demonstrated through the performance of various speech acts, of which the repeated Horizontal Palm gesture was an integral part.

In Chapter 7, the impulse to gesture was situated in embodied interaction as a way to illustrate **interactive constraints**. The configuration of the interactive setting including the number of people, materiality of the physical surround, and concurrent activities has implications for the way people gesture when they speak. Gestures are inflected, coupled, and anchored to the material setting, and they are integrated to the management of multiactivity. The natural bond between real-world actions, gestures, and language in context gives rise to

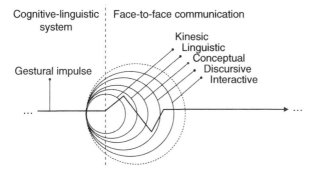

Figure 8.2 The impulse to gesture revisited

recurrent forms of gestures, such as those associated with negation. Similar forms observed in various sign languages suggest this action–gesture–language link is conventionalised in a number of linguistic signs, which may also be used flexibly to achieve pragmatic and interactive functions similar to those observed in spoken language.

These multi-level constraints each offer answers to the question of how, when, and why we gesture. Based on the findings, I therefore propose to visualise the impulse to gesture as a force vector traversing a series of nested circles that reflect the constraints that ultimately determine the shape and organisation of gestures in language use and interaction (Figure 8.2).

The vector is an abstract representation of the impulse to gesture – a constant in human communicative experience because language is multimodal and interaction is embodied. It is abstract because it may result in gesture strokes to phrases, phrases to units, and from units to the bursts, flurries, and patterns that may emerge over entire interactions (hence the ellipses either side of the arrow). The dashed line dividing the cognitive-linguistic system and face-to-face communication presents their separation not as actual but as theoretical – the gestural impulse is integral to language, which cannot be understood in isolation of context. No sequentiality in the production or perception of a gestural impulse is assumed. The diagram instead offers a snapshot of interacting constraints and forces: the inseparability of different influences operating on any one given impulse, be this an individual gesture, a gestural sequence, or a broader pattern of gesturing. The outer circle is unlabelled and dashed, reflecting the possibility of constraints additional to those included within the scope of this book. Lastly, the unavoidable imposition of the circles 'onto' the diagram suggests that constraints have only a restricting influence. Yet as much as constraints restrict, they also enable (see, e.g., Shogan 2002). It is through these constraints (and only through them) that a gestural impulse acquires its range of communicative potentials and possibilities in actual language use and interaction.

8.1.2   Current Chapter

With our conclusions about the impulse to gesture in mind, the current chapter aims to situate, develop, and extend the Impulse Theory of gesture. To situate our theory, we consider how it relates to other theories in the field, especially cognitive-grammatical approaches to gesture. Next, findings from interview and focus group settings provide an original perspective to evaluate the status of the grammar–gesture occurrences on which this theory has been based. To show how Impulse Theory extends beyond negation, we then illustrate its application to other core areas of linguistic systems with a small-scale study of the expression of progressive aspect through grammar and gesture. The chapter ends by indicating some challenges ahead for work on the impulse to gesture.

8.2   Situating Impulse Theory

The impulse to gesture arises at the intersection between our cognitive-linguistic system and a face-to-face communication setting. Impulse Theory therefore views gestures as a cognitive, linguistic, and social-interactive phenomenon, with the important qualification that cognition is embodied, language is multi-modal, and social interaction is situated. While these are well-established domains of gesture research, this book has documented the centrality of grammar to the cognitive-linguistic dimension of gestures in interaction.

Cognitive linguists hold the view that 'grammar is inherently symbolic' (Langacker 1991a: xv) and cognitive grammar has emerged as 'a framework that recognizes only semantic, phonological, and symbolic structures' (p. 423). A symbolic structure relates a phonological structure (a form) with a semantic structure (a meaning). According to this view, linguistic studies of grammatical negation have established an inventory of symbolic structures that equate a phonological form with a negative meaning (such as *no, not* and *nothing* in English). Most grammars have a chapter on negation that presents this inventory of the language's negative symbols and their functions. However, these inventories have not previously included the gestures associated with negation described in this book.

Cognitive grammar purports to offer an 'integrated account of the various facets of linguistic structure' (Langacker 1987: 1). It takes grammatical analysis beyond a language's syntactic component and opens up to all conventional aspects of symbolic structure. Because gestures are symbolic structures (McNeill 1992), Langacker (2008) has asked 'whether co-occurring gestures –

rather than being extrinsic to language structure – are best considered part of it, hence one aspect of the full characterization of expressions' (p. 249). This pondering is part of a larger *mise en question* of what is linguistic and what is non-linguistic:

For the grammar of a language we must obviously restrict our attention to units that can be considered linguistic in nature. However, it is not at all straightforward to character-ize the difference between linguistic and non-linguistic units. If arbitrary distinctions are to be avoided, we must recognize a core of prototypical linguistic units, and a gradation that leads from this core to structures so distant from it that no practical purpose is served by regarding them as linguistic. This conception has the consequence, once again, that a sharp delimitation fails to emerge between what is to be included in the grammar and what is to be excluded; the linguistic character of a unit is sometimes a matter of degree. (Langacker 1987: 60)

The evidence of specific and recurrent bindings of grammatical and gestural form presented throughout this book would suggest that at least some co-speech gestures can fit this characterisation of unit status. If, as Langacker (1987) has suggested, we 'generalize the notion of a (linguistic) symbol to include cases where the signifier belongs to the visual rather than the auditory region of semantic space' (p. 81fn), and we argue for 'the continuity between linguistic and non-linguistic structures' (pp. 427–8), then gestures associated with negation ought to be seriously considered on the level of the language system. For cognitive grammar, 'the ultimate objective is to understand gram-matical behavior on the basis of a deeper analysis that explicitly describes the internal structure of the participating elements and details the nature of their integration' (p. 277). Our descriptions of grammar–gesture nexus and the grammatical affiliates for gestures sought to describe the participating elements and their internal structure from a multimodal perspective. The findings pro-vide much grist for considering whether or not gestures have unit status and raise the possibility of incorporating at least some gestures to future grammars of negation.

The past decade has seen a number of approaches to gesture that also seek to integrate gesture and grammar, though from different perspectives (for reviews, see Cienki 2013, 2016; Kok 2016; Kok and Cienki 2016). Two such approaches are particularly central to the Impulse Theory of gesture being developed here, namely, *Multimodal Construction Grammar* and *Multimodal Grammar*.

8.2.1   Multimodal Construction Grammar

Several key constructs of Impulse Theory, such as recurrency, convention-ality, and the action–gesture–language link find their home in recent work on Multimodal Construction Grammar (henceforth MCG; Schoonjans

2018; Steen and Turner 2013; Zima and Bergs 2017). Without considering multimodality, first, the original construction approach to grammar was developed from frame-semantic and experiential approaches to language (Goldberg 1995). It was based on the observation that certain lexical and grammatical patterns had an idiosyncratic semantic or pragmatic meaning regardless of the propositional content they were used to structure. As a classic example, the meaning of the verb 'sneeze' in *Sally sneezed the napkin off the table* is not inherent to or predictable from the verb 'sneeze' but rather results from interaction with the 'ditransitive' construction 'X CAUSES Y TO RECEIVE Z' (Goldberg 1995). Goldberg and others observed that the meanings of such constructions were related to 'humanly relevant scenes' or 'conceptual archetypes' (Langacker 1991a), hence positing them as the fundamental building blocks to all linguistic knowledge and communication.

A number of researchers have argued that a construction approach to grammar must be extended to include gestures (cf. Zima and Bergs 2017, and contributions to their special issue). For a construction to be 'multimodal', Zima (2017) argues that 'the combination of a verbal pattern and a given gesture has to be entrenched as a unit in the minds of speakers and conventional in the speech community' (p. 15). One way to identify and analyse multimodal constructions has been by searching large collections of video-recorded samples of spoken language in face-to-face communication, such as made possible by the 'Red Hen' corpus (Steen and Turner 2013). Using this corpus, Zima (2014) has found evidence of entrenchment in motion constructions like '[V(motion) in *circles*], [zigzag], [N *spin around*] and [all the way from X PREP Y]' because they 'show strong associations with recurrent forms of gestures, ranging from 60% to 80%' (p. 27; also Zima 2017). Other work that has identified multimodal constructions includes Schoonjans's (2018) multimodal study of German modal particles such as *einfach* ('simply') and Schoonjans et al.'s (2016) multimodal study of cutting/breaking verbs in Dutch. In both these cases, systematic co-occurrences of verbal and gestural patterns support the view that constructions may be multimodal.

The variety of social, professional, and temporal contexts from which my examples of connections between verbal and gestural negation have been culled also indicate a well-entrenched phenomenon. The recurrent bindings between grammar and gesture that I observed associated with negation could well be candidates for 'multimodal constructions', as already proposed by Andrén (2014) for multimodal patterns involving the negative head shake gesture among Swedish children. Furthermore, Bressem and Müller (2017) have identified a particular 'negative-assessment construction' that involves a 'verbo-kinesic' construction between negative structures in speech and a 'throwing away' gesture similar to some gestures we have described in this book. As the name of their gesture suggests, underlying this verbo-kinesic construction is a 'humanly relevant scene' from real-world interaction, such as those we exemplified for the 'wiping away' gesture with negation in Chapter 7.

Though recurrency in language and gesture is clearly a social and interactive phenomenon, both Cognitive Grammar and Multimodal Construction Grammar point to the possibility that what linguists traditionally think of as 'grammar' could itself be multimodal.

8.2.2   Multimodal Grammar

A broad theorisation of the relation between grammar and gesture through the lens of multimodality has led Fricke (2012) to propose a 'multimodal grammar' (Fricke 2013, 2014a, 2014b). The possibility of grammar being multimodal provides an equally suitable context for us to situate our observations of the impulse to gesture.

Unlike corpus-based Multimodal Construction Grammar, Fricke's approach focuses on the in-depth analysis and theorisation of particular examples, primarily sampled from route descriptions in spoken German. Fricke's main claim is that multimodality is not only a feature of individual utterances or constructions, but also a property of linguistic systems and thus of grammar in general. The multimodality of grammar, for example, means that structures and processes typically identified as 'grammatical' may be more general organisa-tion principles that also determine the form and function of other modes that participate in multimodal expressions too. Focusing on gesture, Fricke (2013) exemplifies, for instance, 'the spoken and the gestural instantiation of the syntactic function of an attribute in a noun phrase' and 'the substitution of a spoken constituent with a gestural constituent in the same syntactic position' (p. 736). Fricke's studies of multimodal attribution and integration underpin her argument that 'co-speech gestures belong at least partially to the subject area of grammar' (p. 734). Multimodal Constructions and Grammar–Gesture Nexus may thus be two among many products of a multimodal grammar, mostly yet to be documented. On a theoretical level, this would support Langacker's propo-sal to avoid categorical exclusions from what is to be considered 'linguistic' based on the nature of the signifier.

Impulse Theory joins these approaches in viewing the connection between gesture and grammar as essential for accounting for recurrency in language and gesture in face-to-face, spoken interaction. But the centrality of grammar, conventionality, and underlying actions to Impulse Theory contrasts with a widely held cognitive-psychological view of gesture.

Table 8.1 *Gestures from a Growth Point and an Impulse compared*

Growth Point Theory (McNeill 1992, 2005, 2016)	Impulse Theory
'gestures . . . are nearly all small' (2016: 4)	Gestures are often large
'certainly not part of "grammar"' (2005: 21)	Inseparable from grammar
'lack of convention is a sine qua non' (2005: 10)	Convention is a sine qua non
'spontaneous creations of individual(s)' (1992: 1)	Recurrent in communities
'(speech) tries to fit the gesture' (2016: 6)	Gesture fits the speech
Fundamentally different to sign (1992, . . ., 2016)	Fundamentally similar to sign
'gestures cannot be deliberate' (2016: 4)	Gestures must be deliberate
'gesture is not purposeful' (2016: 39)	People purposefully gesture

8.2.3   The Growth Point

Psycholinguistics is an interdisciplinary field where linguistics and cognitive neuroscience join forces to understand the role of the brain in producing and perceiving language. One psycholinguistic approach in particular pioneered by McNeill has developed a 'growth point' theory of gesture (McNeill 1992, 2005, 2012, 2016). According to McNeill (2016), a *growth point* is the psychological unit responsible for 'the initial pulse of thinking-for-speaking from which a dynamic process of organization emerges' (p. 21). In a growth point, categorical (linguistic) and gradient (imagistic) modes of thinking interact and give rise to or become unpacked through a multimodal utterance: linguistic content in grammar and imagistic content in gesture. Based on work by McNeill, Table 8.1 summarises the nature of gestures produced by a growth point, compared to those we have examined throughout this book.

A growth point produces gestures that 'are nearly all small' (McNeill 2016: 4). These are gestures that speakers produce in 'a shallow disk in front of the speaker, the bottom half flattened when the speaker is seated' (McNeill 1992: 86). Descriptions of the gestures observed to occur in this region involve movements of the hands and forelimbs that are 'fleeting' and 'unwitting'. Impulse Theory, on the other hand, has been developed from descriptions of gestures that are qualitatively different. Recurrent gestures associated with negation are usually large and tend to be performed in, through, and across central gesture space, where they may also be held prominently either for linguistic or interactive purposes. Speakers often extend their hands beyond the confines of this space when gesturing too, for example, when they orient their gestures towards the addressee or couple them with the environment. In this case, gestures are as much driven by features external to the speaker as by internal processes of thinking-for-speaking.

How we view grammar will also shape differences in theories about the nature of gesture. A growth point produces gestures that are 'certainly not part of "grammar"' (McNeill 2005: 21). This is because grammar in the growth point is included as a 'chunk' of linguistic structure (McNeill 2016: 21). In Impulse Theory, grammar is not restricted to the static structures of language. Grammar is dynamic and embodied with symbolic and functional dimensions, both of which connect explicitly with gesture symbolism and function. Negation, for example, is not limited to the logical operation of 'not', that is, the syntactic switch of an utterance's polarity from positive to negative. The grammar of negation involves dynamic construal operations based on fundamentally embodied notions, such as force, distance, and absence (Sweetser 2006; Lapaire 2006; Chilton 2014). When a speaker uses gesture to construe her negation as an act of wiping away, for instance, the grammar of negation is as central to the form and organisation of that gesture as it is to the negative node and scope organising the co-occurring speech. Grammar in Impulse Theory is multidimensional, with gestures being a salient dimension of that grammar (Lapaire 2013).

Gestures produced by a growth point have been described as fundamentally different to the signs of sign language (McNeill 2005, 2016; cf. Emmorey 2002: 164). Yet the gestures of negation on which Impulse Theory is based are not only articulated and organised similarly to grammatical signs for negation in numerous signed languages (Zeshan 2004), but also performed with pragmatic and interactive functions similar to gestures, such as by the signer we observed in interaction (Chapter 7). Opposing gesture and sign by situating them at opposite ends of a continuum may be useful to contrast some types of gestures with some isolated signs (such as 'HOUSE', 'TREE'). But many signs work by integrating linguistic structure with gestural action, such as pronouns and directional verbs (Liddell 2003). Beyond linguistic signs, a number of linguistic practices in *signing* are fundamentally gestural in nature, such as constructed action (Quinto-Pozos 2007), narration (McCleary and Viotti 2010), pointing (Johnston 2013), and depiction (Liddel 2003). In accounting for the role of gesture in signing, these studies have moved signs and sign languages closer along the continuum towards gestures. In a complementary move, Impulse Theory accounts for *sign-like* properties of gesturing and therefore moves gestures along the continuum towards sign language.

If a growth point produces unwitting gestures that are separate from grammar and fundamentally different to aspects of sign, then the origin of the gestures on which Impulse Theory is based cannot be a growth point. In fact, Impulse Theory is not a psycholinguistic theory and does not view a need to posit any specific, speaker-internal cognitive mechanism as the origin of multimodal utterances in interaction. What Impulse Theory offers instead is a number of key constructs based on observable features of gesture data, such as grammar–gesture nexus, sync points in speech (grammatical affiliation), and the action–gesture–language link.

8.3   Evaluating Impulse Theory

By studying video recordings of people in interaction, Impulse Theory has been built on observable evidence of how, when, and why we gesture (laid out in Chapters 2 to 7). This evidence coheres with a number of other approaches currently being developed in the field of gesture studies (Lapaire 2011, 2013, 2016; Fricke 2013; Müller et al. 2014; Schoonjans 2018; Zima and Bergs 2017). Opinions of experts momentarily aside, people without training in gesture studies often have something to say about gestures as well. Some people say they 'never gesture', for example, while others think that they 'always gesture'. Such statements have become running jokes at gesture conferences, but they offer a starting point to evaluate people's awareness of the impulse to gesture.

8.3.1   Implicit Knowledge about Gesture (Interviews)

Edley and Litosseliti (2010) suggest 'instead of concocting all kinds of weird and wonderful experiments in attempting to track down the causes of human behaviour, why don't we simply *talk* to people' (p. 156; following Harré and Secord 1972). Discussing gesture with participants before a study might influence the way they gesture, but a retrospective interview could be useful to solicit their implicit understanding of gestures. The foreign language students interviewed in Sime's (2008) study, for example, gave clear reasons for why they attend to their teacher's gestures (cf. Smotrova 2014). Young men interviewed as part of Brookes's (2014, 2015) observation studies of group interaction in urban South Africa explicitly acknowledged the centrality of gesture to verbal art and group identity. What would the everyday conversationalists who I have studied say about their gestures?

For reasons of space, insights from only one of two retrospective interviews will be shared. My plan was to show these participants a video of their former selves producing a multimodal utterance that I had analysed and await their spontaneous reaction. The goal was then to probe – '[to] use what the interviewee has said as a starting point to go further and to increase the richness and depth of the responses' (Dörnyei 2007: 138). Selecting what to show and deciding how to probe undeniably 'sets the whole agenda' (Edley and Litosseliti 2010: 161). I acknowledge the social constructionist critique that 'both the interviewee and the interviewer are, during the real time of the interview itself, in the process of creating knowledge and understanding' (p. 160). It is precisely this creation process that has enabled me to ascertain the impressions from speakers in my corpus.

8.3.1.1 'That Gesture that Comes all the Time ... What the Hell is That?!'

We may all have cringed upon seeing ourselves on camera. But my first interviewee's reaction to viewing a video clip of herself was to burst out laughing at the way she was gesturing (bold font highlights expressions of interest):

Example 75 Extract 1.1
1 M Ha ha ha **so funny**
2 S What's funny?
3 M **That gesture that comes all the time. What the hell is that?**
4 S ha ha ha

The speaker here is the communications assistant from the business meeting that I reported in Chapter 6, who I am interviewing seven years after the meeting originally took place in France (and now we are speaking in English). What she refers to as 'That gesture that comes all the time' (line 3) is her repeated performance of the Horizontal Palm gesture with the following utterance that I am showing her a video clip of over our Skype call (Figure 8.3):

Figure 8.3 Segment shared with interviewee of her own gestures

'même des gars comme ça ils ont besoin de gestes pour mieux s'en sortir sinon, mauvaise communication, pas de rendement, nul, zéro'

(*'Even guys like that they need gesture to better get by otherwise, bad communication, no performance, rubbish, zero'*; the English translation was neither shown to nor discussed with the speaker)

In the clip I selected, she performs a six-gesture sequence involving four Horizontal Palm gestures (analysed independently of this interview in Chapter 6). The recurrency of her gesture causes not only amusement but also apparent bewilderment ('What the hell is that?!', line 3). I say the bewilderment was only 'apparent' because before I could ask a second question (line 5, Extract 1.2), the interviewee interrupted to explain what she thought her recurrent gesture may have meant while imitating the gestures she had seen herself perform in the clip (square brackets indicate co-occurrence of the Horizontal Palm gestures; line 6):

Example 76 Extract 1.2
5   S   wh-
6   M   it's really something categorical [like this] is [like that]
7   it's like [that] i can tell you it's [like that]
8   i don't know if it's really the way it was because it's
9   true it's hard to hear but it's so funny i just do it like six times or
10   something (.) never noticed that.

Despite initial bewilderment, her subsequent interpretation of the gestures as 'something categorical' (line 6) is a clear statement about the meaning of Horizontal Palm gestures, one in line with in-depth studies of this gesture in French (Calbris 2011). M also prefaces one of her re-enactments of the gesture with 'I can tell you' (line 7), which suggests that she attributes both communicative intentionality and authority to her former self's performance of those gestures. This supports my independent analysis of her gesture as a marker of identity (cf. Chapter 6). Yet despite her awareness of the potential meaning and function of her gestures, she nevertheless claims to have 'never noticed' that she performs the Horizontal Palm recurrently before (line 10).

At this point in the interview, I provided M with the transcript of her utterance (Figure 8.3) and invited her to scrutinise her gestures more closely. She ran through the transcript and reproduced each gesture again whilst uttering each segment to herself. As she finished, I asked: 'So can you tell me what you think you are doing there? Why do you do that?' (Extract 1.3, line 13). Having paused for a second then acknowledged this as a 'good good question' (line 15), M said 'OK so on some of them it's pretty obvious' (line 16) and began to offer an interpretation of her gestures one by one. In her interpretation of the first Horizontal Palm gesture with 'nul' ('nothing/rubbish'), her

Figure 8.4 Interviewee suggests awareness of a gesture family

discourse suggests that she believes that the gesture she performed belongs to a class of similar gestures. This is revealed through both her speech and gesture, again with square brackets to illustrate timing of the gestures, which this time are illustrated in Figure 8.4:

Example 77 Extract 1.3
13 S   so can you tell me what you think you are doing there? Why do you do
14   that?
15 M   (1) good good question
16   ok so on some of them it's pretty obvious i would say (.) so like
17   ['nul' G1], 'nul' you know like (.) it's a bit like [stop G2] you know
18   so it's a bit one of these gestures that you just you know [. . . G3] i
19   think it's rather logical even though maybe it's my logic and doesn't
20   make any sense to anyone else.

In interpreting a gesture she performed with 'nul', M performs the same gesture again but also explicitly compares it to two other gestures with an Open Hand Prone formation. When she says 'it's a bit like "stop"' she performs a gesture in which the open hands turned palm down move outwards at the neck level. When she then says 'it's a bit one of these gestures that you just you know' she executes several instances of the gesture of cutting through (Morris's 'scissor chop'; cf. Chapter 2). For this speaker, the occurrence of 'these gestures' (and possibly others) with 'nul' is 'obvious' and 'rather logical', though she is keen to acknowledge the potential subjectivity of her logic (lines 19–20).

As M proceeds to scrutinise her own gestures, she exhibits awareness of a gesture family: similarities in the form of gestures relating to her expression of 'nul' ('zero/rubbish'). Her discourse further suggests awareness of a shared meaning that all instances of this kind of gesture seem to express, not unlike what Kendon (2004) called a 'semantic theme'. For example, when it comes to the negative expression 'mauvaise communication' ('bad communication') with a Horizontal Palm gesture, she says:

Example 78 Extract 1.4
24 again same kind of story about mauvais nul zero (*bad, nothing, zero*)
25 i think there's something around that so
26 maybe when I think about something that is either not efficient at all
27 or inexistent in this case
28 when you talk about 'nul' (.) then you have that thing

M reflects on why there is the 'same kind of story' (line 24) behind her repeated use of Horizontal Palm gestures with different linguistic segments. She gives both a conceptual and a linguistic reason for why 'you have that thing' (line 28), meaning a Horizontal Palm gesture. Conceptually, she believes the gestures relate to when she thinks 'about something that is either not efficient at all or inexistent' (lines 26–7). Linguistically, the gesture occurs 'when you talk about *nul*' ('nothing/rubbish'; line 28).

In the last step of the interview, I focused on one of the gestures that the interviewee had related to 'nothing' in her analysis. I wanted to see if M would have a theory about why those gestures connect to those meanings, namely the expression of 'nothingness'. To do this, I first repeated M's analysis of the gesture occurring 'when you talk about nul' and performed the gesture for her again (Extract 1.5, lines 33–4). Then to set the new agenda, I asked 'What are you actually doing with the hands though?' (lines 34–5). During the one-second pause that followed, M clearly looked nonplussed, then said 'huh?' (line 37). Bearing in mind this was potentially the first time she had been asked such a question, I repeated the question (line 38), then tried to clarify by performing the gesture again and saying 'Like how does this relate to nothing?' (lines 38–9)

Example 79 Extract 1.5
33 S   you know you said this one (performs Horizontal Palm gesture) it goes
34   with meaning nothing or rubbish (.) what are you actually doing with
35   the hands though?
36   (1)
37 M   huh?
38 S   what are you actually doing with the hands? Like how does this
39   (S reproduces gesture) relate to nothing?

Readers experienced with interview methodology will be aware that I have given the interviewee a theory to work with here (Dörnyei 2007; Edley and Litosseliti 2010). Furthermore, eliciting metapragmatic awareness from speakers has long been viewed as problematic (Silverstein 1981). But since the explicit connection between a gesture and 'nothing' was made by M, I took the opportunity to ask her to specify this connection *in terms of* doing something with the hands. Within that context, and although M's answer is tentative, it is still revealing to see that she offers 'sweeping something off the table' (line 43) and 'chopping something off' (line 54) as actions she relates to the performance of her gesture:

Example 80 Extract 1.6

40 M (1) yeah it's far from being nothing isn't it errm i don't know to be
41   honest (.) i never really saw that i was doing that kind of stuff so i can't
42   really explain but er either phh i don't know i always think like gesture in
43   concrete (points to head) but like **sweeping something off the table** or
44   something (performs Horizontal Palm gesture) (.) but like
45   i don't really see a logic behind that to be honest
46 S OK
47 M so i don't know why i do that (performs gesture) maybe because it was
48   very dramatic because the way i was saying it was like 'nothing' just
49   really like brutal and right it's not something you want if you want to have
50   communication and you get nothing and it's not good maybe something
51   drastic a bit violent (performs gesture)
52 S so how would this kind of movement (performs gesture)
53   or handshape or whatever how would that turn into or reflect violence
54 M erm it looks like I'm **chopping something off** (performs diagonal
55   downwards) or something (.) i don't know
56 S hahaha
57 M hahaha

The interviewee expresses a lot of uncertainty over this passage and only offers a hedged response. She repeats 'I don't know' several times and even says that she does not 'see the logic behind' the answer she is giving (line 45). Nevertheless, the actions she posits to link the movements of her hands to the expression of a concept are coherent with those posited both in this book and previously by scholars working on similar gestures (not least, Kendon 2004; Calbris 2011; Bressem and Müller 2014a).

The interviewee's first reaction to seeing herself in a meeting on camera performing a series of Horizontal Palm gestures was to burst out laughing. Yet within the space of three minutes, M had offered an interpretation for each one of the gestures, suggested they indexed an authoritative speaker, made connections between similar gestures with a shared form, and allocated them both a general meaning and a specific linguistic context-of-use. Elsewhere in the interview, she also commented on the way she organised the gestures into a sequence as 'maybe it's like a comma and a dot'. Despite such clear statements about gesture form, meaning, function, and kinesic organisation, the interviewee was careful to situate any claims that she made either as speculation or common sense.

8.3.2 Socially Shared Knowledge about Gesture (Focus Groups)

The running joke about people claiming they gesture either obsessively or minimally may occur because of the expert–novice relationship that arises, such as the one that is also engendered by the interview format. I have demonstrated how I was able to move beyond general and unverifiable statements about gestures by soliciting, indeed co-constructing, an interviewee's aware-ness of her gestures through the interview format. If you are as curious as me about gestures, then you may also be interested in eavesdropping when the word 'gesture' is uttered within your earshot. In such cases, people are dis-cussing gesture in absence of attested sources of gesture expertise. How might everyday people discuss gesture among themselves?

Two focus groups were conducted in order to explore how people express their understandings of gestures in a group discussion format. The originality of the focus-group format, according to Dörnyei (2007), 'is based on the collective experience of group brain-storming, that is, participants thinking together, inspiring and challenging each other, and reacting to the emerging issues and points' (p. 144). We wanted to tap into our participants' collective experience of gesturing. We did this by focusing on negation and designing an opening question that could potentially allow the issue of gesture to emerge. The plan was to ask participants first of all to discuss 'the different ways or expressions you can use to say "no"', then to feed this discussion with various scenarios corresponding to different negative speech acts, such as 'a friend offers to pay for your dinner, but you don't want him/her to' (to refuse an offer). If this failed to stimulate the topic of gesture, the follow-up question was set as 'Are you aware of how you use your body with such expressions?' The focus groups each consisted of six second-year under-graduate students from the same cohort at a British university in China. No researchers were present, because both focus groups were convened and moderated by a pair of student interns, who conducted the focus group in Chinese. Our interns had no prior expertise in gesture studies but were trained in the basic skills for moderation, namely, to facilitate discussion, ensure equal participation, and keep discussions on track (Dörnyei 2007; Edley and Litosseliti 2010).

Gesture was openly discussed on numerous occasions during these focus groups, both when it emerged as an issue spontaneously and when the moderators introduced it as a topic. During these discussions, the partici-pants not only showed awareness of the forms and functions of gestures, but they often discussed when and how they would use them. To illustrate this, the opening discussion to one of the focus groups will be considered. This discussion occurred soon after the moderator had posed the opening issue of negation, which did not mention gesture at all but asked 'in what situations do you think there is negation, situations when you use negation, or in what situations do you think, ah, negation?' (lines i–iv) One of the students immediately responded 'mǎi dōng xi de shí hou' ('*when buying some-thing*'). After a request for an example from the moderator (line 2), the student then described a scenario where a market vendor gives an initially high price and exemplified the speech and gestures she would use to bargain down. Specifically, she explains 'nǐ jiù shuō zhè bù xíng' (*'you just say this is not ok'*; line 6), repeating this expression whilst performing a Vertical Palm with oscillation gesture (henceforth the 'Wiping Away' gesture). Then she focused explicitly on the gesture she was performing and explained 'jiù huì zhè yàng zi' (*'would just do like this'*; line 7), before saying how this expression would be needed to avoid a 'tè bié zhí bái de nà zhǒng shuō bù xíng' (*'a sort of direct not ok'*) (Figure 8.5).

Example 81 Extract 2.1 FG1 04.15 refusing an offer
i   ok xiàn zài wǒ men kāi shǐ zài zhōng guó nǐ men jué de dōu yǒu nǎ
ii xiē chǎng he shì yǒu negation cún zài de (.) jiù shì nǐ huì yòng dào
iii negation huò zhě shì shuō dōu yǒu nǎ xiē chǎng he nǐ jué de a
iv negation
    ok, let's start, in what situations do you think there is negation, situations when you
    use negation, or in what situations do you think, ah, negation

1   S2 mǎi dōng xi de shí hou
        when buying something
2   M   bǐ rú shuō ne
        for example
3   S2 jiù bǐ rú shuō mǎi dōng xi de shí hou, bǐ rú shuō wèn zhè ge jià gé shén
4   me, rán hòu tā huì gào sù nǐ, jiù shì yī bān shì zài shì chǎng ma, rán hòu rú
5   guǒ tā men gěi de nǐ jià gé dōu huì hěn gāo ma, dì yī cì de shí shou, rán
6   hòu nǐ jiù shuō **zhè bù xíng, zhè bù xíng bù xíng (gesture)**, jiù huì, jiù
7   shuō, jiù huì zhè yàng zi, huò zhě nòng de kě ài yī diǎn, yīn wéi nǐ yào
8   gēn tā kǎn jià ma, suǒ yǐ shuō kěn dìng bú shì tè bié zhí bái de nà zhǒng
9   shuō bù xíng, jiù zhǐ shì shuō ai nǐ néng pián yi yī diǎn ma huò zhě zěn
10   me yang, jiù huì jiàn jiē yī diǎn nà yàng shuō, duì
        for example when buying something, for example you ask the price or
        something, and he would tell you, usually in the market, and they give you
        *a high price, in the first time, and you just say this is not ok, **this is not ok***
        ***not ok (gesture)**, just can, just say, just like this, and, or be a bit cute, because*
        you want to bargain, so you can't use a sort of direct 'not ok', just say can
        you lower the price just a little bit or something, say that indirectly

Figure 8.5 Participant reports VP gesture as resource for bargaining

Following this example, another student now offers a view that contrasts with her peer. She begins by saying that her peer has 'qǐ fā le' ('inspired') her, because she personally 'hěn tǎo yàn' ('hates') sales assistants. She evokes a different kind of market place interaction now and reports how she says 'bié bié bié gēn zhe wǒ' (*'don't don't follow me'*). With this negative utterance she rotates her wrist from a Palm Up position to a hybrid Vertical/Horizontal Palm gesture, effectively showing a different form-function relation of gesture appropriate to that context (Figure 8.6). While one student shifts eye-gaze to this gesture, a different student begins to agree (line 13).

Example 82 Extract 2.2 04.15 refusing an offer
11　S1　wǒ jué de nǐ qǐ fā le wǒ, jiù bú shì yī bān dǎo gòu ma, jiù hěn tǎo yàn dǎo
12　　　gòu duì zhe wǒ, rán hoù wǒ jiù shuō **bié bié bié gēn zhe wǒ (gesture)**
　　　　You inspire me, sometimes a sales assistant, I don't like the sales assistant
　　　　*facing towards me, and I say, **don't don't follow me (gesture)***
13　S6　duì duì duì, shāng chǎng lǐ dǎo gòu, hái yǒu lù shàng fā chuán dān de
　　　　yes yes yes, sales assistants, and those who distribute leaflets on city
　　　　streets

Figure 8.6 Participant suggest alternative form-function pair to her peer

Readers may be wondering why the conversation turned so quickly to the topic of gesture. One of the participants may also be wondering this, because she now extends her hand Palm Down in front of her and says 'lái bǎ shǒu shì xué yī xià' (*'let's try learning this gesture'*; line 14, Figure 8.7 top). The student next to her now explicitly asks the moderator 'yào xué shǒu shì mǎ' (*'need to learn (i.e. discuss) the gesture?'*; line 15), and the moderator confirms this is ok (line 16). Over the next few turns, all the students now perform the Wiping Away gesture (Figure 8.7 bottom). While S6 and S5 perform the gesture without speaking (lines 18 and 22), S4's co-occurring speech is inaudible and S3 links her gesture to the meaning of 'suàn le' *'forget it!'* (line 20).

Example 83 Extract 2.2 04.15 refusing an offer
14 S5 lái bǎ shǒu shì xué yī xià
        let's try learning the gesture
15 S4 yào xué shǒu shì mǎ
        need to learn (i.e. discuss) the gesture?
16 M   kě yǐ a kě yǐ a
        yea why not
17 S2 jiù zhè yàng ma dà gài jiù
        like this
18 S6 (only **performs wiping away**)
19 S4 (inaud., **performing wiping away**)
20 S3 wǒ jué de jiù **suàn le jiù suàn le ba zhè ge yì si (gesture)**
        I think just forget it just forget it, something like this
21 ?? dui dui dui
        yes yes yes
22 S5 (only **performs wiping away**)
23 M   qí tā ne, hái yǒu shén me qí tā chǎng he
        any other situations

Discussion of a context for negation led to the topic of gestures. Two participants gave examples that showed how they might gesture to achieve different functions in the same context. Once gesture was confirmed as a legitimate topic for discussion, all students performed the particular form that was originally introduced and appeared to agree on its meaning, engaging in a shared experience of performing the gesture together. Examples of students showing awareness of gesture form and function like this abound in the Focus Groups, such as when one student explains a difference she perceives between Horizontal and Vertical Palm gestures (the latter being more 'hěn huì róu hé de', that is, *'gentle'*), or when students disagree with each other about whether or not they would use the Wiping Away gesture when refusing a teacher.

Figure 8.7 Participant questions the focus on gesture (top); numerous students in the group perform the gesture together (bottom)

8.4   Extending Impulse Theory

Impulse Theory is based on the case of negation to show how speakers integrate grammar and gesture in multimodal negative utterances. Not only does it demonstrate the multimodality of a notion that is central to the grammar of all languages, but Impulse Theory also helps in understanding how speakers use gesture in a range of contexts, including everyday conversations, business meetings, and situated activity. This section seeks to extend Impulse Theory by illustrating how the connections observed for negation are also characteristic of other central linguistic concepts and grammatical processes.

8.4.1   Beyond Negation

Summarising research on multimodal interaction, Mondada (2016) writes that 'no aspect of language escapes a multimodal perspective' (p. 340). Impulse Theory is similarly not restricted to negation and negative utterances. It provides a framework to address linguistic notions and structures mutlimodally. Any linguistic level, notion, or particular structure could be investigated through the multiple lenses of Impulse Theory. While this book has used

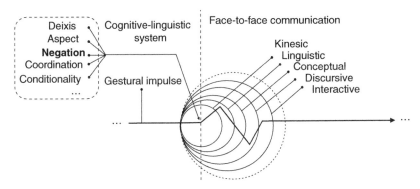

Figure 8.8 Linguistic notions as starting points for Impulse Theory

negation, other core cognitive-linguistic notions such as deixis, aspect, coordination, and conditionality could be taken as the starting point. This possibility can be visualised with a dashed box of such notions in our diagram of the impulse to gesture, situated clearly within the realm of our cognitive-linguistic system (Figure 8.8).

As a brief case study, let's take the notion of grammatical aspect and focus on progressive aspect – another linguistic notion with clear grammatical and gestural manifestations (Harrison 2009). Grammatically, the main tool that speakers use to encode the progressive aspect in English is be + -ing, known simply as 'the progressive' form. Huddleston and Pullum (2005) define this form as a '[c]onstruction marked by auxiliary **be** taking a **gerund-participle** complement' (Huddleston and Pullum 2005: 305; original emphasis). They offer the example *She was writing a novel* and state that the progressive 'usually represents a situation as being in progress' (p. 305). Elsewhere, they note that 'duration' and 'dynamism' are key properties of such *ongoingness* (Huddleston and Pullum 2005: 52). A number of grammarians have noted how these core properties interact with local factors in individual utterances, giving the progressive form an array of interrelated senses (Langacker 1987; Lapaire and Rotgé 2002; Huddleston and Pullum 2005).

In the literature on gesture, a gestural form with an apparent link to progressivity is the cyclic gesture (Ladewig 2014a). According to Ladewig (2014a), the cyclic gesture involves a loose, open hand in 'a continuous rotational movement, performed away from the body, which correlates with the semantic core of cyclic continuity' (p. 1605; Figure 8.9). However, speakers may perform it in contexts of a word/concept search, a description, or a request, and the form of the gesture varies systematically with its context of use. Ladewig (2014a) has underscored the

Figure 8.9 The cyclic gesture (Ladewig 2014a), drawn by
www.mathiasroloff.de

salience of 'ongoing activity' to this gesture's form and meaning, both
kinesically and cognitively (Ladewig 2011). The gesture's circular motion
is an ongoing activity, and its contexts of use are linked to continuous
processes and repeated actions. Furthermore, the gesture can be iconic of
continual actions, such as scooping.

Three initial parallels between the progressive form and the cyclic gesture
may be observed. First, *be* + *-ing*'s core meanings of duration and dynamism
correspond to the cyclic gesture's *continuous* circular motion. Second, *be* +
-ing has a core meaning with an array of interrelated values, and the cyclic
gesture has a core form with an array of interrelated form variants. Third,
context of use and local discourse factors determine both the specific value of
be + *-ing* and the specific formal variant of the cyclic gesture.

From the perspective of Impulse Theory, these parallels indicate the existence of a grammar–gesture nexus – a systematic binding between linguistic
and gestural form – or to refer to an earlier discussion – a possible 'multimodal
construction' (Zima and Bergs 2017). The following examples illustrate how
this particular nexus is manifest in spoken discourse and help extend Impulse
Theory beyond negation. In the examples, the speakers create multimodal
progressive utterances. They structure their speech using the grammatical
marker *be* + *-ing* and simultaneously perform a cyclic gesture. When they do
so, *be* + *-ing* and the cyclic gesture are linked because speakers use them both
to code progressivity. Progressivity, or 'ongoing activity', is a core meaning

inherent to both the grammatical and the gestural forms. Specific meanings emerge when the core meanings interact with local, utterance-specific elements. On the one hand, local elements in speech affect the grammatical marker's core meaning. And on the other hand, variations in gesture form affect the cyclic gesture's core meaning.

The first example is a relatively straightforward instance of a speaker using the *be* + *-ing* construction to encode ongoingness and performing the Cyclic gesture. D is describing his future plans to travel to Brazil. These have changed recently. He was initially flying directly to Sao Paulo, but now he will be flying to Rio de Janeiro, and then taking public transport from there to Sao Paulo. After describing these new travel plans, he admits that 'it's turning out to be quite expensive' (Figure 8.10).

Example 84 D_A_1 04:48 turning out
1 Lavi wants me to be in the north of Brazil with his friends which is fine they are
2 cool and that and then fly down to Sao Paulo and meet him there and blablabla
3 yeah its ok it's not a problem but it's turning out to be quite expensive

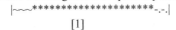

[1]

4 I think the tickets are about 500 euros
   [1] Left-hand cyclic gesture in vertical plane.

Figure 8.10 A one-hand precision grip variant of the cyclic gesture

The motion is continuous and in a central region of the vertical plane. The speaker's hand is closed but not in a fist. His index finger and thumb are touching – as if to hold a delicate object. The standard cyclic motion encodes the basic sense of ongoing activity, while the precision grip feature could reflect the speaker's reference to a specific event (cf. Kendon 2004). Grammatically, *be + -ing* encodes the core value of ongoingness – the journey is 'in the process of' increasing in cost. By swirling the hand round in space, the speaker gesturally construes the idea of increasing cost as a process that has begun and is not yet about to end. The linguistic marker also has a modal value: with *be + -ing*, the speaker expresses a feeling of discontent towards the ongoing activity (Lapaire and Rotgé 2002).

The next example illustrates how, similarly to gestures associated with negation, the form of the Cyclic gesture may be influenced by aspects of the speaker's utterance-related construal. T has been asked by B what she does at the weekend. T gives a list of usual activities and then adds that she leaves her apartment whenever 'there's something going on in the city'. As she says this last phrase, her hands whirl round each other in the horizontal plane above her knees (Figure 8.11).

Example 85 B_T gm 05.09 something going on **2cyc.horiz
1   yeah i don't know i usually have something to do i find something to do like er
2   (2) a concert or like an event or something going on in the city that interests me
                                        |~***********************-.-.|
                                                    [1]
3   either that or i travel
    [1] Two-handed Cyclic gesture in horizontal plane

As the frame grab shows, the speaker's right arm is prone and her left arm is supine. The right arm is above the left arm, the wrists are bent, and a number of fingers are extended. These parameters combine with the core feature of ongoing cyclic motion to create a two-handed cyclic gesture in the horizontal plane in lower gesture space. This variant of the Cyclic gesture synchronises with *be + ing* and the prepositional phrase 'in the city'. The preposition *in* suggests that the speaker has construed the city as a container. This conceptualisation could account for the horizontality of her gesture. Her wrists are placed horizontal and prone, one above the other, so that the hands can whirl round in the horizontal plane, as if they are in a container, that is, the city. Given her conceptualisation, the gesture construes this bounded ongoingness in a palpable space in front of the speaker. The hands encode action that has begun in a specific location but that has not ended. In this instance again, the grammatical marker *be + -ing* expresses its most prototypical value – expansion, ongoing activity.

A third example illustrates the interaction between the progressive form and negation. C asks K to describe his 'ideal weekend'. Because K's weeks are so

Figure 8.11 A two-handed prone/supine variant of the cyclic gesture

varied and unpredictable, he replies that he can 'never truly establish a typical weekend' (line 1). The reason for this he gives is 'because I never know what's gonna change' (line 2). As he says 'never know what's gonna change', his hands cycle around each other in the space immediately in front of him (Figure 8.12).

Example 86 J_B gm1 04:07 what's gonna change
1 I never truly establish a typical weekend
2 because (.) I NEVer know what's gonna change
                |~~*********************-.|
                            [1]
3 (.) and as a student for example
   [1] Two-handed Cyclic gesture in lower-central space

K's forearms are lateral and his palms are facing each other in a lower region of gesture space. The motion is cyclic and in the vertical plane. Grammatically, he uses a *be* + *-ing* marker and negation. With the particle *never*, he negates or opposes the subject predicate relation that his interlocutor thought could be assumed. This use of *be* + *-ing* presents a different dimension of the construction's meaning. The meaning is no longer with standard ongoingness but with the futurate dimension – an instance of the grammaticalised 'go-future' in

Figure 8.12 A two-handed lateral palm variant of the cyclic gesture

which a conceptualiser experiences subjective and abstract motion (Langacker 1991a: 162–3). Nevertheless, the spiralling hands of the cyclic gesture persist, supporting the idea that despite grammaticalisation of 'be going' to indicate futurity, remnants of ongoingness are made salient, construed by the gesture.

These three examples constitute a preliminary study of the link between the grammatical marker *be* + *-ing* and the Cyclic gesture. Speakers synchronise *be* + *-ing* with the Cyclic gesture to encode progressive aspect in speech and simultaneously construe progressivity in gesture. The cyclic gestures exhibit different formal parameters (cf. Ladewig 2014a): one-handed and two-handed variants, as well as variants where the forearms are lateral, or prone and supine. The grammatical marker *be* + *-ing* always maintains its core value of 'ongoing activity', and the gestures always maintain the core feature of repeated cyclic motion of the hand(s) in situ. The variations of cyclic gesture occur with variations of value for the *be* + *-ing* marker; they may be determined by other factors including lexical material and length of utterance. The different values I observed included the core value of expansion, the modal value, negation of the subject–predicate relationship, and a feeling of disapproval towards the relationship (Lapaire and Rotgé 2002).

These 'multimodal progressive utterances' parallel the 'multimodal negative utterances' on which Impulse Theory is based. They suggest the existence of a grammar–gesture nexus that could now be pursued further on linguistic, conceptual, discursive, and interactive levels, as we have done for negation. Not withstanding the results of those further studies, we still see that grammar and gesture converge at a central point in the linguistic system. The examples in this section reiterate that grammar and gesture are linked on symbolic, functional, and conceptual grounds.

Such an approach would likely prove fruitful in studying linguistic notions such as negation and aspect. But also, the approach could be applied to studying connections between gesture and the different clause types (asking, exclaiming, and directing), linguistic categories (e.g. nouns, verbs, prepositions, adjectives, adverbs), and specific syntactic operations (e.g. subordination and relativisation) that reference grammars typically distinguish (e.g. Huddleston and Pullum 2005).

8.4.2   The Diversity of Recurrency

In the context of broadening Impulse Theory – an explanation of recurrent patterns in language and gesture – a particular challenge concerning the gestures and gesturing described in this book arises before concluding the book. The widespread distribution of gestures associated with negation, and potentially all recurrent gestures (Ladewig 2014b), should be apparent from the languages analysed and the research cited so far in this book. But instances of a particular recurrent gesture, and more specifically, of a grammar–gesture nexus, are not necessarily produced, perceived, or used identically across different communities of language users. As I have noted previously, even within one particular language such as English, 'no two tokens of a gesture are ever identical' (Harrison 2009b: 82; cf. Schoonjans 2017 for a discussion).

Though relatively stable in form and function (Ladewig 2014b), recurrent gestures such as those studied in this book exhibit great diversity in how, when, and why they are used. This diversity is manifest at various levels, as shown through the various chapters of the book. Diversity may manifest at the level of individual gestures in terms of kinesic variants and discursive contexts-of-use, as shown in Chapter 2 and demonstrated elsewhere for the 'Palm Presenting' gesture (Kendon 2004; Müller 2004) and the 'Cyclic' gesture (Ladewig 2014b). It may also be manifest at the level of grammatical structures in a particular language, not only as shown in relation to negation here (Chapter 3) but also as evidenced by the array of 'multimodal constructions' that have recently been identified and described for English and other languages (see contributions to Zima and Bergs 2017). Beyond kinesic and cognitive-linguistic variation, diversity is observed at the level of the individual speaker, regarding his or her communicative aims in a particular discourse community. I showed this for Horizontal Palming in a business meeting (Chapter 6), building on findings for the 'Ring' gesture in political debate (Lempert 2011). Furthermore, repertoires of recurrent gestures may be established for specific linguistic communities (e.g. Bressem and Müller 2014b), which presumably also exhibit variation according to the importance they play in the communicative repertoires of each community.

How may this diversity of recurrency be further explored and better understood? One relatively unexplored aspect is how larger cultural norms of communicative practice and interaction might impact the form and function of multimodal bindings. Future avenues may include the study of recurrency in language and gesture cross-linguistically. This will involve comparing instances of a recurrent gestural form and its organisation across different languages (e.g. a comparison of Horizontal Palm gestures in English and French, Harrison and Larrivée 2015). Comparing the use of such gestures intralinguistically will also be valuable, attending to accents, dialects, and varieties; its usage among mono-, bi-, and multi-linguals; and the role of such gestures in lingua francas. Recurrent patterns in language and gesture could be further examined from a cross-cultural perspective, such as to evaluate the impact of cultural-specific cognitive models or gesture taboos on the form, function, and distribution of gestural usage (Kita 2009). An intercultural perspective on grammar–gesture nexus may also help understand the forms and functions of the impulse to gesture in interaction. This would mean examining the role of recurrency in gesture not only when speakers from different linguistic backgrounds interact in a lingua franca, but also including interactions at the level of different social groups (age, gender, background) and different social practices (as potentially distinguishable for different professions and communicative domains). To initiate these comparisons now, however, would be beyond the scope of this book.

8.5   Concluding Impulse Theory

This book began with the widespread belief that when people speak and interact, they experience an impulse to gesture. Some people claim immunity to this impulse (they '*never* gesture'), while others claim to be overwhelmed by it (they '*constantly* gesture'). Our focus has been the steady stream of recognisable gesture forms that people coherently organise and systematically deploy in relation to the linguistic concepts structuring their speech. Our case has been based on negation and the collection of gesture forms that people perform when they express negation in spoken interaction.

So what is the impulse to gesture? The impulse to gesture is the bodily dimension of the concepts, structures, and processes in language use and interaction. The impulse to gesture arises at the interface between a cognitive-linguistic system and a face-to-face communication context, with the important qualifications that cognition is embodied and language is multimodal; face-to-face communication is interactive and situated. Depending on what we want to say, to whom, and in relation to which aspects of our environment, our impulse to gesture is shaped and organised by the relevant kinesic, linguistic, conceptual, discursive and interactive constraints. The impulse to gesture is a spontaneous impulse, but it is characterised by constraints and conventionality too.

The impulse to gesture is a constant in human communicative experience. It is a constant in conversing, narrating, debating, sharing, and negotiating discourse in interaction. The grammar–gesture bindings observed in this book emerge as a fundamental feature of language. Certainly, some people use gestures more; others use them less. But the impulse to gesture will continue to arise whenever language, minds, and bodies intersect.

Bibliography

Andrén, M. (2010). Children's gestures from 18 to 30 months. Lund: Centre for Languages and Literature, Lund University.

(2014). Multimodal constructions in children: Is the headshake part of language? *Gesture* 14(2), 141–70.

Bavelas, J. B., Chovil, N., Lawrie, D. A., and Wade, A. (1992). Interactive gestures. *Discourse Processes*, 15, 469–89.

Beate, H. (ed.). (2005). *From perception to meaning: Image schemas in cognitive linguistics*. Berlin and Boston: De Gruyter Mouton.

Beattie, G. and Shovelton, H. (1999). Mapping the range of information contained in the iconic hand gestures that accompany spontaneous speech. *Journal of Language and Social Psychology*, 18, 438–62.

Beaupoil-Hourdel, P., Boutet, D., and Morgenstern, A. (2015). A child's multimodal negations from 1 to 4: The interplay between modalities. In P. Larrivée and C. Lee (Eds.), *Negation and polarity: Experimental perspectives, language, cognition, and mind* (pp. 95–123). Cham, Switzerland: Springer.

Bergmann, K., Aksu, V., and Kopp, S. (2011). The relation of speech and gestures: Temporal synchrony follows semantic synchrony. *Proceedings of the 2nd Workshop on Gesture and Speech in Interaction (GeSpIn 2011)*.

Bhatia, V. (2004). *Worlds of written discourse: A genre-based view*. London: Continuum.

Boutet, D. (2010). Structuration physiologique de la gestuelle: modèles et tests. *Lidil*, 42, 77–96.

Bressem, J. (2012). Repetitions in gesture: Structures, functions, and cognitive aspects. Ph.D. diss., Europa-Universtität Viadrina, Frankfurt (Oder).

(2013). A linguistic perspective on the notation of form features in gestures. In C. Müller, A. Cienki, E. Fricke, S. Ladewig, D. McNeill, and S. Teßendorf (Eds.), *Body – Language – Communication: An international handbook on multi-modality in human interaction* (pp. 1079–98). Berlin and Boston: De Gruyter Mouton.

Bressem, J. and Müller, C. (2014a). The family of Away gestures: Negation, refusal, and negative assessment. In C. Müller, A. Cienki, E. Fricke, S. Ladewig, D. McNeill, and J. Bressem (Eds.), *Body – Language – Communication: An international handbook on multi-modality in human interaction* (pp. 1592–604). Berlin and Boston: De Gruyter Mouton.

Bressem, J. and Müller, C. (2014b). A repertoire of German recurrent gestures with pragmatic functions. In C. Müller, A. Cienki, E. Fricke, S. Ladewig, D. McNeill and J. Bressem (Eds.), *Body – Language – Communication: An international handbook on multi-modality in human interaction* (pp. 1575–91). Berlin and Boston: De Gruyter Mouton.

Bressem, J. and Müller, C. (2017). The 'Negative-Assessment-Construction' – A multimodal pattern based on a recurrent gesture? *Linguistics Vanguard*, 3(s1). https://doi.org/10.1515/lingvan-2016-0053

Bressem, J., Ladewig, S., and Müller, C. (2013). Linguistic annotation system for gestures. In C. Müller, E. Fricke, S. Ladewig, D. McNeill, and S. Teßendorf (Eds.), *Body – Language – Communication: An international handbook on multi-modality in human interaction)* (pp. 1098–124). Berlin and Boston: De Gruyter Mouton.

Bressem, J., Stein, N., and Wegener, C. (2015). Structuring and highlighting speech – Discursive functions of holding away gestures in Savosavo. Proceedings of the GESPIN 2015 Gesture Conference, September 2015, Nantes, France.

Bressem, J., Stein, N., and Wegener, C. (2017). Multimodal language use in Savosavo: Refusing, excluding and negating with speech and gesture. *Pragmatics*, 27(2), 173–206.

Brookes, H. (2014). Gesture in the communicative ecology of a South African township. In M. Seyfeddinipur and M. Gullberg (Eds.), *From gesture in conversation to visible action as utterance* (pp. 59–73). Amsterdam and Philadelphia: John Benjamins.

(2015). The social nature of cognitive-semiotic processes in the semantic expansion of gestural forms. In G. Ferré and M. Tutton (Eds.), *Proceedings of Gesture and Speech in Interaction 4*. www.gespin4.univ-nantes.fr

Calbris, G. (1990). *The semiotics of French gesture*. Bloomington, IN: Indiana University Press.

(2003). From cutting an object to a clear-cut analysis: Gesture as the representation of a preconceptual schema linking concrete actions to abstract notions. *Gesture*, 3(1), 19–46.

(2005). La négation: son symbolisme physique. Paper presented at the Interacting Bodies, Corps en interaction. http://gesture-lyon2005.ens-lyon.fr/IMG/pdf/Calbri sFinal.pdf

(2011). *Elements of meaning in gesture*. Amsterdam and Philadelphia: John Benjamins.

Calbris, G. and Porcher, L. (1989). *Geste et communication*. Paris: Credif-Hatier.

Carter, R. and McCarthy, M. (2006). *Cambridge grammar of English: A comprehensive guide: Spoken and written English grammar and usage*. Cambridge: Cambridge University Press.

Celce-Murcia, M. and Larsen-Freeman, D. (1999). *The grammar book*. Rowley, MA: Heinle & Heinle.

Cheshire, J. (1999). English negation from an interactional perspective. In I. Tieken-Boon van Ostade, T. Gunnel, and W. van der Wurff (Eds.), *Negation in the history of English* (pp. 29–53). London: Longman.

Chilton, P. (2006). Negation as maximal distance in discourse space theory. In S. Bonnefille and S. Salbayre (Eds.), *Negation: Form, figure of speech, conceptualization* (pp. 351–78). Tours: Publications universitaires François Rabelais.

(2014). *Language, space and mind: The conceptual geometry of linguistic meaning*. Cambridge: Cambridge University Press.

Chui, K. (2005). Temporal patterning of speech and iconic gestures in conversational discourse. *Journal of Pragmatics*, 37, 871–87.

(2009). Conversational coherence and gesture. *Discourse Studies*, 11(6), 661–80.

(2015). Mimicked gestures and the joint construction of meaning in conversation. *Journal of Pragmatics*, 70, 68–85.

Cibulka, P. (2015). When the hands do not go home: A micro-study of the role of gesture phases in sequence suspension and closure. *Discourse Studies*, 17(1), 3–24.

Cienki, A. (2012). Usage events of spoken language and the symbolic units we (may) abstract from them. In K. Kosecki and J. Badio (Eds.), *Cognitive processes in language* (pp. 149–58). Bern: Peter Lang.

(2013). Cognitive Linguistics: Language and gesture as expressions of conceptualization. In C. Müller, A. Cienki, E. Fricke, S. H. Ladewig, D. McNeill, and S. Teßendorf (Eds.), *Body – Language – Communication: An international handbook on multimodality in human interaction* (pp. 182–201). Berlin: De Gruyter Mouton.

(2016). Cognitive linguistics, gesture studies, and multimodal communication. *Cognitive Linguistics*, 27(4), 603–18.

Cienki, A. and Müller, C. (Eds.). (2008). *Metaphor and gesture*. Amsterdam and Philadelphia: John Benjamins.

Coupland, N. (2007). *Style: Language variation and identity*. Cambridge: Cambridge University Press.

Cuffari, E. and Jensen, T. W. (2014). Living bodies: Co-enacting experience. In C. Müller, A. Cienki, E. Fricke, S. Ladewig, D. McNeill, and J. Bressem (Eds.), *Body – Language – Communication. An international handbook on multimodality in human interaction* (pp. 2016–25). Berlin and Boston: De Gruyter Mouton.

Cutting, J. (2008). *Pragmatics and discourse: A resource book for students* (2nd ed.). Routledge: Routledge English Language Introductions.

de Brabanter, P. (2007). Uttering sentences made up of words and gestures. In E. Romero and B. Soria (Eds.), *Explicit communication: Robyn Carston's pragmatics* (pp. 199–216). Basingstoke: Palgrave.

de Ruiter, J. P. (2000). The production of gesture and speech. In D. McNeill (Ed.), *Language and gesture* (pp. 284–311). Cambridge: Cambridge University Press.

Dahl, Ö. (1979). Typology of sentence negation. *Linguistics*, 17, 79–106.

Dahlmann, I. and Adolphs, S. (2009). Spoken corpus analysis: Multimodal approaches to language description. In P. Baker (Ed.), *Contemporary corpus linguistics* (pp. 136–50). London: Continuum International Publishing.

Debras, C. (2015). Stance-taking functions of multimodal constructed dialogue during spoken interaction. In G. Ferré and M. Tutton (Eds.), *Proceedings of Gesture and Speech in Interaction 4*.

Dörnyei, Z. (2007). *Research methods in applied linguistics*. Oxford: Oxford University Press.

Dosse, F. (2010). *Gilles Deleuze and Félix Guattari: Intersecting lives*. New York: Columbia University Press.

Downing, A. and Locke, P. (2006). *English grammar: A university course*. Abingdon: Routledge.

Duffley, P. and Larrivée, P. (2012). Collocation, interpretation and explanation: The case of *just any*. *Lingua*, 122, 24–40.

Edley, N. and Litosseliti, L. (2010). Contemplating interviews and focus groups. In L. Litosseliti (Ed.), *Research methods in linguistics* (pp. 155–79). London: Bloomsbury.

Emmorey, K. (2002). *Language, cognition, and the brain: Insights from sign language research*. Mahwah, NJ: Lawrence Erlbaum Associates.

Enfield, N. (2009). *The anatomy of meaning: Speech, gesture, and composite utterances*. Cambridge: Cambridge University Press.

Fauconnier, G. (1997). *Mappings in thought and language*. Cambridge: Cambridge University Press.

Fauconnier, G. and Turner, M. (2000). *The way we think: Conceptual blending and the mind's hidden complexities*. New York: Basic Books

Ferré, G. (2010). Timing relationships between speech and co-verbal gestures in spontaneous French. *Proceedings of Language Resources and Evaluation, Workshop on Multimodal Corpora, Malta*.

Fricke, E. (2012). *Grammatik multimodal: Wie Wörter und Gesten zusammenwirken*. Berlin and Boston: De Gruyter Mouton.

(2013). Towards a unified grammar of gesture and speech: A multimodal approach. In C. Müller, A. Cienki, E. Fricke, S. H. Ladewig, D. McNeill, and S. Teßendorf (Eds.), *Body – Language – Communication. An international handbook on multimodality in human interaction* (pp. 733–54). Berlin and Boston: De Gruyter Mouton.

(2014a). Kinesthemes: Morphological complexity in co-speech gestures. In C. Müller, A. Cienki, E. Fricke, S. H. Ladewig, D. McNeill, and J. Bressem (Eds.), *Body – Language – Communication. An international handbook on multimodality in human interaction* (pp. 1618–29). Berlin and Boston: De Gruyter Mouton.

(2014b). Syntactic complexity in co-speech gestures: Constituency and recursion. In C. Müller, A. Cienki, E. Fricke, S. H. Ladewig, D. McNeill, and J. Bressem (Eds.), *Body – Language – Communication. An international handbook on multimodality in human interaction* (pp. 1650–61). Berlin and Boston: De Gruyter Mouton.

Gee, Paul (2014). *How to do discourse analysis: A tool kit*. Abingdon: Routledge.

Givón, T. (1993). *English grammar: A function-based introduction*. Amsterdam: John Benjamins.

(2001). *Syntax. Volume 1*. Amsterdam: John Benjamins.

Goffman, E. (1974). *Frame analysis: An essay on the organization of experience*. Boston: Northeastern University Press.

Goldberg, A. (1995). *Constructions: A construction grammar approach to argument structure*. Chicago: University of Chicago Press.

Goldin-Meadow, S. (2003). *Hearing gesture: How our hands help us think*. Cambridge, MA: Harvard University Press.

Goodwin, C. (2000). Action and embodiment within situated human interaction. *Journal of Pragmatics*, 32(10), 1489–522.

(2007). Environmentally coupled gestures. In S. Duncan, H. Cassell, and E. Levy (Eds.), *Gesture and the dynamic dimension of language. Essays in honor of David McNeill*. Amsterdam: John Benjamins.

Green, J. (2014). Signs and space in Arandic sand narratives. In M. Seyfeddinipur and M. Gullberg (Eds.), *From gesture in conversation to visible action as utterance: Essays in honor of Adam Kendon* (pp. 219–43). Amsterdam: John Benjamins.

Hadar, U. (1989). Two types of gesture and their role in speech production. *Journal of Language and Social Psychology*, 8(3–4), 221–8.

Haddington, P., Keisanen, T., Mondada, L. and Nevile , M. (Eds.). (2014). *Multiactivity in social interaction: Beyond multitasking*. Amsterdam and Philadelphia: John Benjamins.

Handford, M. (2010). *The language of business meetings*. Cambridge: Cambridge University Press.

Harré, R. and Secord, P. F. (1972) *The explanation of social behavior*. Oxford: Blackwell.

Harrison, S. (2009a). The expression of negation through grammar and gesture. In J. Zlatev, M. Andrén, M. Johansson Falck, and C. Lundmark (Eds.), *Studies in language and cognition* (pp. 421–35). Cambridge: Cambridge Scholars.

(2009b). Grammar, gesture, and cognition: The case of negation in English. Ph.D. diss., Université de Bordeaux.

(2010). Evidence for node and scope of negation in coverbal gesture. *Gesture*, 10(1), 29–51.

(2013). The creation and implementation of a gesture code for factory communication. *Proceedings of GESPIN 2011: Gesture and speech in interaction*, Bielefeld, 5–7 September 2011.

(2014a). The organisation of kinesic ensembles related to negation. *Gesture*, 14(2), 117–41.

(2014b). Head shakes: Variation in form, function, and cultural distribution of a head movement related to 'no'. In C. Müller, A. Cienki, E. Fricke, D. McNeill, and J. Bressem (Eds.), *Body – Language – Communication: An international handbook on multimodality in human interaction* (pp. 1496–501). Berlin and Boston: De Gruyter Mouton.

(2014c). Gestures in industrial settings. In C. Müller, A. Cienki, E. Fricke, D. McNeill, and J. Bressem (Eds.), *Body – Language – Communication: An international handbook on multimodality in human interaction* (pp. 1413–19). Berlin and Boston: De Gruyter Mouton.

(2015). Organisation of kinesic ensembles associated with negation. *Gesture*, 14(2), 117–41.

Harrison, S. and Larrivée, P. (2015). Morphosyntactic correlates of gestures: A gesture associated with negation in French and its organisation with speech. In P. Larrivée and L. Chungmin (Eds.), *Negation and negative polarity. Experimental and cognitive perspectives* (pp. 75–94). Dordrecht: Springer.

Harrison, S. and Williams, R. F. (2017). Monitoring the swimzone whilst finding south. Sustained orientation in multiactivity among beach lifeguards. *Text & Talk,* 37(6), 683–711.

Hassemer, J. (2015). Towards a theory of gesture form analysis: Principles of gesture conceptualisation, with empirical support from motion-capture data. Ph.D. diss., RWTH Aachen University.

Heine, B. (1997). *Cognitive foundations of grammar*. Oxford: Oxford University Press.

Heritage, J. (1984). *Garfinkel and ethnomethodology.* Cambridge: Polity Press.

Holmes, J. and Stubbe, M. (2003). *Power and politeness in the workplace. A sociolinguistic analysis of talk at work.* Harlow: Longman.

Horn, L. R. (1989). *A natural history of negation.* Chicago: University of Chicago Press.

(Ed.). (2010). *The expression of negation.* Berlin and Boston: De Gruyter Mouton.

Horn, L. R. and Wansing, H. (2017). Negation. In E. N. Zalta (Ed.), *The Stanford encyclopedia of philosophy* (Spring edition). https://plato.stanford.edu/archives/s pr2017/entries/negation/

Hoza, J. (2008). The discourse and politeness functions of HEY and WELL in American sign language. In C. B. Roy (Ed.), *Discourse in signed languages.* Washington, DC: Gallaudet University Press.

Huddleston, R. D. and Pullum, G. K. (2002). *The Cambridge grammar of the English language.* Cambridge: Cambridge University Press.

(2005). *A student's introduction to English* grammar. Cambridge: Cambridge University Press.

Hutchins, E. (1995). *Cognition in the wild.* Cambridge, MA: MIT Press.

(2005). Material anchors for conceptual blends. *Journal of Pragmatics*, 37, 1555–77.

Hutchins, E. and Nomura, S. (2011). Collaborative construction of multimodal utterances. In J. Streeck, C. Goodwin, and C. LeBaron (Eds.), *Embodied interaction: Language and body in the material world* (pp. 289–304). Cambridge: Cambridge University Press.

Jensen, T. W. and Cuffari, E. (2014). Doubleness in experience: Toward a distributed enactive approach to metaphoricity. *Metaphor and Symbol*, 29(4), 278–97.

Jespersen, O. (1924). *The philosophy of grammar.* London: Unwin Brothers.

Johnson, M. (1987). *The body in the mind: The bodily basis of meaning, imagination, and reason.* Chicago: University of Chicago Press.

Johnston, T. (2013). Towards a comparative semiotics of pointing actions in signed and spoken languages. *Gesture*, 13(2), 109–42.

Johnston, T. and Schembri, A. (2007). *Australian sign language: An introduction to sign language linguistics.* Cambridge: Cambridge University Press.

Jones, J. H. (1994). *All together now. Managing people in the business world in the 90s.* London: Heinemann.

Kendon, A. (1980). Gesticulation and speech: Two aspects of the process of utterance. In M. R. Key (Ed.), *The relation between verbal and nonverbal communication* (pp. 207–27). The Hague: Mouton.

Kendon, A. (1988). How gestures can become like words. In F. Poyatos (Ed.), *Cross-cultural perspectives in nonverbal communication* (pp. 131–41). Toronto: Hogrefe.

(1994). An agenda for gesture studies. *Semiotic Review of Books*, 7(3). www.univie .ac.at/wissenschaftstheorie/srb/srb/gesture.html

(1995). Gestures as illocutionary and discourse structure markers in southern Italian conversation. *Journal of Pragmatics*, 23, 247–79.

(2002). Some uses of the head shake. *Gesture*, 2(2), 147–82.

(2004). *Gesture. Visible action as utterance.* Cambridge: Cambridge University Press.

Kirchhof C. (2011). So what's your affiliation with gesture? In: C. Kirchhof, Z. Malisz, and P. Wagner (Eds.) *GeSpIn.* Bielefeld.

(2017). *The shrink point: Audiovisual integration of speech-gesture synchrony.* Bielefeld: Universität Bielefeld.

Kita, S. (2009). Cross-cultural variation of speech-accompanying gesture: A review. *Language and Cognitive Processes*, 24(2), 145–67.

Kita, S., van Gijn, I., and van der Hulst, H. (1998). Movement phases in signs and co-speech gestures, and their transcription by human coders. In I. Wachsmuth and M. Fröhlich (Eds.), *Gesture and sign language in human-computer interaction* (pp. 23–35). Berlin and Heidelberg: Springer.

Klima, E. and Bellugi, U. (1979). *The signs of language.* Cambridge, MA: Harvard University Press.

Kok, K. (2016). The grammatical potential of co-speech gesture: A Functional Discourse Grammar perspective. *Functions of Language*, 23(2), 149–78.

Kok, K. and Cienki, A. (2016). Cognitive grammar and gesture: Points of convergence, advances and challenges. *Cognitive Linguistics*, 27(1), 67–100.

Krysthaliuk, A. (2012). The image-schematic dimension of English negation. In K. Kosecki and J. Badio (Eds.), *Cognitive processes in language* (pp. 99–108). Bern: Peter Lang.

Labov, W. and Waletzky, J. (1967). Narrative analysis. In J. Helm (Ed.), *Essays on the verbal and visual arts* (pp. 12–44). Seattle: University of Washington Press.

Ladewig, S. H. (2011). Putting the cyclic gesture on a cognitive basis. *CogniTextes*, 6.

(2012). Syntactic and semantic integration of gestures into speech: Structural, cognitive, and conceptual aspects. Ph.D. diss., European University Viadrina, Frankfurt (Oder).

(2014a). The cyclic gesture. In C. Müller, A. Cienki, E. Fricke, S. Ladewig, D. McNeill, and J. Bressem (Eds.), *Body – Language – Communication: An international handbook on multi-modality in human interaction* (pp. 1605–17). Berlin and Boston: De Gruyter Mouton.

(2014b). Recurrent gestures. In C. Müller, A. Cienki, E. Fricke, S. Ladewig, D. McNeill, and J. Bressem (Eds.), *Body – Language – Communication: An international handbook on multi-modality in human interaction* (pp. 1558–74). Berlin and Boston: De Gruyter Mouton.

Lakoff, G. (1987). *Women, fire and dangerous things. What categories reveal about the mind.* Chicago: University of Chicago Press.

Lakoff, G. and Johnson, M. (1980). *Metaphors we live by.* Chicago: Chicago University Press.

(1999). *Philosophy in the flesh: The embodied mind and its challenge to western thought.* New York: Basic Books.

Langacker, R. (1987). *Foundations of cognitive grammar. Vol. 1: Theoretical prerequisites.* Stanford: Stanford University Press.

(1991a). *Concept, image, and symbol: The cognitive basis of grammar.* Berlin and New York: De Gruyter Mouton.

(1991b). *Foundations of cognitive grammar. Vol. 2: Descriptive application.* Stanford: Stanford University Press.

(2008). *Cognitive grammar: A basic introduction.* Oxford: Oxford University Press.

Lapaire, J.-R. (2005). *La grammaire anglaise en mouvement.* Paris: Hachette.

(2006a). Negation, reification and manipulation in a cognitive grammar of substance. In S. Bonnefille and S. Salbayre (Eds.), *La négation* (pp. 333–49). Tours: Press universitaires François-Rabelais.

(2006b). From sensory to propositional modality. Towards a phenomenology of epistemic modal meanings. *Corela*, 4(1).

(2007). The meaning of meaningless grams – or emptiness revisited. In W. Oleksy and P. Stalmaszczyk (Eds.), *Cognitive approaches to language and linguistic data* (pp. 241–58). Frankfurt: Peter Lang.

(2011). Grammar, gesture and cognition: Insights from multimodal utterances and applications for gesture analysis. *Visnyk of Lviv University*, Philology Series 52, 88–103.

(2013). Gestualité cogrammaticale: de l'action corporelle spontanée aux postures de travail métagestuel guidé. *Maybe* et le balancement épistémique en anglais. *Langages*, 192, 57–72.

(2016). From ontological metaphor to semiotic make-believe: Giving shape and substance to fictive objects of conception with the 'globe gesture'. *Santa Cruz do Sul*, 41(70), 29–44.

Lapaire, J. R. and Rotgé, W. (2002). *Linguistique et grammaire de l'anglais*. Tours: Presses Universitaires du Mirail Toulouse.

Larrivée, P. (2017). Negation and polarity. In E. Stark and A. Dufter (Eds.), *Manual of Romance morphosyntax and syntax* (pp. 449–71). Berlin and Boston: De Gruyter Mouton.

(2001). *L'interprétation des phrases négatives: portée et foyer des négations en français*. Paris: Duculot.

Larrivée, P. and Lee, C. (Eds). (2016). *Negation and polarity: Experimental perspectives*. Berlin: Springer.

Lawler, J. (2005). Negation and NPIs. www-personal.umich.edu/~jlawler/NPIs.pdf

Leech, G. and Svartvik, J. (1994). *A communicative grammar of English* (2nd ed.). London and New York: Longman.

Lemmens, M. (2016). Idiogests: Semantically motivated gestural idiolects. Paper presented at the 7th Conference of the International Society of Gesture Studies. Paris, 18–20 July.

Lempert, M. (2011). Barrack Obama, being sharp. Indexical order in the pragmatics of precision-grip gesture. *Gesture*, 11(3), 241–70.

Lewandowska-Tomaszczyk, B. (2006). A cognitive-interactional model of direct and indirect negation. *GRAAT*, 35, 379–402.

Licoppe, C. and Tuncer, S. (2014). Attending to a summons and putting other activities 'on hold': Multiactivity as a recognisable interactional accomplishment. In P. Haddington, T. Keisanen, L. Mondada, and M. Nevile (Eds.), *Multiactivity in social interaction: Beyond multitasking* (pp. 167–90). Amsterdam and Berlin: John Benjamins.

Liddell, S. K. (2003). *Grammar, gesture, and meaning in American sign language*. Cambridge: Cambridge University Press.

Liskova, E. (2012). Negation of KNOW, WANT, LIKE, HAVE, and GOOD in American Sign Language. Master's diss., University of Texas at Austin.

McCleary, L. and Viotti, E. (2010). Sign-gesture symbiosis in Brazilian sign language narrative. In F. Parrill, V. Tobin, and M. Turner (Eds.), *Meaning, form, and body* (pp. 181–201). Chicago: University of Chicago Press.

McNeill, D. (1992). *Hand and mind: What gestures reveal about thought*. Chicago: University of Chicago Press.

(1998). Models of speaking (to their amazement) meet speech-synchronized gestures. http://cogprints.org/665/1/McNeill_Catchments.html

(2005). *Gesture and thought*. Chicago: Chicago University Press.

(2012). *How language began: Gesture and speech in human evolution*. New York: Cambridge University Press.

(2016). *Why we gesture*. Cambridge: Cambridge University Press.

Mondada, L. (2016). Challenges of multimodality: Language and the body in social interaction. *Journal of Sociolinguistics*, 20(3), 336–66.

Morgenstern, A., Beaupoil-Hourdel, P., Blondel, M., and Boutet, D. (2016). A multimodal approach to the development of negation in signed and spoken languages: Four case studies. In L. Ortega, A. Tyler, H. Park, and M. Uno (Eds.), *The usage-based study of language learning and multilingualism* (pp. 15–36). Washington, DC: Georgetown University Press.

Mori, J. and Hayashi, M. (2006). The achievement of intersubjectivity through embodied completions: A study of interactions between first and second language speakers. *Applied Linguistics*, 27(2), 195–219.

Morris, D. (1994). *Bodytalk: A world guide to gestures*. London: Jonathan Cape.

(2002). *People watching: A field guide to human behaviour* (rev. rpt edn). London: Vintage.

Müller, C. (2004). Forms and uses of the Palm Up Open Hand. A case of a gesture family? In R. Posner and C. Müller (Eds.), *The semantics and pragmatics of everyday gestures* (pp. 234–56). Berlin: Weidler Buchverlag.

(2010). Wie Gesten bedeuten. Eine kognitiv-linguistische und sequenzanalytische Perspektive. *Sprache und Literatur*, 41(1), 37–68.

(2013). Gestures as a medium of expression: The linguistic potential of gestures. In C. Müller, A. Cienki, E. Fricke, S. Ladewig, D. McNeill, and S. Teßendorf (Eds.), *Body –Language – Communication: An international handbook on multi-modality in human interaction* (pp. 202–17). Berlin and Boston: De Gruyter Mouton.

(2014). Gestural modes of representation as techniques of depiction. In C. Müller, A. Cienki, E. Fricke, S. Ladewig, D. McNeill, and J. Bressem (Eds.), *Body – Language – Communication: An international handbook on multi-modality in human interaction* (pp. 1687–702). Berlin and Boston: De Gruyter Mouton.

Müller, C. and Tag, S. (2010). The dynamics of metaphor: Foregrounding and activating metaphoricity in conversational interaction. *Cognitive Semiotics*, 10(6), 85–120.

Müller, C., Bressem, J., and Ladewig, S. (2013a). Towards a grammar of gestures: A form-based view. In C. Müller, A. Cienki, E. Fricke, S. Ladewig, D. McNeill and S. Teßendorf (Eds.), *Body – Language – Communication: An international handbook on multi-modality in human interaction (HSK)* (pp. 707–33). Berlin and Boston: De Gruyter Mouton.

Müller, C., Cienki, A., Fricke, E., Ladewig, S., McNeill, D., and Teßendorf, S. (2013b) *Body – Language – Communication. An international handbook on multimodality in human interaction*. Berlin and Boston: De Gruyter Mouton.

Müller, C., Cienki, A., Fricke, E., Ladewig, S., McNeill, D., and Bressem, J. (2014) *Body – Language – Communication: An international handbook on multimodality in human interaction*. Berlin and Boston: De Gruyter Mouton.

Neidle, C., Kegl, J., MacLaughlin, D., Bahan, B., and Lee, R. G. (2000). *The syntax of American sign language: Functional categories and hierarchical structure*. Cambridge, MA: MIT Press.

Nobe, S. (2000). Where do most spontaneous representational gestures actually occur with respect to speech? In D. McNeill (Ed.), *Language and gesture* (pp. 186–98). Cambridge: Cambridge University Press.

Oakley, T. and Hougaard, A. (Eds.). (2008). *Mental spaces in discourse and interaction*. Amsterdam and Philadelphia: John Benjamins.

Olsher, D. (2004). Talk and gesture: The embodied completion of sequential actions in spoken interaction. In R. Gardner and J. Wagner (Eds.), *Second language conversations* (pp. 221–45). London: Continuum International Publishing.

Oxford Concise English Dictionary, 9th ed. Oxford: Oxford University Press.

Parrill, F. (2007). Metagesture: An analysis of theoretical discourse about multimodal language. In S. D. Duncan, J. Cassell and E. T. Levy (Eds.), *Gesture and the dynamic dimension of language* (pp. 83–9). Amsterdam and Philadelphia: John Benjamins.

Parril, F., Bergen, B. K. and Lichtenstein, P. V. (2013). Grammatical aspect, gesture, and conceptualization: Using co-speech gesture to reveal event representations. *Cognitive Linguistics*, 24(1), 135–58.

Poletto, C. (2008). On negative doubling. *Quaderni di lavoro ASIT*, 1, 57–84.

Prieto, P., Borràs-Comes, J., Tubau, S., and Espinal, M. T. (2013) Prosody and gesture constrain the interpretation of double negation. *Lingua* 131, 136–50. http://dx.doi .org/10.1016/j.lingua.2013.02.008

Pruszynski, A. J. and Johansson, R. S. (2014). Edge-orientation processing in first-order tactile neurons. *Nature Neuroscience*, 17(10), 1404–9.

Pullum, G. (2012). A few notes on negative clauses, polarity items, and scope. www.lel .ed.ac.uk/~gpullum/grammar/negation

Quinto-Pozos, D. (2007). Why does constructed action seem obligatory? An analysis of classifiers and the lack of articulator-referent correspondence. *Sign Language Studies*, 7(4), 458–506.

Quirk, R., Greenbaum, S., Leech, G., and Svartvick, J. (2000). *Comprehensive grammar of the English language*. Harlow: Longman.

Reddy, J. (1979). The conduit metaphor: A case of frame conflict in our language about language. In A. Ortony (Ed.), *Metaphor and thought* (pp. 284–310). Cambridge: Cambridge University Press.

Sacks, H. and Schegloff, E. A. (2002). Home position. *Gesture*, 2, 133–46.

Schegloff, E. A. (1984). On some gestures' relation to talk. In J. M. Atkinson and J. Heritage (Eds.), *Structures of social action* (pp. 266–98). Cambridge: Cambridge University Press.

Schoonjans, S. (2018). Modalpartikeln als multimodale Konstruktionen: Eine korpusbasierte Kookkurrenzanalyse von Modalpartikeln und Gestik im Deutschen. Berlin and Boston: De Gruyter Mouton.

(2017). Multimodal construction grammar issues are construction grammar issues. *Linguistics Vanguard*, 3(s1). https://doi.org/10.1515/lingvan-2016-0050

Schoonjans, S., Sambre, P., Brône, G. and Feyaerts, K. (2016). Vers une analyse multimodale du sens. Perspectives constructionnelles sur la gestualité co-grammaticale [Towards a multi-modal meaning analysis. Constructional perspectives on co-grammatical gesture]. *Langages* 201(1), 33–49.

Shogan, D. (2002) Characterizing constraints of leisure: A Foucaultian analysis of leisure constraints. *Leisure Studies*, 21(1), 27–38.

Silverstein, M. (1981). The limits of awareness. Sociolinguistic Working Paper Number 84.

Sime, D. (2008). 'Because of her gesture, it's very easy to understand': Learner's perceptions of teacher's gestures in the foreign language class. In S. G. McCafferty and G. Stam (Eds.), *Gesture in second language acquisition and classroom research* (pp. 259–279). London: Routledge.

Smotrova, T. (2014). Instructional functions of speech and gesture in the L2 classroom. Ph.D. diss., The Pennsylvania State University.

Steen, F. and Turner, M. (2013). Mutlimodal construction grammar. In M. Brokent, B. Dancygier, and J. Hinnell (Eds.), *Language and the creative mind* (pp. 255–74). Stanford: CSLI.

Stivers, T. and Rossano, F. (2010). Mobilizing response. *Research on Language & Social Interaction*, 43(1), 3–31.

Stokoe, W. (1960). *Sign language structure. An outline of the visual communication systems of the American Deaf. Studies in linguistics: Occasional papers* (No. 8). Buffalo: Dept. of Anthropology and Linguistics, University of Buffalo.

Streeck, J. (2009). *Gesturecraft. The manufacture of meaning.* Amsterdam and Philadelphia: John Benjamins.

Swales, J. (1990). *Genre analysis.* Cambridge: Cambridge University Press.

Sweetser, E. (1990). *From etymology to pragmatics: Metaphorical and cultural aspects of semantic structure.* Cambridge: Cambridge University Press.

(1998). *Regular metaphoricity in gesture: Bodily-based models of speech interaction Actes du 16e Congrès International des Linguistes* (CD-ROM).Amsterdam: Elsevier.

(2006). Negative spaces: Levels of negation and kinds of spaces. In S. Bonnefille and S. Salbayre (Eds.), *Proceedings of the conference 'Negation: Form, figure of speech, conceptualization'. Publication du groupe de recherches anglo-américaines de l'Université de Tours.* Tours: Publications universitaires François Rabelais.

(2007). Looking at space to study mental spaces. Co-speech gesture as a crucial data source. In M. Gonzalez-Marquez, I. Mittleberg, S. Coulson, and M. Spivey (Eds.), *Methods in cognitive linguistics* (pp. 203–26). Amsterdam: John Benjamins.

Sweetser, E. and Sizemore, M. (2008). Personal and interpersonal gesture space: Functional contrasts in language and gesture. In A. Tylet (Ed.), *Language in the context of use: Cognitive and discourse approaches to language and language learning* (pp. 25–51). Berlin and Boston: De Gruyter Mouton.

Talmy, L. (2000). *Toward a cognitive semantics. Volume 1: Concept structuring systems.* Cambridge, MA: MIT Press.

Taub, S. (2001). *Language from the body: Iconicity and metaphor in American sign language.* Cambridge: Cambridge University Press.

Teßendorf, S. (2014). Pragmatic and metaphoric – combining functional with cognitive approaches in the analysis of the 'brushing aside gesture'. In M. Cornelia, A. Cienki, E. Fricke, S. Ladewig, D. McNeill, and J. Bressem (Eds.), *Body – Language – Communication. An international handbook on multi-modality in human interactionHandbooks of Linguistics and Communication Science* (pp. 1540–57). Berlin and Boston: De Gruyter Mouton.

Wehling, E. (2010). Argument is gesture war: Function, form and prosody of discourse structuring gestures in political argument. Paper presented at the 35th Annual Meeting of the Berkeley Linguistics Society, Berkeley, CA.

Williams, R. F. (2008). Gesture as a conceptual mapping tool. In A. Cienki and C. Mueller (Eds.), *Metaphor and Gesture* (pp. 55–92). Amsterdam: John Benjamins.

(2011). Coordinating and sharing gesture space in collaborative reasoning. Paper presented in the theme session 'Within and across spaces: Towards multi-dimensional models of gesture space' at the 3rd Conference of the Scandinavian Association for Language and Cognition, University of Copenhagen, Denmark, 14–16 June.

(2013). Distributed cognition and gesture. In C. Müller, A. Cienki, E. Fricke, S. Ladewig, D. McNeill, and S. Tessendorf (Eds.), *Body – Language – Communication: An International Handbook on Multimodality in Human Interaction* (pp. 240–258). Berlin: Mouton de Gruyter.

Williams, R. F. and Harrison, S. (2014). Distributed cognition and gesture: Propagating a functional system through impromptu teaching. In J. L. Polman, E. A. Kyza, D. K. O'Neil, I. Tabak, W. R. Penuel, A. S. Jurow, K. O'Connor, T. Lee, and L. D'Amico (Eds.), *Learning and becoming in practice: The International Conference of the Learning Sciences (ICLS)*, Vol. 3 (pp. 1655–6). Boulder, CO: International Society of the Learning Sciences.

Wilson, R. A. and Foglia, L. (2017). Embodied cognition. In E. N. Zalta (Ed.), *The Stanford encyclopedia of philosophy* (Spring edition).

Xiao, R. and McEnery, T. (2008). Negation in Chinese: A corpus based study. *Journal of Chinese Linguistics*, 36(2), 333–67.

Yerian, K. (2016). The performative 'ring': Semi-conventionalized gesture as a resource for constructing social stance and identity. Presentation at ISGS 2016, Sorbonne Nouvelle Paris, 18–22 July.

Zeshan, U. (2004). Hand, head, and face: Negative constructions in sign languages. *Linguistic Typology*, 8, 1–58.

Zima, E. (2013). English multimodal motion constructions. A construction grammar perspective. *Studies van de BKL* 8, 14–28.

(2014). Gibt es multimodale Konstruktionen? Eine Studie zu [V(motion) in circles] und [all the way from X PREP Y]. *Gesprächsforschung – Online-Zeitschrift zur verbalen Interaktion*, 15, 1–48. www.gespraechsforschung-ozs.de/fileadmin/datei en/heft2014/ga-zima.pdf

(2017). On the multimodality of [all the way from X PREP Y]. *Linguistics Vanguard*, 3(s1). https://doi.org/10.1515/lingvan-2016-0055

Zima, E and Bergs A. (2017). Multimodality and Construction Grammar. *Linguistics Vanguard*, 3(s1). https://doi.org/10.1515/lingvan-2016-1006

Index